The Intention

Based on faculty leadership and administrative experiences, *The Intentional Dean* explores the reasons to pursue a deanship and how to successfully attain a position as an academic dean. Additionally, this accessible guide provides understanding of key activities and responsibilities of the deanship, such as setting positive agendas, budgeting and budget reductions, merit pay determination, and effectively attending to disciplinary issues. Stressing bold action, support for curriculum diversity, and the importance of protecting due process, this book helps prospective and current deans take deliberate steps toward making a positive difference in the lives of students. Unique in the manner in which it defends both faculty rights and important administrative prerogatives, *The Intentional Dean* effectively demonstrates how deans can play a key role in bettering their college, the university, and the communities they serve.

John C. Alessio is a Professor Emeritus in Sociology and has served as an academic dean at two universities during his career.

The Intentional Dean

A Guide to the Academic Deanship

John C. Alessio

NEW YORK AND LONDON

First published 2017
by Routledge
711 Third Avenue, New York, NY 10017

and by Routledge
2 Park Square, Milton Park, Abingdon, Oxon, OX14 4RN

Routledge is an imprint of the Taylor & Francis Group, an informa business.

Library of Congress Cataloging in Publication Data
Names: Alessio, John C.
Title: The intentional dean : a guide to the academic deanship / by John C. Alessio.
Description: New York : Routledge, 2017.
Identifiers: LCCN 2016049708| ISBN 9781138290464 (hardback) | ISBN 9781138290471 (pbk.) | ISBN 9781315266183 (ebook) | ISBN 9781351969376 (mobipocket/kindle)
Subjects: LCSH: Deans (Education)—United States. | Universities and colleges—United States—Administration.
Classification: LCC LB2341 .A48 2017 | DDC 378.1/11—dc23
LC record available at https://lccn.loc.gov/2016049708

ISBN: 978-1-138-29046-4 (hbk)
ISBN: 978-1-138-29047-1 (pbk)
ISBN: 978-1-315-26618-3 (ebk)

Typeset in Perpetua and Bell Gothic
by Florence Production Ltd, Stoodleigh, Devon, UK

Printed in the United Kingdom
by Henry Ling Limited

This book is dedicated to my four wonderful children who have all become strong, honest, and gentle leaders.

Julie Marie Alessio
Joshua Martin Alessio
Jason Albert Alessio
Jeremiah John Alessio

Contents

Tables

Preface

Most professors expect little from the administration. They want an opportunity to find answers to questions related to their fields of study, and foremost, they want to see lightbulbs go on in their students' eyes. The contract signed with a university is not just for a paycheck. It is primarily for the privilege of working in an environment that will support the dreams a faculty member has worked so long and so hard to make real. After 21 or more years of education one hopes it will be possible to find a place to work where one's talents and hard-work will be appreciated and rewarded. Appreciation and reward don't mean large amounts of money or posh offices, labs, and classrooms. For the most part they mean expressions of gratitude for a job well done, and support in whatever ways might be possible given the available resources. There are colleges and universities where this happens, but there are also campuses where it does not.

Who is responsible for shaping the above described reality—whether it is a reality of support or a reality of regret and demoralization? Young scholars typically look to colleagues for support and sometimes the department chair. But that support is not always forthcoming, and when it does appear it sometimes has questionable strings attached. Colleagues and department chairs often have their own challenges revolving around promotion and tenure issues and departmental schisms. Indeed, the department might well be the very entity that is turning one's dream into a nightmare. Serving as a faculty union grievance officer for many years I saw department after department torn apart by petty battles—with junior faculty members often caught in the crossfire.

It was clear to me then, as it is clear to me today, that the responsibility for helping departments and faculty members resolve their differences rests in the office of the dean. While it is likely that many deans rise to this challenge, many do not. After years of being critical of those deans that do not sufficiently act on their responsibility to resolve departmental problems, I decided it was incumbent upon me to determine if positive intentional deaning can actually make a difference within a college. By "intentional" I mean being willing to take a risk and actually get involved. It means speaking out when necessary and taking action when action is needed, even if doing so might jeopardize your job or cause you to lose favor with some segment of the faculty of your college. I've observed too many deans holding back, reluctant to "interfere" while faculty members, both junior and senior, struggle to survive in a toxic environment. Bold action and positive faculty mentoring are important aspects of an intentional dean's work.

Intentional deaning also means having an agenda that is consistent with a set of values that will not only make the college and the university healthier, but also the world a better place. It means when difficult decisions have to be made, important values, hopefully represented by the college's mission statement, are not suddenly abandoned as if they are frivolous or of a lower priority than current events permit. Indeed, it is when decisions become most difficult that institutional values should be front and center as an important guiding force. At no time do we see the importance of this issue more vividly than when financial exigencies require budgets to be cut.

Since much of the foundation for this book was laid shortly after the global economic crisis in 2008, which led to major financial problems for higher education institutions during several years that followed, *The Intentional Dean* is accented with the urgency of that time. While it is probably the case that most of the time on most campuses there is relative financial stability, the reality that hard times are an ever present danger in higher education is important for all administrators to keep at some relatively high level of consciousness. Financial crises do happen, and sometimes happen when least expected. It is within that framework that *The Intentional Dean* deals with budgeting (Chapter 6) and budget reductions (Chapter 11) overtly and with considerable detail. Essentially there is a subtext of caution and emphasis on preparedness that runs through segments of the second half of the book. Indeed, the tone and subtext of Chapter 12 are testament in themselves of the last chapter's general overt message about when to move on. While covering very serious issues throughout, the book is not a gloomy read, offering much in the way of positive advice.

Written to help those seeking a deanship and those in the early stages of holding such a position, this book is not meant to be a treatise on all that has ever been known about deaning. However, based on significant and diverse faculty leadership and administrative experiences, information and advice are offered that could be helpful to deans at all career stages. Chapters 1–3 are focused on helping individuals seek and attain a deanship, while Chapters 4–7 are designed primarily for the recently appointed dean. Additionally, throughout the book information is provided that could be helpful to more seasoned deans, but Chapters 8–12 will be especially useful to those who have greater deaning experience.

The Intentional Dean also draws, where considered appropriate, from the contributions of others who write about deaning. Buller (2013) who refers us to the work of Maslow and Rosario (2014) who reminds us of Greenleaf's concept of servant leadership, are two examples quite relevant to the general spirit of this book.

While this is a book about deaning, one cannot be a successful dean without being an effective leader, and leadership in academia is unique (Gmelch & Buller, 2015: 84). Effective leadership seeks to find solutions to problems that will result in a peaceful and lasting settlement. Such an approach is different than simply trying to eliminate a problem. The "elimination" framework looks at problems as phenomena to be somehow blasted into oblivion as one might blast a major physical obstruction. Most human problems, including those at the university, are far more complicated than that and require some finesse and negotiating ability that will allow one to preserve important infrastructure in the form of a department, program, or student service. Openness to change is essential, but as Buller (2015) points out, positive change requires building on existing foundations and avoiding a disposition of simply removing what is already in place. A building attitude toward change is important when aspiring to serve as an intentional dean.

There are, of course, times when one has to resort to drastic means toward finding a solution to a problem. Ultimately, however, an experienced academic serving as a dean will anticipate what needs to be done to *avoid* problems, rather than waiting around to simply respond to them. "Positive leaders are future oriented and proactive, constantly exploring what's possible instead of being bound by past decisions and disappointments" (Buller, 2013: 13). Anticipating what needs to be done and being courageous enough to act on that assessment in order to make positive change, sometimes against considerable resistance, is what distinguishes one as an "intentional dean."

One of the expressions often used in reference to becoming a dean for the first time is that it is a baptism by fire. That is because typically one does not walk into a dean's office her/his first day on the job with a clear set of instructions and a lot of truly relevant experience. It is my hope that this book, while not an instruction manual *per se*, will provide a useful guide to how one might best set out to attain a dean's position and ultimately become an effective intentional dean. *The Intentional Dean* will not put the fire out completely, but hopefully it will at least reduce the heat.

REFERENCES

Buller, J.L. (2015). *The essential academic dean or provost.* San Francisco: Jossey-Bass.

Buller, J.L. (2013). *Positive academic leadership: How to stop putting out fires and start making a difference.* San Francisco: Jossey-Bass.

Gmelch, W.H. & Buller, J.L. (2015). *Building academic leadership capacity: A guide to best practices.* San Francisco: Jossey-Bass.

Rosario, P. (2014). The case for servant leadership, in L.L. Behling (Ed.). *The resource handbook for academic deans* (pp. 73–77). San Francisco: Jossey-Bass.

Acknowledgments

First and foremost I want to acknowledge the support, assistance, and advice of my wife and best friend, Dr Julie Andrzejewski, whose knowledge of academia and own leadership experiences were extremely valuable throughout this project.

Among the deans that have positively influenced my approach to administration, I would like to acknowledge: Dr Dennis Nunes, Dr Michael Miller, Dr Jane Early, Dr John Frey, Dr Kaye Herth, and Dr Joan Roca.

I also want to express appreciation to a few of the many outstanding department chairs with whom I have worked: Dr Jack Zaums, Dr Matt Povse, Dr Janet Bisset, Dr Marianne Borja, Dr Bill Conlogue, Dr Rosemary Krawczyk, Dr Maria Bevacqua, Dr Joe Kunkel, Dr Tony Filipovitch, and Dr Barbara Keating.

All of the above deans and department chairs share a number of important qualities, but most important among them is the ability to do the right thing in difficult situations where costs could be high for themselves personally. In addition to their high levels of competence they epitomize integrity and good judgment.

I would be remiss if I did not thank those with whom I worked the closest during my deanships: Administrative Assistant and only staff person in my first deanship, Ms Dorothy Trotter, Administrative Assistant Ms Becky Gunderman, Assistant to the Dean Dr Denise Thompson, and Development Officer Dr Susan Taylor. Their superior skills and commitment to high quality work contributed greatly to my success and the smooth operation of the dean's office.

Finally, I am grateful to the administrators who hired me, mentored me, and supported me throughout my work as a dean: Sr Patricia Ann Matthews, IHM, PhD, Sr Mary Reap, IHM, PhD, Dr Scott Olson, and Dr Richard Davenport. They all shared the same high level of stewardship for the institutions they served, and were committed to the growth and wellbeing of the students of their respective campuses.

I take full responsibility for the content of this book, including any errors that may have occurred.

Chapter 1

Taking the Fall into Deanship

Making the Decision

As I reflect on my career, and how significant the decision was to become a dean, I am reminded of an old movie: *City of Angels*. Of course, the general context of the movie is a love story, but the most relevant part for our purposes is that an angel learns he can "take the fall" into a life of being human by jumping off a tall building. Yes, as you can imagine, it is not a pretty sight—albeit he survives. Making the decision to become a dean can be a little like that, if not quite so dramatic or interesting to watch. The fallen angel actually does much better than just survive, and you will also as a dean. However, intentionally breaking into the deaning profession is not easy, even though many people end up in the position of a dean somewhat unintentionally and sometimes even reluctantly. Hopefully, you won't have to jump off a tall building, but it might feel that way at times. This first chapter, and an important part of this book, is about the process of deciding to become a dean: taking the "fall" out of what is typically a fairly comfortable professorship into the sausage making backstage life of administration.

Deaning is a challenging and institutionally important role in that it is often times the first line of administration. Even in higher education institutions where the department chairs are technically the first line of administration, the chairs' first allegiance is to the department that elects them, making them foremost professors rather than administrators. Serving at the pleasure of the President, deans can be dismissed at a moment's notice. Sometimes they have tenure in their college and sometimes they do not. Having faculty tenure status as a dean is helpful, but being fired from a dean's post is painful whether one has tenure or not, just as being fired from any position is typically painful. I have witnessed the firing of dean colleagues and it is typically unexpected and quite disruptive in the person's life. It is also, unfortunately, sometimes necessary in order to save a college from serious damage. Admittedly, this is a fairly dark beginning to a book that is intended to be helpful in a positive way. It would not be helpful, however, if I were to sugarcoat any aspect of this interesting, potentially exciting, but indeed challenging institutional role.

REASONS FOR BECOMING A DEAN

One of the activities I enjoyed as a dean was talking to groups of prospective students and their parents during their campus visits. Invariably I would ask them about their intended professions: "How many of you want to be a music therapist . . . a nurse . . . a police officer . . . a psychologist . . . etc." I would then go on to talk about all of our wonderful programs in the various areas mentioned. One day, to add a little humor, I asked, "How many of you are here today because you would like to become a dean?" Of course, there were no hands and I fortunately did draw a bit of laughter. From this rather spontaneous experience I began to more seriously contemplate how people come into the profession of an academic dean. In my last year as a dean, in anticipation of writing this book, I started asking colleagues how they came to be a dean: How and when they made the decision. Out of the resulting anecdotal responses there seemed to emerge two general categories: those who somewhat unexpectedly fell into the position, and those who intentionally planned a career change into deaning, or possibly administration in general.

Happenstance

The first chapter of this book is focused on those who choose to pursue a career in deaning. Those who are coming into deaning in unusual and/or unexpected ways will most likely have little interest in this chapter and might prefer to skip it. Their journey is one driven by the unexpected death or resignation of their dean, the mentoring of an administration that has picked them for some particular reason or set of reasons, their reluctant acceptance of an "interim" appointment, their desire to protect their department from the person that is likely to be appointed if they don't accept the position, or possibly reasons unknown (see Irvine, 2015). Some combination of these and other inadvertent circumstances frequently represent the basis upon which colleges and schools come to be governed and led. These are usually internal appointments that start out as interims, and when a search is conducted to fill the permanent position the interim candidates often have a clear inside track to maintaining their post in a relatively unchallenged manner. For those who fall clearly into the "interim to permanent" category, Chapter 2 may also be of marginal interest.

The way in which a person comes into their role as dean does not necessarily say anything about their ability to do a good job. Many of the just described faculty members end up being outstanding deans for many years, even though their path may not have been a perfect picture of due process/affirmative action, and in some instances may have been fortuitous or even somewhat surreptitious. Just as there are many advantages to hiring a dean from the outside, there are sometimes important advantages to hiring a dean from within. And not all inside hires are a result of an inside track or inadvertent circumstances. There are internal candidates who independently rise to the top of a national pool of applicants. These are people who typically have been planning a career change and have been applying for deaning positions at other institutions as well.

The Intentional Candidate

It should be pointed out that being an intentional candidate is not a requirement for becoming an intentional dean—nor does it assure that one will become an intentional dean. Assuming that one is thinking about pursuing a career as a dean, what are the possible reasons behind this intention? Here are twenty possible reasons with a note as to whether I believe they are good primary reasons (yes, no, or maybe):

- you are a mid-career faculty member and you are not being paid enough to sustain your desired lifestyle (no);
- you are a mid-career faculty member and you are not really interested in your discipline any longer—you feel you have nothing left to offer your field (no);
- you are at the end of your final term as Department Chair and will have to take a pay cut if you go back to regular faculty status (no);
- you have been told by friends that you would make a good dean (no);
- you like supervising others and are particular about the details of getting projects done (no);
- being a faculty member has not afforded you the status you thought it would and you expect better from being a dean (no);
- you view being a dean as a step toward becoming a higher level administrator . . . a provost and possibly a president (no);
- your aunt was a dean and you aspire to being like her (no);
- you have been disappointed by deans under whom you have worked and you believe you could do a better job than they did (maybe);
- you have been told by people, who are not your friends, that you would make a good dean (maybe);
- you have served "successfully" as chair of a large academic department (maybe);
- you are sufficiently fulfilled as a teacher and scholar and are seeking a professionally enriching experience (maybe);
- you enjoy working with curricula and view being a dean as an opportunity to involve yourself in curricular issues on a regular basis (maybe);
- you have seen changes taking place in higher education that you believe detract from the quality of education for prospective students and the

targeted communities that are supposed to be served by higher education institutions (yes);

- you have effectively demonstrated that you have leadership skills that could be useful to others and to higher education institutions (yes);
- you have been successful at, and enjoy, helping people solve problems (yes);
- you have a lot of knowledge about higher education from your many years of service in higher education and would like to put that information to good use for others (yes);
- you have been a successful teacher and scholar for many years and would like to help others enjoy that same success (yes);
- you have an exceptional sense of fairness and due-process and believe you can put those skills to use in helping a faculty make constructive personnel decisions and resolve student academic concerns (yes);
- you have ideas about how to improve higher education or make higher education a more vital agent for positive change in the world (yes).

By now the reader probably sees the general point being made: The decision to become a dean should be far less about what one wants personally than what one can contribute to others. This notion may seem a little corny to some, but too many people decide to go into administration for some combination of the first eight items listed above. If a person is not happy and successful as a faculty member, it is not likely (s)he will be happy and successful as a dean. If money is the sole motivation, then one is probably making a mistake. Some deanships don't even pay all that well. A combination of the last seven reasons stated above, as well as some of the reasons stated in Items 9–13 should be driving a person's motivation for seeking a deanship. That is, in addition to "other directed" goals one might also be looking for a professionally enriching experience, which could mean, all things considered, less annual income than what a new dean previously earned as a faculty member.

Those who work in faculty leadership positions dealing with administration-related problems are likely to encounter those who choose deaning for the wrong reasons. Faculty members sometimes seek advice from their dean about whether to move into administration. They should be counseled honestly. Highly successful deans are probably not as common as they ought to be because the vetting process doesn't always work as it should.

One might think that low competence and a self-serving disposition would be readily filtered out by the screening committee during the dean's search process, but committees are not always able to select the most qualified candidates. Search processes at the dean's level often become highly politicized activities with deans sometimes being selected for many of the wrong reasons. The goal of this chapter is to help faculty members make a reasonably well informed decision about whether to become a dean. Being a dean, including associate dean (White, 2014), is difficult work if taken seriously (Behling, 2014). Being a frustrated dean who is continually questioned by the faculty and the higher administration cannot be a pleasant experience (Gallos, 2002). If a person is unhappy as a faculty member, becoming a dean will most likely only multiply that unhappiness.

It is important to emphasize that regardless of the motivation and/or the history behind a person becoming a dean, one's background and motivations do not always determine whether a person will become an effective and successful dean. It is possible to redefine oneself and change goals as one learns a particular role. The important point to be made in this chapter is that some backgrounds, motivations, dispositions, and so on, make the movement into deaning more feasible and smoother than others, and increase the probability of success for both the person becoming a dean and for the other people (particularly the faculty and other administrators) with whom a dean must work. This book is intended as a guide to those who, if not at the beginning, at some point along their deanship journey, aspire to some combination of Items 9–20 on the previous list and make decisions accordingly. So begins the life of an intentional dean.

Whether and When?

The answer to the "whether" question is not only satisfied by the motivational issues represented in Items 1–20 identified previously, but also by the extent to which one has the personal skills and disposition to be an effective dean. These are items that a good dean vacancy position description will identify. When one reads a position description for an open dean's spot, (s)he shouldn't ask: "How can I make myself appear to be this way: effective leader, fair decision-maker, good communicator, and so on?" (S)he might ask instead, "Do I have these qualities?" If so, what is the evidence of it? It is important to be able to honestly assess one's own skill set and decide whether one can be an effective dean based on the most fundamental but critical qualities (see Reed, 2014). A prospective dean should read several position descriptions and create a list of all the qualities that faculty members are looking for in their administrative leader. One can then assess oneself on each of those items as honestly as possible.

When?

Assuming the issue of *whether* one should pursue a deanship has been resolved, one can proceed to the question of "when is a person ready to become a dean?" Higher administrators, such as provosts and presidents, are sometimes eager to see a particular person move into a dean's role. So they will find ways of giving the person administrative experience prior to the person becoming fully promoted and before the person has had enough of the "in the trenches" kinds of experiences that sufficiently season one for the difficult situations in which deans routinely find themselves. Taking a faculty member out of the faculty prematurely to do administrative work is probably a mistake most of the time. Deans sometimes make this same mistake by encouraging faculty members to become department chairs before they are fully promoted or possibly even before they are tenured. Fast tracking a person into a dean's role this way is even more serious.

During the 1980s and 1990s taking un-promoted and even untenured faculty members out of their departments to fill associate dean positions seemed to become acceptable practice. The thinking was that these faculty members would learn what they needed to know in order to eventually move into a deanship. They were also lower paid than more senior faculty members, making them more cost effective for the Associate/Assistant Dean role. However, when associates with this kind of background become a full dean, they are expected to make tenure and promotion decisions without having fully gone through those processes themselves. They might lack the confidence or the skills to appropriately make critical decisions. Faculty members will likely grumble about sending their promotion and tenure files to a dean that they do not respect as their academic or scholar equal/leader. A dean with modest credentials might lack the confidence to handle seasoned and aggressive department chairs that are pushing for the tenure of an unqualified faculty member.

Taking a person from the faculty prematurely and putting them into an administrative position that is not in the dean's office can be even more problematic than making that person a dean or associate dean. A provost might appoint a young promising associate professor to an interim assistant provost position which might then turn into a permanent position. After occupying this position for 3 or 4 years, a dean's spot opens. Is this person ready to become a dean? Most likely (s)he is not.

There are a number of possible reasons an administrator would make the above appointment: (1) to give a relatively new faculty members an opportunity to advance in their career in a way that might not have been possible otherwise for a long time; (2) to take advantage of the fresh ideas and energy that newer faculty members sometimes project more abundantly than highly experienced faculty members; (3) to appoint someone who is more pliable and not as set in their ideas as a more seasoned faculty member is likely to be—someone who is more controllable; (4) to save a productive capable faculty member from a caustic departmental environment; (5) to save money; and (6) to appoint someone they truly believe is the best available person for the position. Some of these reasons are more defensible than others, but appointing under-credentialed and/or under-experienced faculty members to administrative positions is probably not in the best interests of the faculty member or the institution—most of the time.

If a faculty member is contemplating leaving her/his faculty position to move into administration (s)he might want to respond to these questions first.

- Are you tenured and fully promoted—will there be no doubt in your mind or the minds of faculty members that you can confidently and honestly evaluate the work of faculty members?
- Are you comfortable with where you are in your research agenda—that you can either leave it now or continue it in some form as a dean?
- Are you at peace with your teaching career—you did a good job, you are fulfilled as a professor, and you can move on without doubt or regret?
- Are the people who are encouraging you to go into administration at this time doing so with your long-term best interests in mind?
- Will the benefits (to you and others) of becoming a dean outweigh the costs?

When one can answer all five of these questions affirmatively, then the answer to when (s)he should apply for dean's positions is "now"—all other issues having been resolved. Number 5 is important. One should benefit in some way as well as benefit others. Becoming a dean for the right reasons (helping faculty, developing/supporting programs, strengthening higher education in the fields related to your background, etc.) does not mean that one must choose a life of suffering and denial. The prospective dean is not going into the monastery. (S)he is choosing to become an academic dean, and if that decision does not work well for her/him personally, it will probably be difficult for her/him to make it work for others.

Honest Self-Assessment

It is important to be able to carefully assess whether one is capable and ready to be an effective dean. One cannot rely on others to provide her/him with this information. A prospective dean must be capable of serious introspection and self-criticism. Search committees are often politically divided, and consensus on the most qualified candidates is sometimes unattainable. The only acceptable candidate might end up being the one who simply has not excitedly given their honest opinion about the most considered important issues. It is thus possible to be selected for a deanship even if not sufficiently qualified. It does happen—far more often than one might think. The reader should not take this comment personally since it probably does not apply to her/him. But the important point being made is that if a prospective dean wants to know if (s)he is going to be successful (s)he will, primarily, have to determine that his/herself or in consultation with trusted others. The vetting process itself is not necessarily an accurate measure. Hopefully the above sets of recommended qualifying criteria will also be helpful in that reflexive process.

EFFECTIVE MENTAL TRANSITIONING TO THE DEAN'S ROLE

Role Models: What Deans Have You Known?

Ask yourself what deans you have known throughout your career. Picture them sitting behind their desk as they review your progress report or give you advice about your dossier. Picture them in your department meeting discussing the external review report and the future of your department. Think about how well they solved the problems of your department and the college. This latter image does not have to be of your dean, but could be of any dean of whom you have some familiarity—possibly through your involvement in faculty governance or possibly through the conversations you have had with the faculty of other colleges. Once this meditative exercise is completed, ask yourself if any of those deans are like the dean you would like to be. If you admire the work of some of those deans, then ask yourself, "why?" What specifically was it about each of them that was laudable? Was it their fairness? How was that fairness executed? Was it their ability to solve problems? What approach did they take? Was it their communication style? How would you characterize that style and how might you emulate it? Continue to ask yourself these kinds of questions and put yourself in the place of the effective deans you have observed. Can you picture yourself there? Do you have, or can you develop, the qualities that it takes to be like those deans?

Learning from Negative Precedent

On the other hand, if some of the deans you are picturing are not admirable and are not deans who have, in your mind, done a good job, again you must ask yourself, "why?" What did they do wrong? What didn't they do that they should have? How would you have handled certain situations differently? What mistakes and shortcomings have you observed from which you might learn something that will help you?

It is possible to learn how to be a successful dean from analyzing the behaviors of both effective deans and ineffective deans. As a faculty member I had more ineffective than effective deans that served as my role models. And I learned at least as much from the ineffective deans as I did from the effective ones. This is partly because, as a faculty president and long-term grievance officer, I encountered more problematic deans than good ones. I saw how deans in other colleges mishandled various situations. The deans I served under in my own college were also problematic in a variety of ways, but I saw them from the lens of a faculty member and not from my various faculty leadership roles. There were also positive role models in my career prior to becoming a dean: an exceptionally effective provost, a long-term graduate dean, and a few others sprinkled in here and there that gave me a well-rounded picture of what deaning and administration should and should not look like. I am grateful to all of them for their influence on my career—albeit some of that influence was a bit painful at the time that it occurred.

As this book progresses, much of what is discussed will be influenced by both positive and negative role models. Many of the successes that I had as a dean were almost direct inversions of the decanal behaviors I witnessed as a faculty member and faculty leader. Deaning is not something you do when you are too tired to do anything else. Deaning is not for the lazy or overly complacent person. Deaning is not for people who are reticent about getting involved and taking a stand. Deaning is not for people unwilling to take the time to read and study the various staff/faculty contracts and institutional documents governing due process. I have known those deans, and the chaos and damage they leave behind can be quite devastating for years to come.[1]

Beneficial Roles: Department Chair

While those in administration generally perceive they are underprepared (Morris & Laipple, 2015), one of the most obvious and beneficial transition roles for a dean's position is that of department chair. According to Wolverton and Gmelch, "more deans have served as department chairpersons than in any other position, and they hold that position longer than other administrative positions" (2002: 17). Many of the chair experiences are good preparation for the role of dean. Department chairs typically have small budgets that are structurally somewhat similar to the larger budgets of a dean. They also have some administrative and supervisory responsibilities—albeit that varies from institution to institution. In some university systems collective bargaining department chairs are not considered part of the administration. They are in the faculty bargaining unit and, therefore, have no real supervisory authority over the faculty in their department—albeit they typically supervise the department staff. Being a chair under these circumstances is a significant challenge. Technically the chair is a coordinator of the faculty and the department, but with no legitimate authority to make sure things go smoothly. This may seem like an impossible situation, but it can be made to work. Collective bargaining systems of this type require more involvement of the dean since it is the dean who is the first line of administration and thus is the first line of real authority. But in some respects, being a chair in this kind of system is better training for deaning than being a chair in a system where chairs have administrative and supervisory authority. The reason for this is not obvious, but it is quite simple.

The Issue of Authority

Department chairs that have no legitimate supervisory authority over the department faculty, if they are to truly be effective chairs, must learn and hone the skills needed to get things done without the actual power to give orders. This involves special communication skills, a sound sense of fairness and due process, and an ability to make others see what is fair and reasonable. Unfortunately, what may happen instead is that chairs in this kind of system use illegitimate means to try to control colleagues rather than work with them. They will use scheduling, committee assignments, or resource distribution as ways of rewarding some and punishing others. This approach serves only to create resentments, dividing the faculty and engendering problems that may not be solvable for a long time. New faculty are hired and somehow become part of the same toxic environment. Often search committees for hiring new faculty members are stacked to pick candidates who will be inclined toward one side of the divide or the other, and so the best applicants are frequently overlooked for political reasons.

In contrast, those chairs that have the finesse and communication/interaction skills to run a department fairly and in a reasonably democratic manner, creating policies and formulae for decision-making, will have the best chance of creating a positive and productive work environment. Why is this chairing system theoretically the best preparation for becoming an effective dean? The answer should be obvious. In order for deans to be effective they must operate in the same way. There is an old expression that goes something like, "when you begin to use your authority you begin to lose it." That is truly the case in academia. Your daily operating procedure as a dean must be one of finesse, good communication, cajoling toward mutual understanding, and sometimes, where appropriate, compromise.

Two Chair Models and One Skill Set

Whether one is a dean at a university where chairs are the first line of administration, or at a university where chairs are members of a bargaining unit with no supervisory authority over a faculty, the advice to chairs should be the same. The first, second, and third approach is always to get everyone who is involved in an adverse situation to participate in solving the problem willingly. Any effort to force someone to do something risks starting a chain of events that could cost everyone a great deal of pain and trouble. This approach is based on the assumption that most people will be reasonable if you provide them with an adequate framework within which they can exercise that reasonableness. We know, of course, that not everyone is reasonable and that is why deans, and sometimes chairs, have the authority to put in place certain procedures that will address the problem directly. Under these circumstances, it is not the person that is exercising the authority, but the position and the processes available to that position. This is where some basic sociological training can be helpful. The more one can separate oneself from the role and let the role and due process run its course, the more effective one will be in the dean's role—or any leadership position.

Broader Faculty Leadership Roles

I spent time as a Sociology Director in a three discipline department where the sociologists were two-thirds of the faculty, and the chair was from one of the smaller programs. This required me to attend the dean's council meetings and actually do much of the work of the chair. I had all of the chair responsibilities at another institution, again with a director title, in a unit where there was no designated chair. I also served as program director for an interdisciplinary program that I started and co-developed. So, other than serving short terms as interim chair, I did not have the title of chair, but had the experiences of chairing: scheduling, budgeting, hiring adjuncts, dealing with faculty problems, and various report and paperwork activities—all valuable. As a faculty member I also served on and chaired many university committees that gave me somewhat of a broad-based understanding of the institution and how it operated.

The above positions contribute significantly to preparation for the role of dean, and they are highly recommended. Most important in my background, however, were the many years spent as a campus-wide and state-wide faculty leader: Faculty Association President, Chief Grievance Officer, State Inter Faculty Organization Board of Directors, State Level Inter Faculty Organization Treasurer, and liaison to various other state organizations and state level committees. As stated by Bright and Richards, "serving in the faculty senate, participating in union activities, and working in other governance structures on campus provide critical knowledge of how the institution works from a faculty perspective" (2001: 16). It is through these kinds of positions that I not only experienced the best of what administrators had to offer, but also much of what can go wrong when administrators do not truly have the institution's and public's best interests in mind when they act. The following are two anecdotal illustrations.

Anecdote: Whose side are you on?

Serious problems arise when administrators decide to defend each other or their friends rather than do what is morally, ethically, educationally, and legally in the best interests of all concerned. When a dean arbitrarily denied a faculty member permission to accept a Fulbright Fellowship and the faculty member accepted it anyway, the Dean and the University President worked together to fire the faculty member. They apparently wanted to give the position to someone they knew, which they eventually did. The Chancellor of the state system, a well-respected administrator, became involved and decided to stand by her/his president. Faculty leadership organized a state-wide boycott of the Chancellor's convocation, a major event that had been in the planning for many months. The boycott was successful and the faculty member was reinstated—albeit by that time (s)he had already found another position and did not want to return.

Anecdote: Golf anyone?

In another situation a dean was funneling a disproportionate amount of the college's positions and resources into a single department. The chair of that department boasted of how they "owned" the dean by inviting her/him to their parties and inviting her/him to play golf. Other departments in the college were far more productive in all of the most important ways, and yet could not get positions and resources from the same dean. After years of frustrating meetings with this dean, faculty in the college sought help from faculty leadership. They were gravely concerned about the futures of their programs. For the above reason and numerous others, a petition of no-confidence was signed by a clear majority of tenured faculty members within the college. The President was informed that the petition would be taken to the media if the dean was not fired. The dean was asked to resign and the petition was never given to the press.

Avoiding Dualistic Thinking?

These are classic cases of what might be considered the worst in university administration. Administration is not about friendship and loyalty. It is about following the established policies and working earnestly to promote a better working and learning environment for the faculty and students. The Chancellor mentioned above was a smart person who knew better, but (s)he seemingly got pulled into the "protect your own" paternalistic way of viewing her/his position. Seeing the university in terms of "us and them" is tempting when one is in a leadership role. This is particularly true in a collective bargaining environment where the faculty leadership and administrators regularly and literally sit on opposite sides of the table to address important issues, a process known as "meet and confer." I went into faculty leadership innocently, as most faculty leaders do, but soon found myself being pressured toward dualistic thinking. It is extremely important to resist falling into the "us-them" disposition of administration, faculty, and student relations. An effective intentional dean will be focused on a large enough view of reality to simultaneously appreciate the importance of all segments of the university and the key variables impinging on all involved actors.

Temporary Diversity, Another Example

Faculty leadership positions provide an opportunity for one to know about and work with broader level institutional goals and initiatives. Sometimes this means holding the administration accountable for an honest commitment to those goals and initiatives. A significant part of my faculty leadership was spent helping the institution diversify its faculty and its curriculum. Yet, when challenged to defend faculty members from diverse backgrounds who also brought a different approach to a departmental curriculum, the administration—time and again—defended the *status quo*. On the one hand they were doing what was expected of administrators at the time by calling for diversity, but on the other hand they did not have the courage to do what had to be done to make diversity happen. They could not truly embrace change in the face of the predictable resistance they encountered from some segments of the faculty. Hence, people from diverse backgrounds, which included women in many instances, were hired and then set up for non-retention—a revolving door type of diversity. One can learn a lot from the experience of working on these kinds of issues as a faculty leader. When one is a faculty leader one also learns how important it is for deans to use their leadership skills to educate the faculty about important administrative goals; and they must be prepared to stand alone when necessary. This lesson doesn't just apply to the goal of diversity but to any institutional goal.

So What Are You . . . a Change Agent?

We can revisit Buller's (2007) question, "What kind of dean are you?" Do you want to be a dean that just goes the way the wind is blowing? Or do you want to be an intentional dean that can make positive change where it is needed? Broad level faculty leadership roles help one see first-hand the consequences of both of those alternatives. Clearly the latter is what is needed, however difficult it might be to consistently act as a positive change agent (Coaxum, 2004).

I was once asked by a provost during an interview, "So, is it the case that you accept positions with the goal of carrying out change initiatives? Is that what you do?" My impression was that the intent of the question was to let me know that someone thought I was inclined toward disrupting the *status quo*. Without hesitation I said something to the effect, "Yes, you found me out. I'm guilty as charged." I sometimes regret not pursuing the matter further. If I could go back in time I would ask, "Would you want to hire someone who is not an active promoter of positive change? Are our colleges perfect just the way they are?" Anyone who has been in academia for any reasonable length of time knows better. Even the best of colleges have problems, and some of those problems have root causes that require serious and well thought out actions on the part of the dean. One aggressive bullying department can make life miserable for the rest of the college if allowed to continue to absorb a disproportionate amount of resources—especially during financially difficult times.

Applied Positions in the "Real World"

Occasionally university presidents and/or vice presidents will decide that a particular college needs a dean that is from the "real world." Why not hire a Business College dean that is from the business community—someone who is well connected with the business world and who will be able to lead the college toward greater and more meaningful partnerships? A similar question can be asked about other colleges and schools: Health and Allied Services, Engineering, and sometimes even Schools or Colleges of Art or Music. But we tend to see this strategy actualized most often in Business Colleges where 31 percent of the appointed deans have had management experience outside of academia (Wolverton & Gmelch, 2002: 16). Under this model the idea is to hire a dean who has actually been successful on the application side of the academic content they will be administering. In theory there is a sound logic to this line of thinking—particularly for highly professionalized colleges and schools. Unfortunately, theory is not always supported by empirical reality. "Real world" experience can sometimes be valuable for successful deaning, but not without other essential ingredients. One must always be mindful of what it is that a dean does primarily. Deans manage the curricula and faculty of their college. Yes, they are also fundraisers, but unless a dean has experience with curricula and with the daily activities of their faculty, they will not be adequately prepared to do their job—no matter how successful they are in the applied world.

Those in academia are sometimes confronted with the expression: "those who can, do, and those who can't, teach." While that may sometimes be true, among people with doctorate degrees, the opposite of that expression might also be true. That is, "those who cannot teach, end up in the applied world." Of course, neither of these expressions does justice to anyone in either the applied or academic worlds, but an important point needs to be made about the applied versus academic issue. Even if someone in the applied world is a good teacher, there is a lot more to being a successful faculty member than effective teaching. At most universities there are three to five general areas of responsibility in which a faculty member must excel to be tenured and promoted. Anyone who has not successfully gone through that evaluation process because they have spent their career outside of academia is in the same potential candidate category as the faculty member who is moved into administration too quickly (discussed earlier). As a dean they will struggle to effectively evaluate the promotion and tenure documents of their faculty, and they might find it difficult to provide the kind of leadership and guidance that newer faculty members need in order to be successful.

Combining Both Worlds Effectively

While not common, there are people who have been successful at both academic positions and applied positions. The reason such a combination is not common is that most people probably do not want to leave the security of a successful career to broaden their experiences. Hence, successful faculty members sometimes moonlight in the applied world in order to gain some of the community experience that the more cloistered environment of academia does not afford them. People working fulltime in the applied world can also get experience in academia by moonlighting as adjunct faculty members. But serving as an adjunct professor does not provide all of the other experiences that are needed for an adequate background to become a successful dean. Adjunct teaching does not prepare one to evaluate a faculty member's promotion and tenure dossier. Nor does it prepare one to evaluate submitted curriculum proposals, or to understand the many possible problems that occur daily between faculty members, and between faculty and students.

From the standpoint of becoming a successful dean, moving fulltime into the applied world after a successful career in academia would be the most promising approach. This is not commonly done, but it does happen, and people from this kind of unusual background are typically highly marketable as deans.

The reason the academic phase would best come before the applied phase is that one's doctoral program is usually the springboard from which one is launched into the academic career: a fresh research agenda, recent teaching exposure and experience, and so on.

To maximize the likelihood of a successful deanship directly out of an applied career, without prior academic experience, it would probably be best to attain the doctorate after or during the applied career. Following the attainment of the terminal degree and an academic position, coupled with a solid history of applied experience, one could then be poised for early promotions and possibly early tenure so that one can move fairly quickly into an administrative role. Given that the professorship, in this case, is her/his "second" career (s)he may have to cram a lot of important experiences into a relatively short timeframe, but it certainly can be done. The importance of academic leadership experience for a deanship seems to vary across discipline areas. For example, Nursing and Business deans in particular tend to be far less likely to have academic leadership experience than deans from other colleges, and they are more likely to have prior management experience outside of academia (Wolverton & Gmelch, 2002: 16–17). Many Engineering deans, about 16 percent, come into their deanship from research or industry positions (Hargrove, 2015). Law schools have also been moving toward hiring applied outside deans (Parker, 2010).

There are other possible remedies to the dilemmas involved in hiring an applied career person for an academic dean's post, but they represent exceptions. One such exception is when the dean that is being hired will have enough associate deans (or deans of schools/divisions within the college) to be able to avoid performing many of the activities typically done by the college dean. There are universities like this. Their deans can be seen at conferences with a string of associate deans following them like little ducklings (perhaps some jealousy here). They introduce their associates by identifying each one's specific responsibility: Associate Dean for Curricula; and/or Associate Dean for Promotion and Tenure Evaluation; and/or Associate Dean for Student Affairs; and/or Associate Dean for Budgeting; and so on. Under these circumstances, the dean's role is largely to set the direction for the college, supervise the associates, and fundraise. Someone from an applied career could possibly fill this role effectively. These deans are sometimes referred to as "corporate deans" (Bright & Richards, 2001: 9).

My deanships did not have any associate deans, so I took care of all of the above listed responsibilities by myself with the support of an assistant dean, a development officer, a half-time student coordinator, and an administrative assistant. Deanships with many associate deans probably represent a minority of the decanal positions currently in existence. On the other hand, the two colleges I administered, given their size and complexity, should have had at least one associate dean assigned to them. The experience of directly covering all the responsibilities of a dean's office is challenging but also fulfilling. It prepares one well for writing a book about deaning.

Serving on a Dean's Position Search Committee

Finally, anyone who is interested in applying for a deanship should serve at least one time on a dean's search committee. The closer this experience is in time to the process of applying for a dean's position, the more helpful it will be. Many of the issues covered in the next chapter will be revealed first hand through the process of serving on a dean's search committee.

CONCLUSION

In summary, there is no effective shortcut to becoming a successful intentional dean. The more miles logged doing all of the things that inform one about how universities and colleges operate, what it means to be a successful faculty member, and how one can best solve problems in the academic environment, the more likely it is that success will be attained in the role of dean. More than a few early to mid-career faculty members came to me (as their dean) wanting to get into administration—good hard working people who were already feeling some of the burnout associated with teaching large and/or difficult classes, and/or who were basically tired of doing what they were doing. They wanted to move on and academic administration seemed like the logical next step. I generally told them to apply for a sabbatical, come back with a refreshed research agenda, get promoted to full professor, and broaden their faculty leadership experience. In my view, only then will they have maximized their readiness for the world of administration. Being an intentional dean requires having a level of confidence that affords one the ability to make independent decisions that might not be popular among other important players at the university. That confidence most likely comes with a price, and that price is multiple experiences that usually take a lot of time.

If one can achieve many of the above mentioned valuable experiences in a short amount of time, one can still be relatively young as a dean. Simply stated, no matter how prepared one is for a deanship there is always much to learn on the job, but the less one has to learn on the job the more likely it is that one will succeed. This may be true of most jobs, but it is especially true of deaning.

NOTE

1 Buller (2007: 16) wrote a chapter titled: What kind of dean are you? Therein he offers 20 questions that help one determine how they will be as a dean. It is a clever and useful exercise.

REFERENCES

Behling, L.L. (2014). Editor's introduction, in L.L. Behling (Ed.). *The resource handbook for academic deans* (p. xix). San Francisco: Jossey-Bass.

Buller, J.L. (2007). *The essential academic dean*. San Francisco: Jossey-Bass.

Bright, D.F. & Richards, M.P. (2001). *The academic deanship: Individual careers and institutional roles*. San Francisco: Jossey-Bass.

Coaxum, J. (2004). Managing people: A guide for department chairs and deans (review). *The Review of Higher Education*, 27 (2), 267–268. Retrieved September 2, 2016 from https://muse.jhu.edu/article/49525

Gallos, J.V. (2002). The dean's squeeze: The myths and realities of academic leadership in the middle. *Acadamy of Management Learning and Education,* 1 (2), 174–184.

Hargrove, S.K. (2015). A survey of career pathways of engineering deans in the United States: Strategies for leadership development. *American Journal of Engineering Education*, 6 (1), 33–42. Retrieved September 11, 2016 from http://files.eric.ed.gov/fulltext/EJ1064649.pdf

Irvine, C. (2015). How—and why?!—does one go from the classroom to the dark side? *The CEA Forum*, (Winter/Spring), 90–96. Retrieved September 12, 2016 from www.cea-web.org

Morris, T.L. & Laipple, J.S. (2015). How prepared are academic administrators? Leadership and job satisfaction within US research universities. *Journal of Higher Education and Management*, 37 (2), 241–251.

Parker, E.R. (2010). The role of law schools and law school leadership in a changing world: On being an "outside dean". *Penn State International Law Review*, 29 (1), 121–128.

Reed, M. (2014). Ask the Administrator: What skill sets do deans need? *Inside Higher Ed.* Retrieved September 1, 2016, from www.insidehighered.com/blogs/confessions-community-college-dean/ask-administrator- what-skill-sets-do-deans-need

White, G.W. (2014). First-year experiences of associate deans: A qualitative, multi-institutional study. *Research in Higher Education Journal*, 22 (Feb). Retrieved September 11, 2016 from http://files.eric.ed.gov/fulltext/EJ1064090.pdf

Wolverton, M. & Gmelch, W.H. (2002). *College deans: leading from within*. Westport: Oryx Press.

Chapter 2

Making the Deanship Happen

Finding the Open Position

Once one has made the decision to "take the fall" there is a lot of work to be done en route to becoming an intentional dean. The first step in the process is to start reviewing advertised positions to find campuses looking for the dean you want to be. While there are numerous places to find dean positions advertised, including in the employment bulletins of academic disciplines related to the dean's position that one seeks, the most comprehensive outlet for dean position ads is the *Chronicle of Higher Education* (CHE) (Marchese & Lawrence, 2006).[1] One might also check the bulletins of the various disciplines typically housed in the college one would administer as dean.

Most reputable colleges and universities, regardless of how many specialized outlets they use, are also going to use CHE, and so if one is searching for dean positions one typically need not look further than that. Ads for positions are run for variable lengths of time depending on a number of factors: university/college budgets; how difficult it is to find a dean for that particular area; whether there is an interim or internal candidate that is expected to fill the position; how much time there is to run the search; and the strategy of the search committee. Finding the right open positions typically requires consistently checking CHE and other appropriate outlets.

SELECTING POSITIONS

As pointed out by Krahenbuhl (2004: 8), there are both healthy and problematic reasons for deanship vacancies. It behooves a prospective applicant to know as much as possible about the conditions surrounding an "open" position for which they might apply. Some of the issues will be addressed under the section on making the decision about whether to accept the offer after having successfully interviewed. But there are other issues that one might want to sort out before even applying.

Interims

When a search seems to be moving quickly (short timelines) it hopefully means they are trying to maximize the use of their defined pool of applicants. However, a rushed search can also mean that the institution already has someone for the job. As for this latter possibility, you can sometimes make a few phone calls and do some web searching to determine if there is an interim or an already handpicked internal candidate applying for the position—what Tucker and Bryan (1991: 17) call a "wired search." Similarly, Vailancourt (2012) refers to such candidates as "anointed" rather than "appointed." If the search is "wired," you do not want to waste your time going to an interview just to help an institution appear to be fulfilling its affirmative action and search procedure requirements (Tucker & Bryan, 1991). One possible exception to that recommendation would be if you have not yet had a decanal interview and would like to practice. Under those circumstances it becomes a symbiotic relationship—however ill-conceived, inappropriate, and possibly illegal its underlying reality.

After finding out the current dean is an interim, it is a good idea to call the search chair to determine if the interim was permitted to apply for the permanent position. The committee chair is probably going to want you to stay in the pool, so (s)he might tell you things that (s)he probably shouldn't. For example, (s)he might tell you there is no policy restriction but that the interim is not a candidate; or they might tell you that the interim is a candidate but that there is a lot of resistance to her/his appointment and that you will have a good chance if you are a finalist. Some schools have policies that prevent interims from applying for administrative positions, or sometimes provosts will simply make it their own policy by only appointing someone as interim who agrees not to apply for the position. You will usually be able to find out what the circumstances are if you make that phone call. It is not impossible to unseat an interim, but typically the odds are significantly against the external candidate.

Is the Interim Really an Interim?

While not all interims retain their position permanently (Crocker, 2013), many do, which begs the question of whether they are truly "interim" appointees. Perhaps another word should be invented for this circumstance: "dean-to-be," or "dean in waiting." It is a waste of time and money to conduct a national/international search when everyone involved knows the interim has already been chosen as the permanent dean. Interims can use the dean's office to win the favor of important people in the college—people likely to be on the search committee, and they can also develop a good working relationship with the provost. Many national searches are really a façade for appointing someone already picked for the position. Affirmative action and equal opportunity policies have done a great deal for fairness and for making sure the most qualified people get hired, but unfortunately, they still have a long way to go. Some authors argue that education should follow the model of private companies and hire predominantly from within the institution (Wolverton, Gmelch, Montez, & Nies, 2001). Such a position tends to work against efforts to integrate and diversify leadership.

Non-Interim Internal Candidates

A non-interim internal candidate does not, necessarily, have as much of an unfair advantage as does an interim. In fact, non-interim internal candidates represent an interesting mixture of both advantages and disadvantages. On the advantage side, the internal candidate knows the institution and will most likely find out what questions are going to be asked. It is also highly likely that they have friends on the search committee, and that they will have friends present at nearly every step in the interview process. If this person has been relatively quiet and unobtrusive thus far in their career, they might sail through the process pretty easily.

On the other hand, anyone who has dared to take a stand on anything in academia, or who has built successful programs, knows that it sometimes takes nothing more than doing your job well to produce enemies. Jealousy and competitive resentment lurk around many corners within the academy. All it takes is having one such person on the search committee, someone who is vigilant and reasonably believable, and an internal candidate's chances of success could be doomed. Indeed, sometimes people will make sure they get on a search committee because they heard that someone they do not like might apply. Their sole purpose on the committee is to block a particular person's appointment.

An effective search chair will be looking out for this kind of behavior and will try to ferret out biases and assessments not based on the search criteria, but it is not easily done. There may, in fact, be a tendency for interims to be either quickly eliminated or glide through, depending on the preconceived notions of friends or enemies. But all combinations are possible with internal candidates, including being given a fair and unbiased review. On occasion a committee will decide that an internal candidate should be left in the pool to interview as a courtesy to that person, as someone who has spent their career at that university. One would be hard pressed to find this provision in any of the equal opportunity, affirmative action, or search guidelines of any college or university. It is not an appropriate step to take, and sometimes leads to even more hard feelings and resentments than if the committee had simply done everything possible to treat internal candidates no differently than the external candidates. What an external candidate must realize is that they might be walking into a volatile situation without knowing it until they get to the interview. If upon arrival to campus you start noticing strange and/or unusual behaviors—like someone pulling you aside to let you know something "before you hear it from the 'wrong' person," you might be in for an interesting 2–3-day experience.

Four Experience-Based Anecdotes

What follows are four separate situations involving internal/interim candidates. I played a role in each: as an external finalist against an interim; as an internal appointee; as a member of a search committee involving an interim candidate; and as an external candidate interviewing against an internal candidate.

Anecdote #1: But I promised . . .

Somewhat reluctantly, I interviewed at a small Midwestern University. The provost, a quite senior administrator, picked me up at the airport, which is highly unusual. By this time in my short dean position search career, I already had a sense that the issue of internal candidates applying and interims being allowed to apply was important, and had determined that there was an interim in the position for which I was interviewing—hence, the reluctance. So, I asked the provost if the interim was permitted to apply and he somewhat nervously confirmed that the interim was the other finalist. Determined not to be denied, I gave what I still view as the best 2-day interview of my career.

The provost drove me back to the airport, obviously somewhat agitated. He said, "You have really put me in a jam. I have been getting phone calls all afternoon from the faculty to hire you and I have basically promised this position to the interim. There might be other positions open soon, and I hope you will apply." Of course, my first reaction was that I had somehow been sucked into a 1960s episode of the Andy Griffith show. But actually I was nowhere near North Carolina and the year was 2000. We all know that nepotism and favoritism of various sorts still exist in academia, but we rarely find someone in relatively modern times quite so honest about it. I could have made an issue of it, but decided that it was not a good time to exercise my activism. It is important to be able to stay positive and move on.

Anecdote #2: Ghosts from leadership past

In 2004, not long after returning to teaching from my first dean's position, I was asked by a highly regarded colleague to serve as her/his interim associate dean for 2 years, after which (s)he planned to retire. Her/his thinking was that, after the 2 years as Associate, I would be able to apply for her/his position. When I received her/his call I was already beginning a sabbatical that included 6 months in Italy. I was . . . not interested. Her/his college was not the primary college of my discipline and I knew there were some contentious characters in that college—people I had to deal with as a grievance officer a number of years earlier—cases that involved sex discrimination and workplace harassment. (S)he knew I had a reputation for being resilient and tough under stress and (s)he needed that kind of help. I told her/him that appointing me would be welcomed by many, but would most likely also raise objections among some of the people in the college—mostly people who were on the losing side of my grievance work. (S)he said she could handle it and I eventually relented, agreeing to postpone my sabbatical 1 year, with the possibility of serving a second year if all went well. (S)he was happy. I wasn't, but I felt like it was a good thing to do for someone who had served the university well.

The salary was negotiated, my appointment was announced, and there was nothing left to do but wait for the contract. However, instead of a contract I received a very apologetic phone call from my colleague. As I predicted, there were many people delighted at my appointment, but there were also people who were extremely upset—people who had sat across the table from me under uncomfortable circumstances. And as it turns out, the many complements the dean received for appointing me could not mitigate the significance of the threats that were made if my appointment was not reversed. As an active faculty leader on campus I had won the respect of many, but I had also taken the fun out of, and possibly ended, some unfortunate and illegal behaviors. Those people did not forget and came back to haunt me, as I knew they would.

Therein lies the potential fate of an internal candidate. If you have truly been a leader and have had to deal with difficult circumstances, the chances of someone seeing you as an enemy are generally pretty good. On the other hand, if you have not had to take any hard stands to defend what is right for others and the institution your appointment might go smoothly. What is important to realize is that it takes far fewer people to wreck your chances of appointment than it does to support your chances of appointment. In this case my colleague felt badly about asking me to step aside, but I was happy not to have to serve in that position, and blissfully happy to continue my sabbatical in Italy.

Anecdote #3: Bribery and sabotage

Serving on a dean's search committee where the interim dean was a candidate for the permanent position turned into a nightmare. The interim had sufficient time to win the support of the key players in the college, and that was done (whether intentionally or not) through granting positions and distributing resources in a particular way. Unfortunately, it seemed clear that the interim, while a competent person in many ways, did not have the qualifications needed to withstand a national search. There were a number of candidates who had excellent administrative and leadership experiences and who had much more impressive scholarship, fund raising, and grant writing successes as well. But the committee had enough of the interim dean's supporters on it that a compromise was reached to add the interim as a "gratis" extra interviewee (in case the other three finalists all fell flat on their face or refused to accept)—a huge mistake. What happened after that was both amazing and sad. The beneficiary departments sent their members to all of the open forum interviews with the explicit intent of sabotage—that is, of course, except for the interview of the interim.

External candidates were asked impossible questions and were openly ridiculed when they responded. They were questioned heavily as to why they might want to come to that particular university and were told negative things about the campus. I remember driving the number one candidate back to her/his hotel at the end of the second day and (s)he could not contain her/himself. (S)he wanted to know what was going on and I tried my best to put a positive spin on it without telling outright lies. Despite how difficult the faculty of certain departments made the interview, this candidate was head and shoulders above the interim and the entire committee agreed that (s)he should be given the offer. (S)he turned us down based on her/his negative interview experience. The other two candidates received such negative scores on the faculty evaluation forms that the higher administration did not feel comfortable giving either of them an offer—regardless of the Committee's recommendation. By this time, having witnessed overtly unprofessional behavior on the part of certain departmental faculty members, the Committee was prepared to recommend anyone but the interim. Even the interim dean's supporters on the committee were incensed by the behaviors of their colleagues. But it was too late, and the interim was handed the permanent position against the strong objections of the entire search committee.

The important lessons represented by this anecdote are: (1) from an institutional standpoint, do not appoint interims who will apply for the permanent position; (2) from the standpoint of a prospective candidate, if an interim is an applicant for the permanent position put your energy into applying for other positions; and (3) if you are serving on a search committee, and especially if you are chairing one, do not agree to allow "courtesy" candidates to be included for an interview. Follow the criteria as strictly as possible and let the chips fall where they will.

Anecdote #4: A tale of an internal non-interim candidate

When air travel became nearly unbearable in the months following the 9/11/01 destruction of the World Trade Center, I started looking for positions within weekend driving distance of my spouse. Since I was serving as a dean on the east coast, we had been flying halfway across the country to see each other about every 2 or 3 weeks, and it got increasingly difficult with the added airport security and reduced flights. This story is about another small Midwestern University, but it is different than the earlier story in an important way. The "other" finalist was a professor at the university where I was interviewing, but not an interim dean. (S)he was, however, well liked and highly favored by a group of people in the college—some of whom were on the search committee. Because of state funding pressures, the president and provost were looking for a quick appointment and did not want to have to deal with any negotiation problems or squabbles among the faculty.

The interview went quite well until about the middle of the second day when I was interviewed by a small group identified as a curriculum committee that also had two members of the search committee on it. We were eating a box lunch and I was asked one question: "If you had your career to do over what would you want to improve?" While my scholarship record was strong, I responded as honestly as I could and said that I have always taught at universities with heavy teaching loads, but would have liked to be able to do more scholarly work (my scholarly record was actually quite good for that institution). They then turned to each other and engaged in an extended conversation about insider personal and parochial issues that I knew nothing about. They never asked me another question. It literally was as if I was not there.

At dinner that evening with the chair of the committee (a dean), things came together and I could see that, similar to the circumstance where the other candidate was an interim, I had created some confusion about who should be hired. The committee chair wanted to recommend me, but the "curriculum committee" that interviewed me was a filter for the supporters of the internal candidate. Their job was apparently to come up with one piece of negative information that could be used against me in the search committee deliberations. I was vastly more experienced than the other candidate and more qualified. Additionally, I had a very good interview with the exception of that one mysterious session where the faculty members acted as if I was intruding on their lunch.

The odds of being appointed when interviewing against a non-interim internal candidate are not typically as bad as they are when interviewing against an interim candidate. I have interviewed against non-interim internal candidates and have been offered the position. One should not necessarily avoid interviewing against non-interim internal candidates, but should be prepared for unusual events to occur, because it is highly likely that they will.

Other Decanal Search Considerations: Location

Attaining the first dean's position is not typically easy. Hence, location compromises might have to be made if one is serious about moving into administration (Bright & Richards, 2001: 29–30). This is especially true for couples with duel professional careers. It used to be easy for universities to find positions for professional spouses of administrators. If they didn't have a position open they simply created one. Indeed, there was also sometimes a belief that the institution was getting a double benefit by hiring two qualified people, basically out of one search. That is no longer the case. Institutions will promise to "do what we can" but once you sign the contract, that promise weakens a little more each day. Affirmative Action, Equal Opportunity, Human Resource, and collective bargaining requirements most often make appointments of administrators' spouses difficult. Unless your spouse/intimate partner is in a high demand field whereby attaining a job will not be a problem regardless of where you end up, you may be forced to restrict your applications to nearby institutions, or you might be looking at a long-distance commuting relationship. Alternatively, one can apply solely to large cities where the possibilities for one's spouse are much greater than in smaller cities. Both of my positions as a dean involved commutes for my spouse and me: the first 1,400 miles (every 2–3 weeks), and the second 115 miles (every weekend).

Hence, how far an open position is from "home" or a large city could be a deal breaker. This gives the significance of "location" a completely different spin than simply what kind of weather or terrain a person likes. For people with dependent children, commuting is probably not even an option, and thus becoming a dean might not be an option either, unless the intimate partner is ready to give up their career. Protecting retirement programs also becomes a serious consideration at this career stage.

Desirability of "Place" as a Cost

Beyond the logistics of finding a convenient location for your family relationships, places to live have variable desirability levels which affect pool sizes and selection potential. For example, certain parts of Colorado, various locations on the west coast, and New York City will draw large application pools for their open decanal positions. If you are hoping to be a contender for such positions it is extremely important that your background is an airtight fit to the position description. You must also realize that the desirability of the location could become part of your compensation package. In fact, I interviewed at one such university where I was told that they estimated the value of living there to be worth about 15 percent of the dean's salary. I thought they were joking. They weren't. And the cost of living in that area was very high.

Politics

Generally administrators are supposed to keep their politics pretty close to their chest, but the extent to which you experience shared values with those around you is going to be an issue that will affect your relationship with the community in which you find yourself and the university as well. The ideological leanings of the university are extremely important to you as a dean if you expect to have a positive impact on curriculum development. If there is a critical mass of faculty in your prospective college that is simply and clearly incompatible with your values and corresponding priorities, then you are probably not applying to the right place. Your interview will have to be restrained and overly cautious, and if you get the job you will be hitting your head against the wall a great deal of the time. You can never expect the job to be easy—even under the best of circumstances—so why start out with the odds stacked heavily against you. Investigate the writings of the faculty in the college. Take some time to read articles written by key people in the college. Study the courses within some of the most important programs, and be honest with yourself about what you might be getting into and what you can expect to accomplish within the existing environment. If it isn't right for you, scratch it off your list.

Is the campus stable and healthy? Before applying for a position, one might want to do online searches to see if the university has been in the news recently. Are there lawsuits, ongoing problems of racism, sex discrimination claims, corruption charges, sports scandals, and/or financial problems? You may find some stories that will make you pause, especially if they represent a pattern, and particularly if they involve the college you will be leading. In some instances you may be chosen as a finalist because you have skills in the area within which they need to solve their ongoing problem. If they are upfront about that then you need only consider whether that is what you want your mission as a dean to become. Being a dean is not for the faint of heart, but you might have other agendas that you would rather pursue as dean, and being bogged down in the long-term problems of a particular university might not allow that to happen.

When attending an interview, take a good look around. In what condition are the buildings and grounds? How is the morale of the faculty, students, and other administrators? I once interviewed at a campus where it was clear to me that there was a serious deferred maintenance problem, and the morale of the faculty was among the lowest I had ever seen. Faculty and student relations were unusually tense. When I returned home I wrote a long letter to the president explaining my withdrawal from the search. It turned out that my observations were correct: they were having serious financial and personnel problems. I had great respect and affinity for this institution so it was with considerable regret that I withdrew, giving the president the best advice that I could. I suspected it would not help, and about 3 years later the campus, once a vibrant and excellent place of learning, closed. Presidents can sometimes help save failing universities, but deans are not positioned to do that. If the campus is seriously failing, don't go. This situation puts deans in perpetual crisis mode with few, if any, opportunities to create a positive intentional agenda.

Religious-Based Campuses

Don't jump to conclusions when you learn that a university has a religious background. Some colleges and universities are still run by a particular religious group, but do not have much in the way of religious requirements for their administrators and faculty. Some of my experience comes from Catholic campuses. One typically no longer finds much in the position ads about the Catholic background or Catholic expectations of Catholic universities, and that is because they do not want to discourage qualified people of all faiths from applying. Catholic doctrine is alive and well in these institutions and available to people who are Catholic, but it is generally no longer forced on anyone. Typically, more than half of the students and faculty members at these institutions are not Catholic.

Some of the schools run by Catholic religious orders are among the most progressive campuses in the United States. This is especially true of the schools run by the Sisters of St. Joseph of Carondelet and those run by the Jesuits. Each order tends to have its own focus and strengths. The Sisters of the Immaculate Heart of Mary (IHM), for example, are well known for their ability to effectively and efficiently run institutions. They sometimes find themselves in top leadership positions of institutions belonging to other Catholic orders because of their strong organizational and financial management skills. Most, but certainly not all, Catholic colleges and universities have a progressive mission based on principles taken either from Catholic social teaching as developed in a nineteenth-century papal encyclical, or from the work of a particular saint who did good works during their life. Catholic universities have come a long ways on LGBT issues, but continue to struggle with the issue of abortion.

While there are probably more Catholic higher education institutions than of any other one religious denomination (over 250 in the United States), there are also many colleges and universities run by other religious groups. Some are quite progressive, such as those run by the Quakers, and some are likely to be more conservative, such as some of the schools run by Mormons, Southern Baptists, or evangelical talk show hosts. Some church affiliated schools will seek out only "Christian" faculty and administrators—sometimes advertising open positions in Christian journals and other religious outlets. Whatever your interest you can probably find it, but if your target is too specialized it might take some time. For most schools with a religious affiliation it is not critical that the dean be of that religion. It is important, however, that the dean can operate effectively within overt institutionally promoted ideological or religious principles. While these principles may not be forced on anyone, a dean's intentional behavior will hit a brick wall if it is outside of the general canopy within which the campus is housed.

Levels of Status

It is important to be realistic. If you did not have a research-one (R-1) record as a professor it is not likely that you will be a dean at an R-1 University. Faculty search committees looking for a dean are interested in finding someone with a record that matches their culture and expectations. So it would be viewed as a mistake for a committee at a Comprehensive University with a fairly heavy teaching load to interview someone whose background up to that point was from a research oriented, low teaching load institution. They would be concerned that the candidate would not be able to effectively adjust their expectations to meet the needs of the more comprehensive local expectations. The general point being made is simple: look for positions that are compatible with the person you have been as an academic. That is most likely what the search committee is going to be looking for, that is, someone who is consistent with their particular culture and corresponding expectations. The best time to recreate yourself is probably not at the stage where you are moving into administration.

Sometimes higher administrators, provosts and/or presidents, decide to try to change the campus culture. They may be trying to elevate the visibility and status of the institution and want to encourage more scholarly work. So they may specifically charge the committee with the task of finding a dean who is a "cut above" the current campus norm in terms of scholarly productivity. When this is done correctly, the position ad will say something to the effect that the college is looking for a dean who will help move the university toward a higher level of scholarly activity. This kind of change should be done openly and with an understanding that it will involve a gradual transition with faculty members having enough time to adjust without feeling threatened or betrayed. It is under these circumstances that one might find themselves deaning at an institution that is not the same as the one in which they spent their career. This situation is the exception and not the norm.

MAKING THE APPLICATION

University Human Resource Offices have converted to electronic application processes. These electronic forms typically require part of the information from one's Curriculum Vitae (CV) and other relevant documents, with the rest of the materials attached. They create another step, but nothing substantive has changed.

Cover Letter: First Encounter

The first experience the committee members will have with you is your cover letter.[2] Your challenge is to address everything that is in the position announcement in about two-and-a-half pages with twelve point font and near 1 inch margins. If you go beyond three pages you run the risk of losing people. You want the reader to clearly and easily note that you have covered all of the areas identified in the position description. It is likely, if the committee is well chaired, that the committee members will be required to score the candidates on each of the mentioned items. If there are ten items and you miss one of them, you get a zero on that item, and thus you are already automatically at 90 percent without even considering the other scores. If the committee members miss one of the items because you were too verbose (and it could be different items for different members), then your score takes a nose dive. There is no appeal process here. You simply get a letter wishing you well.

The cover letter is supposed to make the reader look forward to reading your CV. If the cover letter is done well then committee members will search the CV for further evidence of what their first impression, the cover letter, told them. If they find information in your CV that enhances and verifies what you say in your cover letter, your scores will most likely go up. On the other hand, if the cover letter appears to be incomplete or done as an afterthought, the reader is likely to spend less time on reviewing the CV to find supporting evidence of your ability to cover the position description items. Some conscientious committee members might try to read the CV more carefully to compensate for what is missing in the cover letter, but that probably won't be the norm. If even one of the committee members is turned off by your cover letter, your application is probably not going to see a lot of daylight.

Trying to be clever or dramatic is not advisable. You want to be as straightforward and professional as possible. Even humor can be tricky. If someone does not get "it" then you might come across as simply looking goofy. You don't want that to happen. There are a lot of straight laced people out there who are easily offended. Don't waste your time applying for deaning positions unless you are prepared to meet those people—not half way—but 100 percent of the way. There might be some space for humor in the interview, but probably very little in the cover letter.

It is also a good idea to let the reader know that you took the time to look something up about the college and the university. This information, gleaned from web searches, might also be worked into your discussion of some of the position items you have to address: such as what you noticed about the diversity of the campus, or what you noticed about the interdisciplinary programs in the college.

Finally, if you reuse parts of your letter for multiple positions, please make certain that all references to the institution have been properly changed for the position at hand. This mistake happens fairly often and you do not want to be the subject of humorous comments at the first search committee meeting.

Curriculum Vitae

One of the most important features of a CV is its organization. Members of deans' search committees, and provosts in particular, are most interested in an applicant's leadership and administrative experience. That information should be up front–right after the educational background (see Bright & Richards, 2001: 39). Use clear bold subtitles. Detail the important leadership and administrative activities in which you engaged. What did you accomplish as chair of the University Curriculum Committee for 5 years . . . more efficient review of proposals, shorter and fewer meetings, initiated an appeal process for departments, and so on? What did you accomplish as chair of a department or director of a program? All of this can be done in bullet form within the appropriate subtitles.

It is important to keep in mind that it is not a faculty position for which you are applying (Buller, 2015). Most deans positions do not allow time for teaching, and some provosts and/or presidents won't permit it. Hence, one does not need to provide much information about their teaching. The committee will need to know that the applicant has been successful as a teacher and toward that end one can give some general summary data, such as stating that one's teaching evaluations have always been within a certain range on a certain scale. If the ad specifically requires demonstrating a history of being a successful teacher, that can be addressed in the cover letter with a comment that data from classes can be provided if the committee requests them. They won't. They just need to make sure that candidates can address their teaching competence. Deans are supposed to be complete role models for newer faculty members and that includes sharing ideas, largely based on experience, about how faculty members might improve their teaching.

How Long Should It Be?

Some people let their CV grow indefinitely so that by the time they apply for a dean's position it might be well over twenty pages. Adjusting and reorganizing your CV for an administrative position will, in itself, add length to your CV. I recommend setting a maximum length for your CV and then following the rule that the only way you can add something is to take something away. Tucker and Bryan (1991: 18) recommended a maximum length of six double spaced pages. Six pages today would stand out as being unusually short. I kept my CV at fifteen pages for approximately the last half of my career. Fifteen is not a magic number and any amount between ten and twenty pages will work. What is important is that your CV looks reasonably well managed and is not overly cluttered with information that isn't as relevant as it once was in light of new developments in your career.

References, Who Should I Ask?

Institutions will ask for anywhere between three and seven references—typically five. It is not advisable to provide more references than the ad requires (Bright & Richards, 2001). The reason for this is simple. The committee is not likely to call all of the references they request. They will come up with some scheme for deciding who gets called, and most likely it will be either following the list top to bottom until someone answers or calling the first two or three on the list until a connection is made or until a certain number of attempts have been made—then moving on to the next name on the list. Your goal is to have the committee only speak to your strongest references. If your strongest references are your required top four and you provided three extras, it is quite likely that at least one of the extras will be called. We all know how busy academics can be. That might end up working against you if the "extra" person does not deliver as strong a recommendation as the others would. You want to make sure the committee will call referees who can effectively communicate their support for you across all of the areas of questioning.

It is never possible to know for certain whether someone will give you a completely positive recommendation, and anything less than that could be the kiss of death. Choose your referees carefully. When you ask them to be a referee don't be bashful about it—ask them straight out whether they think they can give you a completely positive recommendation. Ask them if they have any reservations about your work or anything that you have done. Ask them what they think they might say if asked to identify your greatest weakness, because that is almost certain to be one of the questions—or some variation of it. Don't hesitate to take someone off your list if you have the slightest doubt that they would give you a glowingly positive recommendation. Why is it so important that your references be so positive? It is because the references of your strongest competitors will likely be completely positive. All it takes is one negative comment to give those on the committee who are favoring someone else enough ammunition to have you eliminated. This is where you hear comments like, "Yes, but Reference #3 said his office was messy so he must be disorganized." Or you might hear, "She can't be a good communicator because Reference #4 said she was soft spoken."

Work your reference list carefully. You might have different lists for different types of institutions. For example, if you are applying for positions at private religious schools and public schools, you might want to have clergy on the list for the private school applications, but not necessarily for the public school applications. I agree with Bright and Richards' recommendation of having about ten referees altogether "who can speak in varying combinations depending on the nature of the deanship" (2001: 9). All referees should be people who know the applicant well, and who can thus speak to all of the questions that will be asked—not just one particular area of the applicant's work.

Calls to People Not on the List

Once you are a finalist it is almost certain that calls will be made to people not on the list. Whether these calls are consistent with institutional due process or not won't prevent them from occurring. Finalist lists are made public, and once your candidacy is public information, anything goes. People on the search committee may be calling colleagues they know in the department of their discipline at your college or university. They may call the chair of your department—whether that person is on your reference list or not. Even faculty members who are not on the search committee will be calling their friends at your institution. It is also likely that the provost will be making calls, typically to administrators under whom you have worked. Administrative assistants sometimes call each other to find out how a candidate treats office staff. The president of your campus faculty organization might get a call by someone on the search committee who is in faculty leadership. I received a number of such calls when I was president of the faculty on my campus, and for some time afterward.

At this stage of the game there isn't a lot you can do except hope that your friends really love you and that your enemies hate you enough that they will seize the opportunity to get rid of you by suppressing their true feelings or saying as little as possible. The good news is that there is no systematic way of processing all of this "extra" information that is being collected about you, and most likely 95 percent of it will simply die on the grapevine. However, if key members of the committee come up with something pretty damning, that could hurt you. Otherwise, the most important "extra" information, and the main extra information you need to be concerned about, is what is collected by the provost or president of the institution of your candidacy. They need to know that you will be a manageable team player. The slightest information counter to that will have to be offset by some strong attributes that the provost or president badly needs in a dean, like an ability to help solve specific ongoing personnel disputes, the ability to help diversify the faculty, or the ability to move curricula in a particular direction.

It is a good idea to anticipate the extra calls and, long before you apply for any dean positions, start repairing some of those bridges you burned back when you were a hot headed pup. Remember the colleague you blasted while serving as chair of the University Curriculum Committee? That person is now president of the faculty. And remember the dean you openly pounded on for violating governance procedures? Well, that person was just appointed interim provost. It is important to always be diplomatic about your activism/leadership activities, and to rebuild damaged bridges as quickly as circumstances permit without compromising your integrity.

Professional Search Agencies

I have never contracted with a professional search agency, but I have been contacted by many over the years. In a few instances they have brought me together with institutions and interviews, including one that went as far as an offer. When contacted by a search agency, it is important to remember that they are working for the institution they represent and not necessarily for you. It is up to you to protect your time and yourself in general. The role of the search agency is to perform all of the filtering steps mentioned above, but on behalf of the college or university that has the open position. This process could also work for you, but that is not the actual goal. Search agencies are sometimes faced with getting candidates to places where few people want to go. As stated by Krahenbuhl, "Most commonly, institutions hope that the firm will help to attract a strong pool of applicants" (2004: 9). That is more difficult to do in some locations than in others.

Potential applicants working with a search firm need to be cautious about being oversold on an institution. Generally people who work for search agencies try to be honest, but it is also their job to put a positive spin on a position so prospective applicants will be interested.[3]

The good thing about search agencies is that when contacted by one you can be reasonably sure that there is a truly open position on the other end. Typically institutions will not contract with search agencies if they already have a pretty good idea of who they want in the position. There are exceptions to this principle however. Early in my searching I was pulled into an airport interview by a search firm and it turned out to be a way of providing a second interview for a search where all but the lead finalist dropped out just before the interview stage.

How Many?

Tucker and Bryan (1991) argue that the number of applications sent out should be kept to a minimum—possibly no more than three or four. Their argument is based on the belief that word will get out into the relatively small academic community and it will not look good to have a lot of applications out. While that is a concern at the level of president, it is not likely to be an issue at the dean's level, especially for those seeking their first appointment. While it is important that one chooses positions for which to apply according to the above discussed criteria, it is also important to keep one's CV moving. The core application season runs from about September 1 through the end of March, and seasons are not all the same in terms of opportunities. If it is a good season, one should be able to keep five to seven applications in play at all times—possibly more if positions are truly plentiful. It is helpful to keep a list of the applications that are out and a record of what stage they are in. One might also jot down brief notes about each position, such as their strengths and weaknesses, to remind oneself of the current state of the possibilities.

Universities create a static pool of possible applicants as soon as their position is announced with a closing date. Efforts are sometimes made to avoid closing dates, but that approach can create problems for the search committee. For the applicant, however, the pool of positions is dynamic and thus rolling. Today you might have five applications out, but in 2 weeks you might have eight. In 2 more weeks you might be back to six. The time gap between your applications could be a problem, but ordinarily it is not. The reason it tends not to be a problem is because search committees do not operate at the same rate of efficiency. For my second dean's position I had some very good positions in play when an excellent opportunity emerged. I was reluctant to apply because I was so far along in some of the other searches in which I had a significant interest, having already had phone interviews for a couple that were promising. As it turned out, the search for the newly announced position was chaired by a very astute well-seasoned dean who was able to bring her/his search around the other searches in which I was already a semi-finalist. By the time I started getting campus interview calls for the other positions for which I had applied earlier, I had an offer from the more recently advertised position. I was well situated to actually have choices if I had wanted to slow things down a bit, but I was as interested in accepting the offer as they were to give it me.

HOW IMPORTANT IS "CHANCE"?

While I'm not a great believer in "chance" as a force in the world, I do know enough about search processes to realize that there are many exogenous variables that contribute to whether a person survives a search. You can call it luck or chance if you like, but basically what goes on in a dean's search often times stretches the bounds of sanity. If you have done everything you were supposed to do and you are still eliminated, just remember two important pieces of information: (1) It does sometimes happen that there are people out there who have done even more than you have, and (2) sometimes strange things happen in searches that eliminate the best candidates, of which you could be one.

Number 2 obviously has nothing to do with whether you are qualified, and probably isn't about you at all. It is about some strange bias, fear, prejudice, or misperception that one or more committee member(s) have about you, or about other candidates in the pool. How do they arrive at these erroneous conclusions? It would probably be scary to know. What is most important is that you don't waste time mourning the loss of any one position. It isn't some sort of jinx and it is not necessarily related to the appropriateness or quality of your credentials. Sometimes people of questionable abilities and/or motives make decisions that eliminate, and/or keep, the wrong candidates. Most people on search committees are serious competent people, but all it takes is one or two who are following a different light and the entire search can be derailed. Effective search chairs will try to minimize the likelihood of this happening, but they cannot always be successful. As an applicant you have to expect that this phenomenon will sometimes occur and simply move on.

NOTES

1 Marchese and Lawrence (2006) address a number of the issues covered in this chapter, but from the standpoint of hiring administrators rather than the standpoint of helping someone attain an administrative position.

2 See Krahenbuhl (2004) and Bright and Richards (2001) for additional discussions of the importance of the cover-letter.

3 Bright and Richards (2001) provide a positive view of search firms which tends to be more from the standpoint of the institution than the applicant.

REFERENCES

Buller, J.L. (2015). *The essential academic dean or provost.* San Francisco: Jossey-Bass.

Bright, D.F. & Richards, M.P. (2001). *The academic deanship: Individual careers and institutional roles.* San Francisco: Jossey-Bass.

Crocker, P.L. (2013). The paradox of being an interim dean: The permanent nature of a transitory position. *University of Toledo Law Review*, 44(winter), 319–327. Retrieved July 31, 2016 from http://engagedscholarship.csuohio.edu/cgi/viewcontent.cgi?article=1281&context =fac_articles

Krahenbuhl, G.S. (2004). *Building the academic deanship: Strategies for success.* Westport: Praeger Publishers.

Marchese, T.J. & Lawrence, J.F. (2006). *The search committee handbook: A guide to recruiting administrators.* Sterling, VA: Stylus Publishing, LLC.

Tucker, A. & Bryan, R.A. (1991). *The academic dean: Dove, dragon, and diplomat.* New York: Macmillan Publishing Company.

Vailancourt, A.M. (2012). Were you appointed or anointed? *The Chronicle of Higher Education* (July 5). Retrieved July 31, 2016 from http://chronicle.com/blogs/onhiring/were-you-appointed-or-anointed/32259

Wolverton, M., Gmelch, W.H., Montez, J. & Nies, C.T. (2001). *The changing nature of the academic dean.* New York: Jossey-Bass.

Chapter 3

Getting the Call

There are few moments in my career as exciting as getting that first call from a dean's search committee chair. When the first call occurs it is most likely to let the applicant know (s)he is on a short list and to find out if (s)he is still interested in the position. They may also want to know if it is alright for the committee to start calling references. The "list" at this point could be a list of finalists, a list of semi-finalists, or a fairly long "short" list that the committee is struggling to whittle down to a manageable number. In most instances it will be a semi-finalist list, and the caller will ask for information needed to set up your first phone interview. The first phone interview could be conducted by a full or partial committee with a goal of reducing the remaining candidates down to two to four finalists. Sometimes a second phone interview occurs as an additional filter and possibly to reduce the pool even further.

NON-CAMPUS INTERVIEWS

What to Expect in the Phone Interview

In the phone interview one can expect any number of a long list of possible questions. Here are some of the more common question issues a candidate should be ready to address:

CHECKLIST:

1. Examples of most important leadership experiences
2. Most difficult decision
3. Procedure for cutting a budget
4. Approach used for budgeting
5. Example of a decision you made against your own personal interests
6. How to handle a decision where the faculty and higher administration disagree

7. Why you want to be a dean
8. Why you are interested in *this* university
9. Opinion about some aspect of their curriculum
10. Where higher education is heading
11. Identification of future growth areas within the college
12. Principles you believe should be used in college resource distribution
13. Principles you believe should be used in making promotion and tenure decisions/ recommendations
14. Your view on merit pay
15. Your view on collective bargaining and/or tenure
16. How you would make decisions to distribute merit pay
17. How you would handle a particular "hypothetical" situation
18. Identify an area where you need to improve
19. What you see as your long term career plans
20. Questions you have of the committee.

Some of these issues will be addressed later in this book. However, many of the corresponding questions have no actual "correct" answer, and might also be politically charged. Under those circumstances, your challenge is to give an answer that will allow each person on the committee to hope/expect that you might follow what they, each committee member, believe is the correct response. That means answering in a way that leaves openings for different behavioral possibilities. On the other hand, being vague can cost you points as well. It is sometimes helpful and generally safe to give different responses for different scenarios. That way you are demonstrating your flexibility and willingness to look at all sides of a situation. For example, budget cutting can be done differently if the amount to be cut is large than if the amount to be cut is small. It is also generally a good idea to include consultation with your chairs and other administrators as part of your discussion about your decision-making process.

Whatever the questions and your corresponding answers it is extremely important to remember that there are most likely people on the committee who have already made up their minds about you one way or the other, and to those who already oppose you it is possible that nothing you say will be considered in your favor. That is, there is always some way to twist a response around to make it seem negative. On the other hand, you would not be experiencing the interview if there were not people who supported your application. Your most important job is to not let those people down. They need credible evidence to take to the next search committee meeting that justifies why they ranked you high in the first place. Give them something with which to work: some enthusiasm; some sharp quick crisp answers; be thoughtful at times, but without belaboring; be consistent with what you have provided in your application; and be sure to have done your homework.

Homework

What are the current trends in higher education and higher education administration? Do some reading on these issues. What are some of the interesting characteristics of the university to which you have applied? Go beyond the information provided in the announcement. What are the programs of the college you would be administering and what are some of the important issues related to those various curricula? Surprise the committee with what you have noticed and be prepared to comment on particular courses or program idiosyncrasies within the college. The more work you do early on, the less work you will have to do when it comes time for the in-person interview if you are fortunate enough to get that call.

If things are going well you will eventually be in a position to turn down phone interviews. Do not hesitate to pull out of a search if you have other interviews coming up that are more important to you. These are decisions you can only make once you see how well you are doing in the position arena, which is not just determined by your background, but also the backgrounds of the pool of prospective deans who are your competitors. It is also determined by the field of positions at that particular time. There are good dean position seasons and bad ones—most likely affected by the economy and a host of other unknown variables.

Greatest Weakness

The search process is designed so that candidates can be eliminated at any step along the way based on accurate "negative" information.[1] So it is likely that you and/or your references will encounter a question like: "Everyone has weaknesses, and thus everyone has a greatest weakness, so what is yours?" If you or any of your referees answer that question candidly and in an unqualified manner, you had better make sure that all of the other candidates' and their referees do the same. Of course, we all know that we cannot be sure of how that question is being handled by others, so our best option, unfortunately, is to "avoid" it. A referee might simply say, "I cannot think of any weaknesses that are relevant to the successful execution of this position." This is an honest answer if the referee truly believes in the person being recommended, and one probably shouldn't be recommending someone in whom they lack confidence.

It is, however, difficult for a candidate, to make the above claim. Hence, an alternative is to turn a possible negative into a positive. For example, one might say their greatest weakness is simply the flip side of their greatest strength, and follow with an explanation that would be difficult to construe as negative: "I like to do things thoroughly and with maximum accuracy so I might sometimes take a little longer to complete a project than someone who likes to move quickly. However, I generally compensate for this tendency by starting earlier and putting in more hours than most other people in the same position." Anyone listening to this response might jot down, "candidate is slow." But that would not be an honest interpretation of what was said and others could correct that interpretation easily: "What the candidate said is that (s)he likes to be accurate and thorough and (s)he is willing to put in the extra time to make that happen."

OK, It's Your Turn to Ask

It is generally considered rude for a committee to not give a candidate an opportunity to ask questions. The irony of the great importance placed on this part of the process is that during the phone interview the committee does not really want you to ask a lot of relevant questions. Most likely they have another interview lined up shortly after yours and would like to have a few minutes to catch their breath before proceeding to the next candidate. When a candidate, during a phone interview, starts asking a lot of detailed questions that require long answers, committee members start getting nervous and start making their answers somewhat cryptic. Eyes start rolling in exasperation.

On the other hand, it is important that you ask something—lest you be viewed as disinterested. So the most advisable response to the opportunity to ask questions is to affirm that you do have many questions, but that for now you would simply like to know X. And X should be something low key and yet revealing of your interest and knowledge of the institution/college. For example, you might say something like, "I noticed that the institution's enrollment has been fluctuating over the last 5 years. Is there an official interpretation of these data that would explain what is happening?" Typically what will be taking place after a question like that is committee members silently gesturing to each other to answer the question, since possibly nobody really knows the answer. They might not have known the enrollments fluctuated over the last 5 years if you had not mentioned it. Under those circumstances, someone will probably give you a made-up answer and the committee will be grateful that you will not be asking more questions at that time. There will probably be some joking about it, and you can thank them for the interview and say that you look forward to meeting them in person and asking more questions if given the opportunity to visit the campus. Thus you have shown that you have done some homework, that you are interested in the welfare of the university, and that you are a person who is sensitive to the importance of data. It is also possible that fluctuating enrollments are an important issue on that campus and that someone on the committee can speak directly, and with authority, to your question. It is a positive outcome either way. Generally, it is good practice to keep both your answers and your questions relatively short and to the point.

At the end of an interview you may be exhausted, but hopefully you will also feel pretty good about yourself. One is sometimes inclined to rehash every question and wish they had said something else. It is valuable to learn from an interview so that you might be better prepared for the next, but don't waste time beating yourself up over what you did or did not say in the interview that is now over. Your challenge now is to get ready for the next phone call.

Airport Interviews

Airport interviews are a way for the committee and sometimes certain administrators to see how you handle yourself in person without the expense and time commitment of a full on-campus interview. It is also a less public phase of the search process. In many respects it is like a video interview and serves the same purposes—albeit it could be argued that seeing someone in person is more tangible and authentic than seeing someone on a screen. Airport interviews are another filtering step that is probably used more often for provost and presidential searches than dean searches—although it does sometimes occur in dean searches. The airport interview is somewhat of a tease. Here you are all dressed up and ready to go, but you are somehow quarantined to an airport terminal.

Video Conference Interviews

A more humane and efficient alternative to the airport interview is the video conference interview where you arrange to meet the committee via a high-speed broadband audio-video telecommunications system. Both you and the committee are in rooms with big screens in each of your respective locations. A cost-benefit analysis comparing the video conference with the airport interview would pretty much eliminate the airport interview forever, but airport interviews are still used, and in the search for a dean's spot one must be ready for just about anything. If you are called for an airport interview and you have any doubts about whether you would accept an offer from that particular university, my advice is to not go.

On the other hand, video conference interviews can be quite enjoyable for both the candidate and the committee. The key to effective video conference interviewing is to behave exactly as you would if you were sitting around the table with the search committee. Don't do anything you wouldn't do if the committee was there in the room with you because, in effect, they are there with you. Sit up straight and look around at each of the committee members on the screen. Each person needs to feel as though you are talking to them.

Regardless of the phase of the search process, and which type of interview you are experiencing, the set of possible questions remains basically the same—albeit corporate Human Resource offices are increasingly recommending asking "off the wall" questions in interviews just to see how prospective employees handle themselves in ambiguous situations. It might take a while for that practice to catch on in academia, if it ever does. Notwithstanding, your goal is to make a positive enough impression that you will make the cutoff for the finalist list, thereby earning a call for a campus interview.

THE CAMPUS INTERVIEW

Sometimes committee members will do everything they can during the phone interview to let you know that you are a highly ranked candidate, which leads you to anticipate that you will be getting another call. On other occasions the call for the campus interview might be a total surprise. You thought you blew a couple of the phone interview questions and the committee didn't seem all that receptive to your responses. Yet, here you are, being invited to the campus. However it happens, the invitation to campus typically means that you are one of two to four candidates that theoretically have a fresh start in attaining the sought after dean's position. In some respects the campus visit means the same thing that your campus visits for faculty positions meant: you are a finalist, all evaluation meters are supposed to be reset to zero so that all finalists have an equal chance from this point onward, and it is the job of both you and the institution to impress one another.

Of course we know from our earlier discussions about interims and internal candidates that it is not always possible, and probably unlikely, that all finalists will have the same chance of being selected for the position. It is difficult for committee members to let go of their rankings—whatever the bases for those rankings.

Accepting the Interview: Recency and Primacy Effects

Before further discussing the campus interview content, it is important to mention the process of accepting the interview. There are two important issues to consider: (1) whether this is an interview you actually want to attend—given the expenses, and given other opportunities you may have; and (2) if you do accept the interview, when should you agree to go.

The first question was answered, for the most part, in Chapter 2 in discussing the application process. Since new information periodically emerges, the same issues related to applying for a position must be continually revisited to determine whether one should continue with a particular search. Unless your goal is simply collecting frequent flyer miles, if the odds of accepting a position become low and you have other interviews, you may want to focus your energy elsewhere.

In response to the second question, if you decide to accept the interview you might want to be strategic about when you will agree to go. Search chairs should work to minimize the interview order effect as best they can. The research on the relevance of interview order among candidates is mixed, with the early research showing that interviewing last increases ones chances significantly (recency effect) and the more recent research refuting that position. The notion that interviewing first gives one an advantage is referred to as the primacy effect. Zackal (2015) provides a good summary of this issue and corresponding findings. Given the conflicting evidence, one must choose to either ignore the issue altogether or pick a preferred argument: is it recency or primacy that most influences the candidate selection process? While space limitations prevent addressing all of the arguments herein, candidates might do well to investigate this issue and act accordingly. My observations have led me to be most concerned about the recency effect, whether as a committee chair or as a candidate. Interviews for dean's positions can be pretty grueling. Whatever candidates decide regarding this matter, it is important that they make sure they are not disadvantaged by the interview schedule. Whether one wants to interview earlier or later might also be impacted by whether one has had, or expects to have, other interviews. Keeping interviews close together increases one's chances of having more than one offer to entertain.

Attending the Interview

Campus interviews for dean's positions are seldom less than 1.5 days. The longest interview I had was 3 days, but typically they are 2 relatively full days. The night before your first full day of interviewing you will typically fly into a major city within a couple hours' drive of the campus, and be met at the airport by a search committee member. If the search chair is careful, (s)he will want to pick up and return all the candidates in order to make sure they are all given the same treatment. Search committees want to assure that all candidates are given a positive greeting and leave on a positive note. As a candidate, that is what you should expect and if you receive anything different you should ask yourself, and possibly the search chair, why that was the case. Since you are going to be picked up by someone from the search committee, you will want to make sure that you look nice upon arrival. Your arrival attire can be casual, but not too casual.

It is common that someone, usually the search chair, will take you to dinner the night that you arrive and brief you on what to expect over the next couple of days. There may have been some last minute changes in the schedule that was sent to you in advance. This is also where you are likely to hear about some surprises that they don't really want to be surprises—someone on the committee read your book and thinks you are too quantitative—the provost is a bit absent minded—they forgot that the students are on study break for midterms and there might not be anyone at the scheduled student session—one of the faculty members is obsessed with budgeting theory and will undoubtedly ask you several questions in the open faculty session—you are likely to sense some hostility from certain faculty members who feel they have not been treated fairly—the president is typically late and sometimes doesn't show up for his/her appointments and so on. Your challenge is to not appear to be surprised or derailed in any way by anything that is said. Take it all in stride as if it is normal because, as all academics should know . . . it is normal. These things happen on college campuses and you need to be ready for anything, especially when you arrive for an interview.

You will want to eat heartily during this meal because it might be the last time you will be permitted to do so. The search chair will be doing most of the talking and you will not be asked a lot of questions. That changes the next day when the formal interview begins, and typically all of your meals will be part of the interview process, thereby involving a lot of questions. It is not a bad idea to have some nutritional snacks with you that you can retrieve during any breaks you might have. It would be foolish for you to expect to enjoy your meals, but some campuses actually do make sure that candidates enjoy that part of the interview process in order to enhance the "guest's" overall experience, especially if they are proud of the restaurants in their community or possibly even their campus food service. The more positive the experience of the candidate, the more likely it is that the candidate will want to accept the position. It is amazing how many institutions fail to appreciate this simple fact. They spend a lot of money and time to bring someone to their campus seemingly so they can mistreat them. Your job as a candidate is to sort all of that out and stay focused on what is most important to you.

How to Dress

There are different opinions about how a candidate should look when interviewing for a dean's position. Some believe that you should look scholarly and professorial. Others argue that you should look comfortable and casual. I believe you should look as sharp as possible. If you don't have a couple of nice suits (female or male), buy them. If you are serious about getting a dean's position you could end up spending a lot of money on clothes since you will want to have at least two notably attractive well-fitted outfits for your interviews. Getting nice clothes for your interview provides you with part of the relatively expensive wardrobe you will need once you have settled into your first deaning job. As a dean it will be important for you to command as much respect as possible from all of the constituents that you encounter. Looking sharp gives you an edge of respect that you might not attain otherwise, and sometimes that slight edge is all you need to prevail in a particular situation. This issue is especially important for candidates who aspire to the intentional dean model, a model that puts being an effective leader above being a good soldier—albeit deans must expect to receive and follow "orders" from higher administrators.

It all starts with the interview. There have been books written about dressing for success and an article recent to this writing appeared in the Wall Street Journal (Smith, 2016). The goal is to look especially nice by relatively normative standards—however you can make that happen. A candidate doesn't want to be self-conscious about how they look when visiting a campus. It doesn't matter how big or small a person is, or how they are shaped, making sure clothes are of high quality and fit well is very important. For men the tendency is to wear a fairly dark suit with a white shirt and tie. That is not necessarily the best option today.

Shirts that have some color to them and ties that were not purchased for a funeral bring some life to the moment and make a candidate stand out. Looking professional does not necessarily mean looking drab. This is the candidate's chance to make an impression. Looking exceptionally ordinary might not be the best route to that goal.

Differences in Dress for Women and Men

Men are more fortunate than women when it comes to finding an appropriate wardrobe for a dean. Men's suits have some important variations but generally that is the only reasonable option for men—a suit. Women, on the other hand, can wear a suit, a dress, or simply a blouse and skirt. Women's suits can have a skirt or pants, and sometimes they can be purchased with both.

Dress in academic administration is still gendered and racially/ethnically biased. If anyone thinks that sex discrimination no longer exists, they are probably from another planet. The more a woman can mitigate that effect, the better her chances of being hired, however unfortunate that circumstance might be. Hence, a suit is probably the best option for a woman. In addition to her choice of clothing, it seems that short, crisp, and tailored looking hair is one of the means by which women administrators may try to conform to traditional Western male appearance codes.

On the other hand, it is important for men to appear non-threatening to other men. Male candidates want to look fairly traditional, but not intimidating. The last thing you want to do is frighten anyone by your appearance. There are also ethnic stereotypes that can come into play. Despite dressing sharp in well-fitting clothing, as the son of immigrants from Southern Italy with corresponding physical features, I would occasionally receive godfather references and other related comments about my appearance—by colleagues who probably spend too much time watching television.

A "harder" appearance requires a softer demeanor and a "softer" appearance requires a harder demeanor. What is meant by harder and softer in this case is whether one has a physically strong and/or forceful appearance or whether one's self presentation seems reticent and/or reserved. One can deny that looksism, racism, and sexism still exist, but that will not help an applicant, who might be affected by those isms, get the job (s)he would like.

The First Day

Candidates are usually met bright and early for breakfast, sometimes as early as 7 AM, and this meal will probably take place in the hotel in which the candidate is staying. While not always the case, it is possible that this first activity on your first full day is an important part of the interview. The person(s) who has breakfast with the candidate could be someone from the committee or the search chair who is simply charged with making sure the candidate gets breakfast and is successfully brought to campus. It sometimes happens, however, that general scheduling difficulties leave this time slot for someone like the provost, a dean who cannot make the meeting later in the day, or possibly the president, who is on his/her way out of town. Presidents are not always part of the interview process for deans, but they sometimes are. It is important to remember that the dean technically works at the pleasure of the president—albeit a dean might not have much actual interaction with the president during the regular performance of their job.

As with all meals during the interview, it is important to try to eat as much of the meal as possible without being rude or without avoiding the many questions people have. It is not likely that the candidate will be able to finish any of the meals. Breakfast is important, so one might best order something that is sustaining and easy to eat. Candidates don't know when they will be able to eat sufficiently throughout the interview, so it is a good idea to have a plan that keeps one's blood sugar and general disposition relatively stable.

Once the interview schedule begins, the candidate experiences a whirlwind of interviews that will be over in a flash. Each interview will be approximately 50 minutes to an hour, depending on how much time is left to get from one interview to another. There may be glitches in the scheduling process that will leave the candidate with some brief breaks. These are bathroom and nutrition bar opportunities. Candidates should consider having a low sugar nutrition bar available.

Remember the Questions?

During the campus interview, candidates can expect some version of the same questions they were asked during the phone interview. Some of the questions will be asked more than once and the candidates' task is to provide consistent (non-contradictory) content while at the same time showing refreshed interest and vigor in their responses. The tendency is to do the opposite, saying something like: "Well, as I said in response to this question yesterday and again this morning . . . " And then the candidate might go into an apologetic, short, and wanting version of the same response given previously. That is a mistake. It is important to face each question as if it is the first time you heard it and give it a fresh and more interesting twist each time.

Candidates shouldn't think of questions strictly in terms of a specific set of possible answers from which they must choose. Yes, whoever asks the question does have a preferred answer in mind, and there are probably other possible answers that would be perceived as negative. This is true even during the Search Committee interview where the questions are predetermined and approved by the committee members. Candidates should think of each question as successful politicians think of questions: an opportunity to say something about themselves that they want others to know. It isn't sufficient to simply give a pat answer to a question. A dynamic candidate uses their response to each question, no matter how many times it has been asked, as a vehicle to carry some important message about them and their accomplishments that they have not yet had an opportunity to convey, or that they would like to reemphasize.

While they probably won't occur often, it is important to be prepared for unusual questions designed specifically to catch one off guard and see how one handles her/himself under such circumstances. Open faculty forums are the most likely place where such questions will occur. They could be questions related to your published work, but asked in a way intended to provoke rather than elicit an answer. In other words, you might find yourself being baited in some way. Since such questions rarely directly address qualifications necessary to be an effective dean, it is sometimes best to initially handle them with a non-answer, or possibly another question, that shows some quick wit and a little humor. These situations can be tricky so you need to give yourself a few seconds to shape an answer, whether it is to the question you were asked or one of your own, that will show you are well informed and reasonable.

Who Are the Players?

The configuration of interviews candidates encounter during a campus visit varies from institution to institution. There are, however, some core players that candidates should expect to meet sometime during their interview. Of course, there is the Search Committee, which is usually made up of a representative from each department within the college you will serve and a staff person from the Dean's Office. There may also be students appointed to the committee. The search committee will typically be chaired by a dean from another college. The dean chosen to chair the Search Committee could be significant in some important way and candidates might want to look up that person's background. It could tell candidates something about the kind of person the provost is looking for to fill that particular position. What kinds of works has this person published, and how does this person compare with your interests and background? Candidates usually meet with the search committee twice: once early the first day and then again as part of an exit interview on the last day.

There will most likely be a separate interview scheduled with the Dean's Office staff. Candidates must not underestimate the importance of this meeting. Since these are people with whom the dean will be working every day, they have a substantial investment in who is hired. They will, understandably, use whatever influence they have, which could be considerable, to make sure candidates they perceive to be unsupportive or unappreciative of their rolls are not selected. In addition to the Dean's Office staff a candidate might be interviewed by the current dean, depending on the circumstances. If the sitting dean is leaving under positive circumstances, you will most likely interview with this person. Likewise, if the interim dean is truly an interim and nothing more, (s)he might also be on the schedule. If the interim dean is returning to the faculty this will be an important interview since this is someone with whom you will have to work in the future.[2]

In addition to a meeting with the dean of that college, there will be a meeting with all of the deans of the university. There will also be a meeting with all of the department chairs, some of whom will be on the search committee. These meetings are typically pretty uneventful unless there is a contentious issue simmering—like the issue of a preferred candidate. That does not mean these interviews are not important. The chairs and other deans will be working with the new dean on a regular basis and have a lot at stake. The provost will most likely take recommendations from the existing deans pretty seriously.

The provost will most likely interview the candidate the first day and then might take her/him to dinner or lunch one of the days thereafter. As suggested above, it is possible that the president will want to meet the candidate, but that is not always the case. If the president has a lot of confidence in the provost, an interview might not be considered necessary—particularly since presidents are off campus a lot with their fund raising and political activities. Keep in mind that each candidate is supposed to have exactly the same arrangement, and scheduling higher administrators for all three or four finalists for two dean's searches that might be taking place at about the same time could be a logistical nightmare.

Interview the Provost

When visiting a campus candidates are doing more than simply interviewing for a job. They are trying out the campus and seeing how they might fit there. They are, in effect, interviewing the campus. One of the most important parts of the campus interview is the interview of the provost. One shouldn't be afraid to think of it that way. Candidates should not let the provost pick them; they should pick the provost. It is appropriate to ask others direct questions about the provost. What is her/his management style, how does (s)he behave under pressure, does (s)he accept blame for her/his own mistakes, and so on? Is this a provost that will support your efforts to be an intentional dean, a dean who is unafraid to take risks and promote positive change?

One can ask direct questions of the provost as well. What are the provost's priorities and how does the dean factor into those priorities? Candidates can contact people at other campuses where the provost previously worked. How was this person as a dean? What kind of job did they do and so on? Deaning is a stressful job even when all goes well. One should not accept a position if there is a good chance they are going to be subjected to unnecessary discomfort. The provost can have a significant effect on a dean's life. They can also have significant control over a dean's ability to leave if that dean doesn't have previously arranged options.

Assessing the Interview

By the time the last campus interview session is over it is likely that a candidate will have a pretty good idea of what their chances are of getting the job. That isn't always the case, but it is more often than not. Part of that "good idea" is governed by how well the candidate feels (s)he did in the various interview sessions, which is not completely under the candidates' control. Those doing the interviewing will sometimes give pretty strong signals in various ways that might either help or hurt a candidate in the interview. If there is a lot of controversy on the campus about this position candidates might receive mixed signals, and sometimes that isn't bad. Candidates might be able to adjust to these signals or possibly inquire as to why they are occurring.

If a candidate doesn't receive a call from anyone within a couple of weeks of the last candidate being interviewed, it is likely that someone else has been made an offer and the institution is waiting for a response or trying to negotiate an agreeable salary and other terms of employment. There is no shame in being the third ranked of the three candidates. One typically starts as one of twenty-five to sixty candidates, depending on the school/college and the nature of the institution. It is often the case that the first choice candidate or first and second choice candidates will not accept the position. If it is still early in the season, they may be holding out for what they believe could be a better offer somewhere else.

Whether the call comes within 2 weeks of the last interview or a month afterwards, if it is from the provost it will most likely be an offer. While some provosts will also make the negative calls, that task is sometimes relegated to the search chair. It is also the case that candidates sometimes simply receive a letter along with everyone else who was not selected. When the provost calls, (s)he may want to meet with the candidate again before actually going into the details of the offer.

MAKING THE DECISION

Anticipating the possibility of getting an offer, it is important for a candidate to decide whether this institution is the right one. In addition to the issues discussed above and in Chapter 2, there are some interview experiences that will help candidates decide whether they would accept an offer from a particular university. One such experience is the open faculty forums, which are among the most important parts of the campus interview. They sometimes reveal important divisions among the faculty, and they often let candidates know what some of the most serious problems are on the campus. For example, if a candidate is asked questions about how they would handle pay disparities, or how they would handle harassment complaints, or how they would handle grade inflation, these are all telling questions and probably represent broader discussions taking place on that campus. It is a good idea to follow those questions with a few questions of one's own—if not during that session, during the exit interview with the committee or during the interview with the provost.

As candidates go from one interview session to another, how have the people seemed? Are there signs of vitality in their gait and in their greetings, or are there signs of low morale? Are there signs of enthusiasm and joy at this institution? If it is clear that part of the new dean's job will be to somehow bring enthusiasm and joy to their college, candidates need to know that up front and have a pretty clear sense of how it could be done—or if it is even within the realm of possibility. A new dean does not want to be set up for failure. (S)he wants to have the best chance possible of being successful.

Negotiating the Contract

It is advisable to not show too much emotion in any particular direction when first receiving an offer. The salary and other conditions of employment still need to be negotiated. The offeree may want to let the provost know they are pleased to receive the offer, but they may also want to maintain the composure of a serious negotiator. It is important to ask for sufficient time to think about the offer. While an offeree doesn't want to appear to be unreasonable, it is important to think carefully about what will be needed to do the job and not be afraid to ask for it.

If there are other possible interviews or offers in the works, offerees shouldn't be afraid to ask for more time. The offeree might let the provost know that (s)he is interviewing, or has interviewed at other institutions, but that if X, Y, and Z are included in the offer (s)he will drop out of the other searches immediately. The provost will most likely try to accommodate the offeree unless the requests are outside the range of what is possible for that particular institution—and there are institutional/system parameters that are sometimes difficult to transcend. Even under those circumstances the provost can request special permission from the system office to go beyond the system parameters based on factors like previous administrative experience.

IMPORTANT ISSUES TO CONSIDER BEFORE SIGNING

Taking a Leave

Many institutions have an administrative or general leave clause in their faculty operating manual or their faculty collective bargaining contract. Offerees should find out if the institution in which they are currently working has such a contractual provision and apply for it. One is well advised to request as long a leave as the policy permits. An offeree might feel like (s)he never intends to return, but that might not be how (s)he is feeling 6 months into the new job, or possibly 2 years later. One should always take the leave if available. It is foolish to give up hard earned rights. Having some protection gives a new dean the ability to act with more assertiveness for the faculty and students of their college.

Tenured Full Professor

Being appointed dean as a tenured full professor gives one equal status with the most advanced faculty members and allows one to feel freer to take risks as needed—for the faculty, students, or for the institution. Being appointed with full professorship may require a separate interview with, and subsequent approval from, a department. Departments are not likely to reject candidates, but not being accepted within the department does not mean the dean cannot continue to claim her/his full professorship status earned at the dean's previous institution. If there is any doubt that the department will approve full professorship status for the dean, it might be strategically best to withdraw the request.

It is not advisable, however, to accept a dean's position without tenure or a leave of absence from a previous position. Some institutions do not grant tenure to deans. Neither of the institutions for which I was a dean allowed deans to have tenure, which made the leaves of absence I attained even more critical. At the first institution there was ambivalence on the part of both the faculty and the administration to grant tenure to deans. In my last year there I was able to convince both the administration and the faculty that they were making a mistake. My primary argument was that the administration would continue to have difficulty recruiting good deans (since not all institutions provide leaves of absence for their faculty), and the faculty would not have deans that could be strong advocates for them when they most needed it.

At the institution of my second deanship, where there was a formal collective bargaining agreement, tenure for deans was prevented primarily by the faculty. Because of the protections provided by collective bargaining the faculty didn't feel it needed strong deans, and the administration was not willing to offer anything sufficiently tempting for the faculty to relent. While candidates from within the system can retain their faculty tenure through an administrative leave, external hires cannot be given tenure. This policy reduces greatly the ability of the institution to hire strong outside dean candidates. Recent research has demonstrated the significance of having a dean who can support the faculty and the college/school programs (Hoffman, 2016; Dowling & Melillo, 2015; Wilkes, Cross, Jackson, & Daly, 2015).

Other Items to Negotiate

There are other possible issues to consider that may or may not enter into the negotiation, such as office space, the college budget, and staff support. How important is it to have assistant/associate deans? How big is the college? What is the provost expecting from the dean and how will the dean make time to comply? Offerees should pay attention to the position percentage breakdown of the dean's primary activities and make sure it is consistent with their strengths and interests. One should pay particular attention to the percentage of time that is designated for fundraising, since that is a growing expectation of deans. Do the dean's responsibilities require someone to take on some parts of the college operation to give the dean more time for fundraising, as the provost and/or president have indicated they would like the dean to do?

When thinking about requesting additional support, it is important to think carefully about the kind of help that will be needed. This decision will, in part, depend on how many faculty members and how many departments there are in the college. What are the expectations placed on the dean from above and what are the dean's greatest strengths? If the offeree is comfortable and efficient in doing all of the typical deaning tasks, an assistant dean might be advisable over an associate. Assistants can come from a wider range of backgrounds and can be hired for a wider range of skills—typically at a lower cost than associates. Associates are more likely to be faculty members aspiring to be deans, and that alone can sometimes be problematic. If the college has more than 100 faculty members and is reasonably complex, the dean should probably have at least 1 assistant and 1 associate dean. Larger colleges sometimes have more, especially if the dean has heavy fundraising responsibilities.

Will the dean need her/his own development officer? Does the office need another administrative assistant? These are all issues that should be addressed before signing the contract because that is when offerees have the best chance of getting what they will need. It is important to realize, however, that the provost will not want to give one dean a great deal more than what other deans in the university have. So it is advisable to have a good understanding of what the current practices are at the university and adjust one's requests accordingly. There is a fine line between raising the bar a little relative to decanal resources and drawing resentments (especially from other deans) that might more than offset the value of what one has gained by making heavy demands. It is, of course, also possible to negotiate oneself out of an offer. Hence, it is important to negotiate with finesse, carefully differentiating deal breakers from soft "demands."

CONGRATULATIONS!

Once you've accepted the position and your contract has been signed, treat yourself to a shopping spree and buy yourself a new wardrobe. You are now on your way to Pleasant Valley University. Congratulations! But now what?

NOTES

1 Krahenbuhl (2004: 8–9) distinguishes between searching by recruitment or by screening. Some campuses use a combination of the two, but it seems that most use a screening approach.

2 For a valuable discussion of the issue of working with a former dean see Ryan (2014). In an interview with a former dean you might want to try to get a sense of what it will be like to work with that person afterwards, as well as any information you can attain about the current dean's budget and the current provost.

REFERENCES

Dowling, J.S. & Melillo, K.D. (2015). Transitioning from departments to schools of nursing: A qualitative analysis of journeys by ten deans. *Journal of Professional Nursing*, 31 (6), 464–474. Retrieved September 11, 2016 from www.sciencedirect.com.libproxy.stcloudstate.edu/science/article/pii/S8755722315000538

Hoffman, D.E. (2016). The importance of including the dean. *The Journal of Law, Medicine & Ethics*, 44 (Suppl.), 81–86. Retrieved September 11, 2016 from http://eds.a.ebscohost.com.libproxy. stcloudstate.edu/eds/pdfviewer/pdfviewer?vid=2&sid=645c4cd7-2d58-4553-9a7f-4dbb8675ecf2%40sessionmgr4008&hid=4208

Krahenbuhl, G.S. (2004). *Building the academic deanship: Strategies for success*. Westport: Praeger Publishers.

Ryan, K. (2014). Working with a former dean, in L.L. Behling (Ed.). *The resource handbook for academic deans* (pp. 51–55). San Francisco: Jossey-Bass.

Smith, R.A. (2016). Why dressing for success leads to success. *Wall Street Journal*. Retrieved February 23, 2016 from www.wsj.com/articles/why-dressing-for-success-leads-to-success-1456110340

Wilkes, L., Cross, W., Jackson, D. & Daly, J. (2015). A repertoire of leadership attributes: An international study of deans of nursing. *Journal of Nursing Management*, 23 (3), 279–286. Retrieved September 11, 2016 from http://eds. a.ebscohost.com.libproxy.stcloudstate.edu/eds/pdfviewer/pdfviewer?vid=3&sid=645c4cd7-2d58-4553-9a7f-4dbb8675ecf2%40sessionmgr4008&hid=4208

Zackal, J. (2015). Is it better to interview first or last? *HigherEdJobs*. Retrieved February 14, 2016 from www.higheredjobs.com/articles/articleDisplay.cfm?ID=662

Chapter 4

Teach Me My Job, Andrea

We can pretend it isn't so, but we are only fooling ourselves. When we walk into an office for the first time, an office we have not run before, what we don't know most likely far outweighs what we do know. Hence, it should not have come as a surprise to my secretary and office manager (both the same person) when I walked in on the first day of my first deaning position and said, "OK Andrea, teach me my job." One can pretend they don't really need to be taught anything and fake their way in hopes that osmosis will eventually take over, but there are far more interesting ways of making a fool of oneself. By being honest and forthright with one's staff, it is possible to establish a working relationship that, especially in the early stages, depends heavily on the staff's acute awareness of the timelines, deadlines, and the idiosyncrasies of that particular office. As a result of quickly learning these important behavior patterns, it is then possible to more quickly take advantage of one's own skills and thus operate more effectively and efficiently.

At a small to medium-sized university it is possible for the dean (in my case a dean who supervised 90 percent of the faculty on campus) to survive with one staff person if that person is as efficient a worker as Andrea. (S)he kept her/his office area immaculately clean and orderly at all times. (S)he almost never got behind in her/his work, and often still had time to read a novel, which would have been a concern if (s)he had not been so amazingly effective . . . and paid so poorly. Getting her/him a raise was extremely difficult and even then the pay was still lower than it should have been given her/his effectiveness.

There was an assistant dean's position in some faraway location handling mostly student affairs work, so it was literally just Andrea and me running the college. Whatever the existing arrangement when you arrive for your first deanship, it is wise to take advantage of the knowledge of those who have been working in that office. It can be done in a positive way without loss to your self-esteem or authority.

This chapter is about what deans are expected to do. The sooner one learns the basic protocol of her/his office, the easier these tasks will be. The expected behaviors of a dean will vary somewhat across universities, but there is also a considerable amount of overlap. The information of this chapter is based primarily on deaning experiences at two quite different institutions: one a relatively small private university of about 3,500 students and the other a larger state university currently of about 19,000 students.

IRREGULAR/UNSCHEDULED RESPONSIBILITIES

There is probably about a 75–80 percent overlap between the activities required of a dean at the two universities mentioned previously. Depending on the amount of support a dean has in the way of staff and assistants/associates, the 75–80 percent overlap can most likely be found for college deans' positions across the vast majority of universities. The overlap with community college deaning positions will probably also be substantial, but somewhat less than at the university level. The following list will be used as a springboard for moving into a fuller discussion of what deans do on a planned and unplanned (irregular) basis, focusing on some of the activities that are most important. The discussion will include comments about some differences between the two types of schools mentioned previously, and how those differences might impact on the dean's role.

CHECKLIST: Let's Make a List

1. Approve student overloads in special cases
2. Approve undergraduate students taking graduate courses
3. Settle complaints from students that chairs cannot resolve
4. Settle complaints from parents that chairs cannot resolve
5. Conduct investigations of serious complaints—such as faculty member mistreatment of students, faculty member mistreatment of another faculty member, student mistreatment of faculty member, and harassment of all types
6. Negotiate settlements to grade appeals if possible and if not possible make sure due process is followed throughout the appeal
7. Attend various social and professional functions of the college departments and university—some of which are regularly scheduled and some of which are not
8. Respond to requests for activities from the academic vice president (AVP) and occasionally from the president
9. Provide congratulations and condolences to members of your unit as appropriate—especially faculty and students
10. Visit chairs occasionally to see how they are doing and how things are in their departments
11. Serve on numerous college and university wide committees and attend meetings accordingly:
    a. Policy and Operations
    b. Curriculum

   c. Core Curriculum
   d. Marketing
   e. Promotions and Advertising
   f. Distance Education
   g. Honors and Fellowships
   h. Calendar
   i. Planning Action Committee (PAC)
   j. PAC Goals and Subcommittees
   k. Faculty Development
   l. Admissions
   m. Orientation
12. Review part-time faculty member requests for advancement in lecturer status and prepare a recommendation to be given to the Academic Affairs Council
13. Meet with faculty members who seem to be struggling in some way and encourage them to make changes that will make their work more satisfying
14. Meet with faculty members who are doing far more than is expected and get them to adjust their priorities to maximize satisfaction from their work
15. Meet with new faculty members occasionally to make sure they are doing alright and adjusting to their new position
16. Periodically review the dean's role in fulfilling the university's Strategic Planning Committee goals and activities to make sure that the dean's designated activities are getting done
17. Serve as a decision-maker when called upon
18. Carry out disciplinary actions as needed
19. Attend system-wide meetings and workshops as they arise
20. Meet with prospective donors and other community members when called upon

There would not be enough space in this book to fully discuss all of these responsibilities, and by no means is this list intended as an exhaustive set of activities—among all universities of any type, or even the ones mentioned above. What is the responsibility of a dean at one school might be the responsibility of a different office at another school. For example, smaller private universities require deans to have much more contact with students and parents of students than do larger state universities where a student affairs office is more likely to handle most student/parent concerns. With higher cost and campus smallness comes student and parent expectations of greater access to the administration.

The above list does, however, give the reader a pretty good idea of the kinds of irregular activities that a dean can expect to perform. Sometimes these activities will relate to a meeting scheduled on the dean's calendar, but sometimes they will involve unexpected appearances at the dean's door by people who are at the brink of a crisis, or what they perceive at the moment to be a crisis.

Once the dean learns more about all the players in her/his unit (s)he will know which unexpected calls are serious and which are not. There may be some people that the dean will want to ask the administrative assistant to never let into the dean's office without an appointment, while others, such as the chairs, might have relatively open access to the dean. But even chairs can abuse their privilege and require some degree of filtering. This is an area within which an experienced secretary/office manager/administrative assistant becomes very valuable ("administrative assistant" will be used from this point on). They know how to protect the dean from unnecessary interruption, and with some candid conversations between the administrative assistant and the dean a system can be worked out whereby the integrity of the dean's calendar and office efficiency can be maintained.

Complaints

Settling complaints may seem like a fairly simple and relatively unimportant matter—hardly worth discussing. Of course, this is not the case. Students are sometimes wronged by faculty members or other students, which can happen in a variety of ways, and faculty members often have problems with their colleagues. Effectively handling complaints turns out to be one of the most important functions of the dean's office because it is from complaints that greater problems arise if not handled properly: low departmental faculty morale, low student satisfaction, formal grievances filed through the union, presidents and provosts getting calls from disgruntled parents and/or board members who are friends of the disgruntled parents, important significant university financial donors being dragged into the conflict, and so on.

At some institutions, deans have the support of a fully staffed affirmative action office that is separate from the human resources office. When this is the case, a lot of the investigative work revolving around certain complaints can be shifted to that office. The dean still needs to do some preliminary ground work to determine if the case fits the criteria for sending it to affirmative action, but if it does fit the criteria the dean can be grateful for one less investigation to conduct. How grateful one will be is determined in part by how effective the affirmative action office is. The unspoken first priority of the affirmative action office is to protect the university from legal action. However, a good affirmative action officer will understand that the best long-term protection for the university is to take all cases seriously and pursue them all equally within the parameters of the policies governing behavior at the university—regardless of who is involved.

Some smaller institutions, however, do not have a sophisticated plan for dealing with affirmative action related complains, which means that the dean will have to conduct the investigation and make a remedy decision that will be recommended to the higher administration. Drawing directly from my own experience, both with and without an effective affirmative action office, it is the case that the forms of sexual harassment complaints can be quite varied: sexual harassment of female students by male students, sexual harassment of female students by female students, sexual harassment of female faculty members by male faculty members, sexual harassment of female students by female faculty members, sexual harassment of female students by male faculty members, and sexual harassment of male students by male faculty members. Some part or all of these sexual harassment complaints were investigated, as well as many other types of complaints, by me as the dean. The emergence of a literature on bullying has allowed institutions to more effectively define and prohibit it. Bullying has been involved in a number of cases I have had to handle, but typically interconnected with other issues such as those mentioned above. In a number of instances the investigations I conducted led, either directly or indirectly, to individuals, and sometimes departments, being disciplined in various ways, including faculty members being fired and departments losing faculty lines. Some examples will be offered in Chapter 9.

Faculty Competence Complaints

Another fairly common type of complaint is student or faculty member complaints about a faculty member's competence level. In a non-collective bargaining environment the dean has a great deal of latitude to investigate such complaints, sometimes within a set of agreed upon faculty-administration guidelines. Within a collective bargaining agreement, however, there are strict contractual guidelines for faculty performance review with a limited number of opportunities within which the dean can take action. Due process is the quintessential principle of collective bargaining and the slightest violation of due process can rightfully negate an important and otherwise justifiable administrative decision related to poor faculty performance.

Unions have become relatively weak at defending their faculty members from due process violations, but good administrators will want to follow the agreed upon process, as should everyone in academia (Gunsalus, 2006: 150–151). Many administrators unfamiliar with collective bargaining don't bother to study the collective bargaining contract and so they are frequently violating the legally protected terms and conditions of employment, and thus the faculty members' rights. While the collective bargaining system in higher education probably has more forgiveness in it than it should for administrators, deans who are repeat offenders can find themselves in serious trouble once the human resources office gets tired of dealing with the union complaints. Pressure can be placed on the higher administrators to either get this dean in line or get rid of her/him. Typically it is easier to remove deans than to change them after they have developed a career, however short it might be, of contract violations. Sometimes the dean's behavior is unfortunately reinforced at administrative meetings where there might be joking about how Dean X has been taking on the union, and this joking might take place in a way that turns an irresponsible and ill prepared dean into a hero of sorts. At this stage the distance from hero to unemployed is very very short. Seeing deans lose their job in this manner is quite sad.

The best way to deal with faculty competence complaints, as well as any other complaints, is through existing university/college guidelines, whether they are within a collective bargaining contract or otherwise. Deans should learn the proper protocol and due process guidelines before they are needed in order to prevent making costly mistakes.

Unsolicited "Information": Lunch Anyone?

A new dean should be careful about what information (s)he chooses to internalize, especially if it is unsolicited information. The following anecdote speaks well to this point. During my first week in my first position as dean, a member of the search committee approached me about having lunch with another member of the faculty. The implication was that this was a senior member of the faculty and someone of importance to the institution. In actuality it turned out to be a fellow with a large chip on his shoulder. The entire lunch was spent by him waving every piece of institutional dirty laundry that he could find or contrive.

This may seem like a fairly innocent encounter—hardly worth mentioning. It is more important than one might think because the messages that a person receives cannot be erased. If someday an issue arises relative to one of the people mentioned during this luncheon, the dean might unwittingly respond with a bias influenced by the disgruntled faculty member with whom (s)he had lunch. So how does one handle this situation? To whatever extent possible, without being rude, do not believe anything you have heard and try to make the lunch as short as possible. It is also important to make absolutely certain that this person does not pay for the lunch. It is a good practice for deans to be careful not to "owe" anyone on the faculty anything, but especially those who seek their favor.

This advice is not intended to suggest that deans should not listen to faculty complaints with compassion and interest. There is a significant difference between complaints and vicious gossip, and it is the latter that should be avoided. But the broader point is that one should be particularly careful not to confuse "gossip" with "information"—especially in the early stages of one's deanship.

Considering the Source

There are, however, some people to whom a new dean may want to listen. For example, if the outgoing dean is not leaving under negative circumstances, one probably will want to pay attention to any information that this person has to offer.

However, the new dean is in danger of immediately experiencing information overload and will need to make sure (s)he keeps the misinformation and useless information intake to a minimum. Outside of the formal processes deans are required to follow, they are wise to simply take people as they find them on a daily basis: neither good nor bad. To whatever extent possible, deans should behave in accordance with how their position is defined within the existing documents that speak of their responsibilities. Ignoring rumors and innuendos is critical to success.

Who Is in the Basement? A Space and Judgment Story

It is common that deans have serious space issues. Upon arriving at my second dean's position such problems became immediately apparent.[1] A large segment of the college was in the basement of one of the oldest and most problematic buildings on campus. Other departmental stations were also overcrowded, and few had adequate space for graduate assistants, adjuncts, or appropriate labs. There was a special college-wide committee to study the matter, a committee that had been in place for a number of years prior to my arrival and which had produced several reports, including a rather extensive space assessment document in a heavy binder. The dean's office was literally bombarded with complaints by those who had poor to very bad space, and those who had adequate space were sympathetic toward those who did not. Clearly, this was a shared reality within the college.

Yet, the perception of other administrators on campus was that the space issue was the work of one disgruntled faculty member who had a reputation for obsessing about the poor quality of the basement space. The identified faculty member had been located in the basement, but was eventually able to move out. This left her/him separated from her/his entire department, and that was a source of concern as well.

I was later told by others that (s)he yelled at the administration about the poor space conditions—that (s)he was, more or less, a volatile person who was to be either avoided or handled very carefully. Members of her/his own department used her/his name, apparently with prior success, as a weapon of sorts. If I was unable to fulfill their request regarding some matter, they would say something to the effect, "well, Professor X is not going to like this." Or, "I would not want to be the one to tell Professor X about this."

My first encounter with Professor X was in a committee meeting involving faculty members and administrators who were working on developing a doctoral program in Professor X's department. (S)he was on the committee. Professor X's behavior was nothing like what had been described by others. Based on the "information" I had been given up to that point, I expected her/him to monopolize the time and throw fits when (s)he didn't get her/his way. Instead, (s)he spoke only when (s)he had something useful to contribute and was respectful and appreciative of everyone else's comments. I eventually had some frank and difficult meetings with contingents within her/his department that sometimes included her/him, where I laid out some options for them to consider: related to labs, related to graduate assistants, and related to their programs. But Professor X was no more demanding or unreasonable than anyone else, and seemed to be listening to what I had to offer, which was based on what could be done within the constraints of the dean's budget.

In time, two pieces of reality gradually unfolded. (1) The basement which housed Professor X's department turned out to be every bit as bad as Professor X and others claimed. In fact, after the third flooding (parts with 4 inches of water), it seemed clear that the basement was not an appropriate or healthy place for professionals to spend their day. There was also a certain amount of risk for the expensive equipment located throughout that space. Professor X was justified in being upset, and I eventually came to share her/his frustration. (2) The most surprising reality to unfold was that Professor X turned out to be an excellent teacher and one of the most successful scholars at the university. I eventually became so impressed with her/his work that I supported her/him for two prestigious college and campus awards, which (s)he won.

Public identities can be shaped quickly and without sufficient justification. The above anecdotal experience is offered as an example of why new deans cannot afford to accept, without serious question, undocumented or decontextualized "information" about people and/or programs. The best way to avoid making bad decisions based on false realities is to preserve a healthy level of skepticism about everything heard relating to the behaviors and dispositions of the people with whom one works.

Collect Useful Information ASAP

It is within the above context that deans are urged to spend time at the beginning of their first year, which is usually during the summer when things are generally pretty quiet, to investigate the important policy documents for the university and system (if the university is part of a larger unit). Those documents should be easily found online—many from links provided on the Human Resource Office webpage. The first summer is also a good time to review the faculty files to get to know the faculty members a bit before they return for the fall semester. It is nice to be able to talk about a faculty member's work with them during that first encounter. It is also useful to know who is having difficulty in terms of issues like an upcoming tenure decision, student complaints, or being stuck in rank.

Regardless of whatever else the provost and president expect, the dean's primary responsibility should be managing/leading the faculty toward high performance levels so as to better serve the students. That is an ongoing "irregular" expectation. The earlier one can gather the documented information needed to best perform that responsibility, which includes information about due process and handling complaints, the more effective the dean will be as time goes on. Acting with a high level of intentionality requires accurate information. When one takes risks, one cannot afford to be acting on hearsay or the impressions of others.

SCHEDULED ACTIVITIES

In addition to the numerous irregular/unscheduled activities that deans are often drawn into, there are also many structured activities. The lengthy list provided at the beginning of this chapter was clearly not exhaustive and only a few examples could be discussed. That is all space constraints would permit. The independent nature of unscheduled responsibilities makes a dean's day eventful and interesting. Structured activities also have their interesting twists and turns at times, but they are more predictable, allowing the dean to anticipate, plan, and prepare for, the work that needs to be done, and the expected outcomes.

Orientation

Whether one is dean at a small or large university, there are typically a number of orientation events scheduled throughout the year. The dean may sometimes be involved in planning those events via participation on an Orientation Committee (often through student affairs) or via events that the dean's office organizes and which the dean attends. During the first year on campus the dean will be notified by the chair of the Orientation Committee, by the Director of Admissions, or by the College Student Center Director as to what activities one is expected to attend. Some of the expected activities will be campus-wide in nature, such as new-student luncheons, and others will be specific to one's school or college.

One of the more enjoyable college-wide orientation activities is giving welcoming speeches to prospective students and their parents. There are multiple ways of approaching this responsibility, but I preferred using a combination of prepared notes and impromptu comments, with the latter including a lot of time for Q&A. Fielding questions is a lot of fun and usually an opportunity for going well beyond the specific answer to the question. Some faculty members might be present, as well as the Student Center Director, who can also field questions. There may be times when the last thing one feels like doing is an orientation event. There will probably be other times, however, when orientation events will be a welcomed part of an otherwise overwhelming day—a nice relaxing break from difficult problems.

Regardless of how it might seem, orientation activities are extremely important for the campus and for the college/school. There are many small activities in the experiences of a prospective student that add up to that student's campus/college choice. The dean's encounter with them could be one of those activities. In fact, how a student feels after leaving the dean's session might be the deciding factor. When the dean turns the session back over to the Director, (s)he should notice the smiles and comments parents and students are making to each other. Those smiles and comments are students in the fall classes. It may seem obvious, but never too obvious to state, that deans need students in order to be able to support the faculty and college programs. The dean's confidence in the programs of their college will show during orientation sessions and the students and parents will be influenced by that confidence.

College Catalog

Deans are not typically directly in charge of updating the catalog for their college, but it could happen. There are few benefits to having this responsibility, but once in a while good things come from the tedious and mundane (more on that later). Responsibility for overseeing catalog updating in a particular college will most likely fall upon an assistant dean or an associate dean, and it is usually part of a larger academic affairs-wide process spearheaded by someone from that office or possibly someone in student affairs or the registrar's office. Department chairs are expected to have their revisions to the dean's office by a specific date to allow for plenty of time for the copy to be sent to the university editor's office. Whether in the hands of the dean or the assistant dean, the dean's office must make certain that the chairs provide their departmental information on time. The dean's office is responsible for revising the general part of the catalog that pertains to her/his college, and may check the departmental revisions to make sure everything is done as expected. This would especially be the case if the dean was trying to make major changes—otherwise the dean should be able to submit the revisions to the editor almost immediately after receiving them from the departments. When major curricular changes are made (such as with the core or general education requirements) catalog revisions become a major oversight project for the dean's office and submission deadlines must be adjusted accordingly.

Part-Time and Overload (PT/OL)

Along with program and office budgets the chairs submit their requests for part-time and overload pay funds to the dean. This request should be a carefully estimated amount based on the projected number of sections that will need to be taught by part-time faculty members and regular faculty members (full-time and pro rata) on an overload basis. Most experienced chairs are pretty good at this by now and break pretty close to even at the end of the fiscal year. It is also easier to estimate for some departments than for others, so some departments end up short at the end of the year. It also happens that enrollments sometimes increase to where the dean has to add sections that were not anticipated. The registrar frequently requests that certain departments add sections to accommodate overflow demand. Chairs are asked to keep track of these sections so the deans will know why departments are short at the end of the year if, indeed, they run out of PT/OL money.

Toward the end of the fiscal year when chairs are running out of PT/OL money, they will approach the dean for support. The dean does not always have a reserve, but the AVP normally does. The dean, therefore, has two options: ask the AVP to add money to a particular departmental PT/OL budget, or transfer money from somewhere else, such as another department. Typically there are enough funds left in one or more departmental budgets to cover departments that have a shortfall. In institutions where deans have sufficient reserves/discretionary funds, budget transfers between departments are not usually necessary.

One of the issues that complicate the PT/OL budgets is that they are sometimes connected to summer school funds. This is for two reasons. (1) Summer teaching is generally supported by part-time or overload pay because some summer courses are offered by part-time faculty members and summer teaching in general is considered overload teaching for full-time faculty members. (2) In some institutions summer programs are expected to pay for themselves and also be a source of discretionary funds for the dean. Those discretionary funds are then in turn sometimes used to support part-time and overload courses during the regular school year as well. In institutions where summer school budgeting is combined with all of the part-time and overload pay for the college, chairs will sometimes reduce their summer offerings in order to balance their PT/OL budgets—if it looks like they are coming up short. This way of balancing one's books should be discouraged so as to not significantly diminish the summer school program. A reduced summer program diminishes opportunities for students and makes it difficult for the institution to maintain the physical plant during the summer.

In institutions where summer school is self-funding as a separate entity, and summer school tuition is the source of discretionary funds for the college, it is important for the dean to actively manage the summer program. Class sizes have to be above certain limits and courses have to be approved based, to some extent, on demand. Most chairs will work with the dean on this issue, but some may expect full autonomy. Hence, it is important to remind chairs that the dean's ability to help the chairs throughout the year is dependent on a successful summer program and requires that everyone cooperates. If necessary, the dean can refuse to approve requested summer courses that might negatively impact on the summer school budget.

Workload

Workload is usually defined in the faculty manual or in the collective bargaining agreement. Workload is not as straightforward as one might image or hope. There are three sources of confusion. One is release time for directorships and chairs; a second is lighter loads for faculty teaching graduate courses in order for them to do research; and a third is unusual "differential" scheduling arrangements for faculty members in heavy student contact disciplines like art and music. Because of the unusual class structures of disciplines like art and music, deans should do an exhaustive review of the methods used to arrive at faculty workloads in those departments. What exactly are they doing relative to workload assignments? What is the rationale for doing it? Is what they are doing reasonable given institutional resources and needs? Is it "fair" relative to what other faculty members do across the campus and so on? It is easiest, but imprudent, for new busy deans to accept workloads of the past as legitimate workloads of the present without careful examination of all the relevant issues. The same is true of equitable and cost effective workload arrangements relative to graduate and undergraduate teaching responsibilities. Additionally, directorships are not always clearly defined relative to release time compensation, so there ends up being a significant indefensible difference across directorship positions relative to reassigned time. These kinds of discrepancies need to be addressed once the dean has all of the needed information.

Weather

In parts of the country where there are notable weather concerns that might impact driving conditions, the institution must have a method for cancelling classes and possibly even closing the university. In most institutions this responsibility does not fall on the deans. However, it can and does happen, and it is a big deal. Sufficiently before winter the university president sends the responsible vice president (and deans if they are involved) a notice regarding weather-related cancellations and delays. The notice contains the phone numbers and access codes for all of the radio and TV stations in the area. It is thus the responsibility of the vice president's designee (possibly one of the deans) to cancel classes when weather conditions threaten the security of commuting students and the faculty. Cancellations are conducted by putting a message on the university snowline and by calling all of the radio and TV stations. Each station has an access code that has to be provided by the caller in order for the station to broadcast the cancellation or delay. This is to prevent unofficial calls by unofficial people (i.e., student pranks). Snow day duty can be a thankless and surprisingly stressful task.

Student Evaluations

It is common today for universities to expect faculty members to have their classes evaluated by their students. Generally, they are not required to have all of their classes evaluated, but leaving out specific classes does look a bit suspicious. New faculty members are well advised to have all of their courses evaluated since the burden of proof of successful teaching is theirs when they are being considered for tenure and promotion. At some institutions today student evaluations are sent out from the dean's office every term and returned in sealed envelopes to the dean's office. There is an opportunity at that time to look at some of the evaluations if necessary. The evaluations are then sent to the Office of Institutional Planning and Research (or its equivalent) for processing, and are then sent back to the dean's office for review. Quantitative summary information is provided, and student comments are aggregated. Once the dean has had an opportunity to review the summaries the information is returned to the departments for distribution to the respective faculty members. Faculty members whose scores are notably low, or who are drawing a lot of negative student comments should be called in for consultation and advisement, but the exact process for doing this will vary across institutions. Collective bargaining institutions may have a specific set of guidelines under which such meetings can be held.

Accreditation Visits

Many programs are accredited by outside agencies, even in colleges not known for having a lot of "professional" programs. One of the responsibilities of the dean is to make sure the departments are on schedule for preparing for the accrediting body visitations. Along with this comes the responsibility of monitoring, in a general way, the extent to which accreditation standards are being met. When accrediting body teams come to campus for visitations, the dean is expected to participate—usually in the form of interviews and exit interviews—sometimes with the AVP and president.

Another responsibility related to accreditation is to make certain that accreditation "requirements" are not misused. Some departments may use accreditation bodies to get resources they may not actually need, or to pressure the university toward decisions that may not be in the best interest of the entire institution. There are three steps to prevent this kind of manipulation from happening. The first step is to carefully read the accreditation standards for all of the departments that are accredited. This may seem like an easy assignment, but on top of everything else the dean must do it can be a challenge. Some departments might be counting on the dean not being fluent in their discipline's standards. The second step is to make absolutely certain that the department is in compliance with all of the accreditation requirements. And the third step is to let the accreditation body evaluators know when they visit campus that the accreditation guidelines are fully understood and that the college will not be bullied by unreasonable demands. Of course this can and should be done in a congenial manner, but nevertheless it sometimes has to be done and done with a great deal of certitude. Accreditations can be a good thing if they keep a discipline's curriculum current and properly staffed. They become counter-productive, however, when they force deans to assign more resources to a program than needed and thus prevent other departments from received badly needed resources.

Student Academic Appeals

In some institutions, notably smaller private institutions, deans play a role in the student appeal process. In other institutions such appeals are handled by a faculty committee with a final appeal step at either the dean's office or the office of academic affairs. Once each term students who do not maintain the necessary academic standards as per the undergraduate catalog are notified of their academic probation status or dismissal for academic reasons. When dismissal occurs students are notified of their right to appeal the decision, which could be to the dean. The appeal typically should contain two vital pieces of information: (1) What are the extenuating circumstances that resulted in the student's failure to maintain sufficiently high academic performance; (2) What has changed or will change to remove those extenuating circumstances. The dean's response should take those factors into consideration as well as any other information deemed appropriate. The dean should respond in writing to the student and copy the letter to the registrar, advisor, and any other relevant parties who may be legally involved. Student appeals can be quite dramatic and sometimes might include family members who want to verify the extenuating circumstances and assure the dean that their daughter, son, sister, brother, and so on will never let their grades slip again.

Staff Evaluations

Many human resources offices have instituted a continuous evaluation mechanism which involves steps throughout the year. This process is to be used to evaluate staff, which for the dean may include assistant/associate deans, secretary/office managers, departmental administrators/staff, and possibly others, depending on the nature of the institution and college. Annual performance evaluations usually happen at specific times of year, typically in the spring. Pay increase evaluations, which might be separate from performance evaluations, are sometimes on the anniversary of the person's hire. Staff evaluations involve a probationary period following the hire, which may be regulated by a collective bargaining agreement. Staff evaluations should include a step whereby the staff person evaluates their own performance in a number of relevant areas. The dean and the staff person then compare notes and the dean makes recommendations for improvement. They also discuss the previous year's recommendations in terms of whether they were met or not.

Chair Evaluations

In non-collective bargaining environments there are department chair evaluations, and they take place at the end of each appointment term, typically 3 years. In collective bargaining environments, especially environments where the chair is part of the faculty bargaining unit, the chair's evaluation is not usually separated from their evaluation as a faculty member. Notwithstanding, transition to another chair term typically must be marked by another election or at least a departmental opportunity for an election. When the dean performs a separate chair evaluation the dean is most likely expected to include input from the department members. Under those circumstances, the dean sends a letter with an evaluation form to the faculty members of the chair's department, collects and summarizes the data, and then makes a recommendation to the AVP. The evaluation process should begin at the end of the fall semester/quarter of the last year of the chair's term. Many campuses now have term limits for chairs, and it seems the limit is usually three terms. Normally exceptions can be made, but rarely and only in situations where the department and university have no immediately identifiable alternative.

A dean's decision to renew or discontinue a chair's appointment can be a delicate one with many possible ramifications. Buller states it well by raising some important questions.

> When is a chair actually causing harm to a program? What harm is the person doing? If you can't point to specific concerns you have about opportunities that are being missed, work that is not being performed, or successes that are not being achieved, then you really need to reconsider whether you have an ineffective department chair or a simple personality conflict (2007: 296).

Even if a chair's performance is questionable, the dean is well advised to not remove chairs without good reason and without being prepared for the fallout that will likely occur, especially if the chair is reasonably well liked in their department.[2]

Clearing Students for Graduation

In some institutions deans may actually be involved in clearing students for graduation, and going through the graduation ceremony may be contingent upon actually being certified as a graduate. Under these circumstances students are given their actual graduation certificate on stage. It is a practice valued by private schools in particular that aspire to a higher status level than other universities. They want to be able to say that their graduates are truly authentic in every sense. Today most universities have what are called walking rules whereby if a student is within a certain number of credits from completing their program they can go through the graduation ceremony. This form of graduation is made possible by students receiving a blank piece of paper as their diploma, rather than an actual certificate—a practice that makes life much easier for everyone.

In my first dean's position I had to certify the students prior to graduation. Some smaller universities sometimes have only one graduation ceremony—typically in the spring. Students may be graduated, however, at the end of the summer sessions, at the end of the fall semester, as well as at the end of the spring semester. Clearing students for graduation before the graduation ceremony in the spring requires special attention because of the tight schedule involved in making sure students will be able to actually participate in the graduation ceremony. This requires a special session of the chairs and registrar in the dean's office immediately upon completion of the grades for spring semester. Chairs, with the assistance of the registrar, identify any problems related to students being graduated based on their spring grades. When this session is completed chairs sign a form that identifies any students expected to be graduated who will not be able to be graduated as a result of spring grades. All other issues related to the student's graduation should have been taken care of prior to that meeting.

Under the practice of "prior certification" it sometimes happened that family members came from faraway places, even other countries, to see students be graduated and then the student could not participate in the ceremony. Sometimes students would literally be pulled out of the graduation line. It is with great pleasure that I report the successful dismantling of this practice at the institution where I first became a dean.

Strategic Planning Goals

Deans are expected to take part in the ongoing strategic planning process of the university. This process involves a number of steps and the annual production of an operational plan, a rather thick document that identifies all of the actions to be taken throughout the coming year, and who is to be held accountable for the identified activities. The dean is to take note of her/his responsibilities in this regard and act on them to assure their completion. The activities identified for action each year are part of a longer term planning process that includes identifying canopy goals and objectives over a 3–5-year period. It is important for deans to take these goals seriously since they are based on the objectives identified by the president at the beginning of each year, which are typically approved or given some form of blessing by the board of trustees. Deans are frequently asked to chair committees that are for the purpose of overseeing one or more of the planning goals. This is not always an easy responsibility given everything else deans are expected to do.

Outcome Assessment

Whether starting an outcome assessment program or continuing to improve one that exists, it is important for faculty members to be reminded that their programs already exceed internal and external expectations, and that no matter how good their assessment plan would be, it could not reflect the level at which they are currently performing. Assessment should not drive the quality of programs. Programs should always be well above the assessment bar, and most always are. Assessment is simply a way of protecting the public from those rare programs that might slip below a particular minimal standard. It is also a way for departments to identify areas that could be adjusted for improvement or change even if they are already at a high level of performance. And finally, departmental assessment plans are now generally expected by external reviewers.

It should be safe to assume that departmental program assessment exists in most institutions today, but there may still be a few exceptions. It is also possible that some of the early assessment programs were not done well and should be revisited. There were no departmental outcome assessment plans on the campus of my first deanship, and all of the departments had one when I left. Most were excellent, but some were marginal and hopefully have been improved by now. Assessment continues to be somewhat controversial and sometimes difficult to manage.

Measuring Outcomes

Part of the dean's challenge in overseeing outcome assessment is to make sure that departments are measuring "outcomes" and not inputs.[3] Some discipline-based accreditation bodies accept "inputs" as sufficient to fulfill their evaluation requirements. Departments that have been using inputs to fulfill their individual program accreditation evaluation requirements believe they have also fulfilled their outcome assessment responsibilities, and may want to simply turn in their accreditation report as evidence of an outcome assessment. That generally does not work. Outcome assessment requires a methodology that demonstrates either a "before and after effect" of the program (such as an entry and exit exam), or that the program is producing student-based results that meet some external standard—such as a discipline-governed exam, discipline-governed product evaluation, or a discipline-monitored advancement/employment record.

Regardless of what skills the dean might have in this area, it is generally more effective for a faculty to hear an outside voice. Bringing in an outside consultant shows that the dean is serious about assessment and wants to help the faculty in whatever ways are possible. Additionally, there are always new assessment issues emerging that may require respected outside expertise, such as the current issues of assessing online programs and programs that include credits for experiential learning.

Another important part of the dean's challenge regarding outcome assessment is to get the departments on a regular schedule of assessment. Some universities require departments to conduct an assessment and submit a report every year. This is probably not a good use of a department's time. A full assessment and report every 2 or 3 years would be more reasonable and probably more useful, since it could be done with more time and care.

Many universities now require external reviews for all of their departments, typically every 3–5 years. Outcome assessments could simply be coordinated with the external reviews. For example, if the external reviews occur every 5 years then an assessment could be conducted at a midpoint and then again for the external review itself. By carefully integrating the assessment process with the external reviews one maximizes the value of both. This does not mean that there are not pieces of data that should not be collected annually, such as the number of publications, professional presentations, and student awards within each department. These are useful kinds of data that can be easily collected and which deans can use to effectively lobby for their colleges.

External Reviews

While the focus is on programs, external reviewers also address how well the department is operating and what kinds of plans departments might consider for the future, given current trends in the field. Following an extensive self-study and corresponding report, two or three reviewers are brought in from separate universities that have programs similar to the ones being reviewed. Departments that are serious about improving will try to get reviewers from campuses that are at least one cut above them in some way. The hope is that these reviewers will be able to provide some recommendations for improving the department's programs and/or moving the department to a slightly higher level in terms of its reputation and program offerings.

Departments that don't want to change what they are doing will want to invite reviewers from departments that are the same as theirs or possibly not quite at their level. Their goal is to simply have the reviewers applaud them so they can ask for more support from the dean for doing the same thing they have been doing for the last 20 years. Continuing a long departmental tradition is not a bad thing if what they have been doing is at a high level of excellence. As stated by Bright and Richards,

> In short, the department wants to use the review as a club with which to pound on the dean until it gets what it sincerely believes it should have, whereas the dean hopes the process will be more like holding up a mirror to the department so it can see itself more clearly as others see it (2001: 185).

With everything the dean has to do it is easy to get burned on the selection of the external reviewers. It is, however, the dean's responsibility and prerogative to be involved in choosing the external reviewers. This is a bit tricky since deans might not know many people in a particular field outside of their own. The faculty of a department presumably has the most contacts within its own discipline and the most knowledge of its discipline.

So deans that involve themselves enthusiastically in this process can be easily criticized for acting outside of their area of expertise. There are two reasons deans should not be deterred by this possible criticism. The first reason is that deans might be surprised to learn how limited the reviewer contacts are for many departments. It isn't that department faculty members don't know a lot of people in their field. It is more so that they do not know people considered qualified or interested in conducting an external review. The second reason is that it is better to be criticized for going beyond one's area of expertise than it is to have a department bring in two crony buddies that will say only what the department wants them to say. Reviewers typically spend 2 days with a department and the college covers the expenses for those 2 days. A lot of time goes into preparing for the interviews, studying the results, and discussing those results with the respective department. It is a serious waste of time and resources if the external reviewers are not poised to do an honest and serious critique of the programs they have been hired to review. Serving as an intentional dean occasionally requires pushing a blurry line beyond everyone's comfort zone, and this is one of those situations. Asserting administrative prerogative in this instance may be essential to protecting a college program and, hence, protecting the quality of the educational experience for future students.

If a department has been stagnant for 20 years and is refusing to recognize the contemporary demands of its field and the university at large, the last thing a dean wants to happen is for that department to bring in the same two reviewers it brought in 5 years earlier. This does and will occur if the dean is too busy to fully participate.

NOTES

1 As pointed out by Krahenbuhl (2004: 184–185) space problems are eternal in higher education. Everyone claims to have a space problem. So when there is a complaint of a problem it is not always easy to know how real it is. A false claim carried forward by the dean can be embarrassing once debunked.

2 Buller (2007) dedicates an entire chapter to this issue. I recommend reviewing that chapter if the reader would like additional information. Also, see Favazza (2014).

3 For an alternative positive approach to this challenge, see Walton (2014).

REFERENCES

Bright, D.F. & Richards, M.P. (2001). *The academic deanship: Individual careers and institutional roles*. San Francisco: Jossey-Bass.

Buller, J.L. (2007). *The essential academic dean*. San Francisco: Jossey-Bass.

Favazza, J. (2014). The role of the dean in department and program review, in L.L. Behling (Ed.). *The resource handbook for academic deans* (pp. 169–173). San Francisco: Jossey-Bass.

Gunsalus, C.K. (2006). *The college administrator's survival guide*. Cambridge: Harvard University Press.

Krahenbuhl, G.S. (2004). *Building the academic deanship: Strategies for success*. Westport: Praeger Publishers.

Walton, K.D. (2014). "The war of the worlds": Assessment of student learning outcomes of academic majors, in L.L. Behling (Ed.). *The resource handbook for academic* deans (pp. 345–357). San Francisco: Jossey-Bass.

Chapter 5

Setting Your Own Agenda

The responsibilities and duties of an academic dean are endless and can easily consume every moment of one's day if allowed to do so. A dean's success, while dependent largely on fulfilling the expectations of their role, is also dependent upon the unique qualifications of the dean.[1] As with any leadership position, one should only accept a dean's post under the condition of having an agenda that will bring added value to the college/institution—an agenda that will be compatible with that of the higher administration and that will be acceptable to a critical mass of the departments in the college (Krahenbuhl, 2004). A dean's agenda can be built upon an inherited strategic plan, or it can be generated out of a new college strategic plan, the creation of which is led by the dean (Krahenbuhl, 2004; Conboy, 2014). The later circumstance, leading the creation of a new strategic plan, is a major agenda item in itself and could end up being one's most time consuming goal. This chapter identifies possible agenda items deans might consider—assuming that a compatible strategic plan is in place either in the college or in the university overall. It then offers examples of how some of those items were addressed by the author.

CHOOSING AGENDA ITEMS: SOME EXAMPLES

A list of possible agenda items might appear as follows:

CHECKLIST:

1. Increasing the amount and/or level of research/scholarship in the college
2. Improving the overall quality of teaching in the college
3. Increasing the amount of external resources attained by the college
4. Increasing the number of graduate programs and/or graduate students
5. Decreasing the teaching load of the faculty
6. Increasing or decreasing the average class size for the faculty

7. Changing the core teaching scheduling model to more effectively accommodate research time
8. Make better use of existing classroom and office space and/or find new space
9. Increase faculty involvement with external constituents
10. Increase the cultural, racial, and/or gender diversity of the faculty overall or in specific departments
11. Increase the number of interdisciplinary programs
12. Increase diversity within the college curricula
13. Promote and support gender equality
14. Lead a major curriculum change, such as changing a core curriculum.

While all of the above and many other possible items might be important goals for a college, a dean can only expect to accomplish "so much" while in one position—and that means probably not all of the above. Some of the items are interrelated, and working on one goal facilitates working on another. In the following actual examples such interrelationships and their importance are readily identifiable.

Faculty/Student Diversity and Curricula

Many university leaders worked to diversify university campuses in the 1980s and 1990s. At that time this meant encouraging hiring and retaining faculty members from diverse backgrounds, and recruiting diverse students as well. While this initiative succeeded in drawing and retaining highly assimilated people to campus, it was not successful in drawing and retaining people who identified with Non-Western cultural ways of living and knowing. Taking this deeper and richer step toward diversity required transforming the curricula of the campus toward becoming more inclusive.

Toward that objective a state grant was attained and implemented at a fairly large state university. The basic thrust of the grant was to provide released time to faculty members to be able to engage them in seminar type discussions/presentations/workshops. Faculty members were then challenged to critique their own fields of study and become more open to alternative (typically non-Western) explanations of the reality addressed within their discipline. In some cases that alternative explanation involved looking at reality specifically from a woman's perspective rather than the discipline's existing traditional male dominated perspective. Hence, "diversity" was not restricted to ethnic cultural diversity. This was particularly relevant at a university that had just been legally proven, via a major class action lawsuit, to systematically discriminate against women.

The expected end product of the grant was that the participants submit a curriculum transformation proposal for approval through the university's curriculum review process. Overall the curriculum transformation project was quite successful, making the campus more appealing to faculty members and students from culturally diverse backgrounds. Those faculty members and students from various backgrounds were then able to participate in the enhancement of campus diversity beyond their physical presence on campus. By teaching and learning about diverse ways of approaching their subject matter they could participate in the enrichment of the university curricula and feel more welcome than they would have with a completely traditional curriculum (Alessio, 1996).

Fast Forward

Diversity naturally became an agenda item during my deaning. Since diversity was a key part of the president's and provost's goals, they were supportive of initiating a program similar to the one funded by the grant referred to above. A college diversity program was thus developed and in place until the economy collapsed in 2008. This example shows the important relationship between Agenda Items #10 (faculty diversity) and #12 (curriculum diversity). It also shows the importance of having support from the higher administration.

Importance of Curriculum Diversity

The importance of diversity cannot be emphasized enough—within the faculty in terms of cultural identities, but especially within the university's curricula. Universities should not be restrictors of information, but explorers of the broadest range of information possible. Bringing in people as faculty members from different cultural backgrounds or influences can help facilitate curricular diversity, but does not guarantee it, since often times people from diverse backgrounds must become champions of the *status quo* in order to survive in academia. As emphasized above, the academic environment of the university must become one where the status quo viewpoint and/or teaching method is always questioned (Santamaria, Jeffries, & Santamaria, 2016; Wolfgramm-Foliaki, 2016). Under these circumstances flaws in the mainstream thinking are exposed, new paradigms emerge, and new/different and more helpful ways of seeing reality are brought forward.

It is interesting to see how developing this kind of academic environment helps diverse faculty members become more comfortable finding and presenting information about their subject matter from the perspectives of people from their particular ethnic or cultural background. This isn't always a clean and perfect process. For example, one might ask what being gay has to do with mathematics. And if one tried to find literature on gay mathematics *per se*, one might be disappointed. We know, however, that there exists an Association of Lesbian, Gay Bisexual, and Transgendered Mathematicians that, among other initiatives, promotes the contributions of gay mathematicians. Should the information promoted by this organization be required knowledge for all mathematicians? Is it possible that there is something about being gay that contributes to the way gay mathematicians see the world and thus mathematics? Given the callous mistreatment of gays throughout the world and the important contributions gays have made to mathematics, should every mathematics department offer a course or part of a course on the contributions of gays to mathematics?

The above example is used because to most people it will probably seem to be one of the most far reaching relative to diversity. No doubt most mathematicians will balk and bluster at the notion of integrating such information into their curriculum. The importance of such integration, however, cannot be known until scholars are open to new possibilities and are willing to explore those possibilities. One of the most important mathematicians of the twentieth century, Alan Turing, was gay. He is credited as being the inventor of the computer and a significant contributor to the Allies' victory during WWII. Yet, Turing's gay status was prosecuted as a crime, led to his conviction and severe mistreatment, and ultimately his suicide at the age of 41. Perhaps his gay status had nothing to do with his work as a mathematician, but maybe it did. That point notwithstanding, it is known with certainty that Turing's gay status had a great deal to do with mathematics that is missing—that is, the mathematics that was never completed because Turing suffered immensely and committed suicide at a young age. Within the void left by mono-cultural thinking and practices we can find the power and importance of diversity: what we don't know, but could know if we were open to all people and all sources of ideas and information.

All on the Same Page

At a fall college picnic during the first year of my second deanship, I was making rounds to try to get to know the faculty of the various departments. Interactions with one particular department stood out. It was a fairly large department and nearly all of the members were present at the same table. As the discussion progressed a senior faculty member deliberately and with great pride conveyed that all members of the department were "all on the same page." Very little was said by the other members of the department, which continued to be the case throughout my tenure as dean there. Even the department chair seemed quite deferent to this person.

The "same page" comment was not fully understood until excellent students started coming to my office complaining that they were getting a very narrow view of the subject matter being taught in the program of that department, and they didn't know if they wanted to continue with that discipline as their major. Some spoke of transferring. Student references to alternative perspectives in class or on homework papers were quickly discouraged, derided in some instances, and even sometimes punished with low grades. The department in question represents one of the long-standing fields of study in academia, a discipline with a history of many different theoretical, philosophical, and methodological approaches.

But this department had been gradually "weeded out" of most faculty members that did not fit the chosen theoretical and methodological profile, a profile that also represented a particular political ideology. There were only a couple remaining senior faculty members who openly disagreed with this deliberate homogenization and they were ostracized by the rest of the department. Most of the faculty members were yet to be fully promoted and/or were untenured, so they were tightly controlled.

In addition to the serious personnel issues this situation represented, it was also a disaster from the standpoint of curriculum diversity. Resolving the personnel issues was extremely difficult given the fear that prevailed over any efforts to obtain actionable evidence. As dean, however, one is also responsible for the integrity of the various curricula of the college. Upholding this responsibility is tricky if one believes, as they should, that in general curricula belong to the faculty. Efforts were made to advise the chair and others in the department of the need to diversify rather than homogenize their curriculum. Other departments not only responded well to such advice, but greatly appreciated it. This department dug in and became more entrenched in their plan. As a large department their student major numbers were not where they should have been or could have been, dropping over a period when their faculty member numbers had actually increased.

In short, they were not serving the students, college, university, and broader community as well as they should have been and were not open to change. It is my understanding that the department has changed a great deal since my retirement. Hopefully they are now more open and diverse in their view of their subject matter and in their general search for truth.

Research Productivity

One of the ongoing challenges of comprehensive universities is finding ways to support and generate faculty research and corresponding publications (Item #1 on list). Faculty members typically have teaching loads as high as 12 credits per semester/term, serve on several committees, and provide students with various forms of out of classroom advising and mentoring. In many cases even graduate advising and mentoring does not bring a teaching load reduction or classroom assistance.

Putting the issue in question form, however, brings one closer to the heart of the matter: "How can I, as dean of this college, assure that the scholarship of the faculty will increase?" The answer to that question is not imbedded in some added review process or evaluation process; nor is the answer complicated. Most faculty members become professors because they love their subject matter. Certainly they love teaching about it, but they also love studying it and writing about it.

What most faculty members need is the time and resources to make that happen, and that is what most faculty members at comprehensive universities don't have. When that reality is acknowledged the question about increasing scholarship takes on a slightly different form: "How can I help faculty members more effectively do what they want to do?"

Once the question is phrased in this manner several other potential agenda items come into the picture. If a college wants to increase scholarship productivity the dean must reduce the amount of time that faculty members spend in the classroom, which means reducing teaching load (Item #5 in the above list). Reducing teaching load does not necessarily mean reducing the number of students that a department teaches. What it does mean is that faculty members will make fewer trips to the classroom and spend less time preparing for classes.

Hard Choices: Teaching a Specialty or Researching It?

A dean can give faculty members in the college the following choice: Continue teaching the same number of courses or give up your "esoteric" specialty course (probably based on one's dissertation) so that more time can be spent continuing one's research and writing on that subject. Instead of teaching a class with twelve students in it, offer independent study options to two of the best student majors who can then learn from the professor while also contributing to the professor's research activities. Credits from the twelve students who would have been in that class probably won't be lost since those students will most likely find another elective to take in that department. Of course, not everyone in a department can do this at the same time, but a supportive department can find a fair way to rotate such opportunities so that credit production damage is minimized and upper level course options are still available for the students. An obstacle to this approach is that faculty members, when they are hired, sometimes negotiate to be able to teach a course related to their dissertation topic, and they don't want to let that go. This is a mistake if one wants to continue to be productive in her/his field. Having an option to teach three classes instead of four or two classes instead of three during a semester is far more valuable for a faculty member's career than teaching a specialty course.

Bigger = Fewer Trips to the Classroom

A second option a dean can give the faculty of the college is: "Continue teaching the same number of medium-sized sections of introductory level courses or combine some of them into larger venues" (Agenda Item #8 as well as Agenda Item #6). It should go without saying that small classes are better pedagogically than large classes. I have taught all sizes, from 5 to 500, and those who argue that large classes can somehow be better than smaller ones are just selling snake oil.

We know, however, that resources are limited and becoming even more so. So "least harm" alternatives must be sought.

There are size breaks where little is lost when a class is doubled, and that includes credits. In fact, this option could actually be used to increase credit production if a department decided it needed to do so. This is an old idea, but it still works. If a lecture hall is at about 100 seats, combining two sections of 40 into a lecture hall of 100 would open up the possibility of increasing the number of students taught by this faculty member by 25 percent of their previous student load for that course. But that doesn't have to happen and probably should be discouraged if the goal is really to increase scholarship.

If a faculty member has forty students in a class (s)he is probably doing things (s)he should not be expected to do. Forty students, especially if one has three other classes, are too many to evaluate with essay exams, reports, and presentations. It is done, but that does not make it reasonable. Forty students are too many to keep track of in terms of class participation, and they are too many to really get to know on an individual level. Hence, combining two such sections does not have to be a pedagogical loss, and it will most likely benefit the faculty member in terms of organizing and executing their research agenda.

Positive Results

When the above policy changes were implemented, the college began to see significant increases in scholarship within 2 years. The college reached new highs in just about every area of research productivity, including student presentations and publications—since some faculty members were now working more with students one-on-one in exchange for giving up smaller classes. It is also interesting to note that rather than decreasing, credit production for the college increased. The college also saw a notable increase in the amount of external research funding applications and awards (Agenda Item #3), even though it was not one of the dean's set agenda items. It was encouraged and rewarded if faculty members successfully pursued it, but untenured faculty members were advised to focus on what they knew they could successfully accomplish. A lot of time can be spent on an external grant proposal with no tangible results. Increasing external funding in general was a goal for the college, but that was accomplished with the support of an excellent fundraiser for the college. Hence, sample Agenda Item #8 was also fulfilled.

Changing the Scheduling Backbone (Sample Agenda Item #7)

The basic schedule for a semester model is typically M-W-F 50-minute classes and T-Th 75-minute classes. Mixed in with these options are evening classes and sometimes Saturday morning classes. Of course, not everyone is on the same schedule. Some departments find ways of rotating who gets to be on the T-Th and/or evening schedule and other departments use scheduling to reward already successful scholars or those who wield the most political power in the department. Sadly, scheduling is also sometimes used to punish faculty members for not voting for the elected chair or for refusing to serve on certain committees and so on—a bad idea that only serves to reduce morale and decrease productivity.

Four Days a Week

An alternative backbone to the 5-day scheduling model is a 4-day teaching model with the fifth day reserved for meetings, advising, and scholarly activity. The first institution of my deaning experience rejected this idea at every level. At the second institution, however, not only did the faculty of the college support it, but some of the departments had informally adopted such a model already—feigning a 5-day model but really working within a 4-day schedule. Hence, in the spirit of sample Agenda Item #7, the dean's office promoted a discussion of the costs and benefits of changing the college's scheduling core to a 4-day teaching week. The most important argument against the change was that the college would be out of step with the other colleges and students would have difficulty scheduling classes. This argument turned out to have less credence than originally thought because it was discovered that there was so much scheduling variability university-wide that little would change. Indeed, students were already having problems related to scheduling variability and this change, if anything, might give them more predictability—at least within their own college. One department in particular pushed the college conflict argument heavily and ultimately was the only department in the college that refused to fully endorse the change, even though there actually were no conflicts for that department.

The Schedule and Research Productivity

It is uncertain as to whether the scheduling change continued with subsequent deans, but its purpose should be clear. As in the case of reducing teaching load, combining sections and so forth, a 4-day scheduling backbone reduces the number of trips to the classroom and allows faculty members to have longer blocks of time for their research and writing. Moreover, the 75-minute class periods are consistent with contemporary teaching practices of using a lot of media forms: documentaries, multidimensional presentations, online access for on-demand research and so on. So it turns out that Agenda Item #7, changing the scheduling backbone, is also closely related to Agenda Item #1, which is to increase scholarly activity. Number 7 is also related to Agenda Item #5, teaching load reduction, not only because it supports increasing scholarly activity, but also because a residual effect of Agenda Item #7 is to have slightly fewer class-time slots during the course of a normal workweek. While this problem can be mitigated by stretching the day a little, it can also be mitigated by having fewer classes offered, as Item #5 ultimately supports. Changing the scheduling backbone and reducing teaching load also go together in that fewer classes will likely mean increasing the number of larger classes and thus larger classrooms. Larger venues with more students typically require slightly more startup and wind down time, so the 75-minute periods are more practical in a number of important ways.

UNEXPECTED AGENDA ITEMS

Space Issues

Unexpected agenda items will appear, and space issues are likely to be one of them. Upon discovering that departments in the college are literally fighting over who gets the larger classrooms, an incoming dean will recognize they have a long-term problem. Such was the case for my second decanal position. The prior dean created a lottery system to determine who would get to use which large rooms each semester, but that didn't solve the shortage problem. Given the earlier discussed goal of having more large classrooms, this issue was bound to become even more serious. On top of that, there were office space issues with departments in a basement that had water problems. Finding academic space is not an easy matter on an already crowded campus. There is only so much bartering and negotiating a dean can do with dean colleagues, some of whom have space problems of their own. Under these kinds of circumstances one must explore all possibilities and be prepared to think outside of the box.

Unfinished space was found below the sports arena, but the cost of the renovation was beyond a dean's available resources. Additionally, the athletic department wanted the space and was already using it for storage. After 4.5 years of lobbying and negotiating, a compromise was struck with the athletic department and a commitment was secured from the deans' council and the higher administration to use internally reallocated university funds to build out the arena space. There is now a beautiful lecture hall and a classroom in what was previously a storage area, and it is used primarily by the departments of my former college.

Long before the arena space issue was settled, another important "discovery" was made: a movie theater connected to a small strip mall across the street from the university. It occurred to me that much of the space in that theater was sitting vacant throughout large segments of every day. With a few calls to the regional manager of the theater, I successfully negotiated a contract to rent the largest of the movie rooms as a lecture hall 2 days a week from 9 AM to 4 PM. The details of electronic media integration, lapboards, and chalkboards were cleverly worked out by the assistant to the dean. This arrangement was created early in my deanship, and was sufficiently successful that a couple years later the contract was renegotiated to rent the space for 4 days a week instead of 2. The lecture hall space dilemma was thereby solved. The rent for the space was extremely reasonable and could be paid out of the college budget. But eventually the cost was picked up by academic affairs so that other colleges could be encouraged to use the theater space as well.

Back to the Basement: Thinking Outside the Campus

In Chapter 4 there was reference to a water problem in the basement of the main college classroom/office building. The context of that discussion was to advise prospective deans to be careful about what they choose to believe when they first begin a position as dean. As mentioned within that context, however, the basement was a serious problem for the faculty members housed there. It did flood occasionally and it was, in my judgment, an unhealthy and problematic space for offices and labs, especially labs with expensive equipment. There were two large departments housed there and one was the largest in the college. The other had a lot of expensive equipment.

The same strip mall that housed the theater mentioned earlier had some vacant space in it, and the father of the owner of the mall had been a "friend" of the university. A significant part of the solution to the basement problem seemed obvious: take the largest department in the college out of the basement and put it in the mall across the street. This seems like an easy solution but it has two negotiable parts to it. One obvious part is convincing the mall owner to donate the space that was needed. The second part was convincing the department that such a move would be a vast improvement over their existing situation. One would expect the first issue to be the most challenging. It wasn't. There were lab issues. There were issues related to having adequate staff support. There was concern about being isolated from the campus and many other concerns as well. Eventually, Professor X saw the potential in this move and probably played a key role in convincing others to agree to it. The experience of convincing this department to consider coming out of the basement, which they complained about incessantly for years, was interesting. It was like convincing someone who had just spent the last 10 years in a dark cave to come out into the light. They weren't sure their eyes could take it and it was just too scary.

Out of the Basement at Last

The "ask" was made and the donor generously gave us free rent for 3 years. With a bountiful summer school CSBS surplus it was possible to plan, design, and complete an excellent facility with classrooms, labs, and enough office space for all who wanted to move, which was most of the department. As it turned out, the department faculty was giddy with delight in moving into this new facility. It was a perfect venue for their new doctoral program and one other of their well-known programs that required a great deal of contact with the public. The donor has since extended the free-rent agreement and as of this writing there is a positive solution to a very difficult situation. Eventually the university will probably have to give back that space, but hopefully not until there is a new building to replace it.

With one department essentially moved out of the basement it was possible to convert basement office and lab space to large classroom space. Fewer walls, more openness, and state of the art technology made for some very nice classrooms. With that accomplished it was possible to convert older classrooms above the basement into office and lab space for the second department to be moved above ground. This process was not without resistance as well, with many of the same kinds of comments that were heard from the first department to be freed from the caverns. But they now enjoy great offices and departmental visibility. The basement might still flood, but the possibility for dampness issues is greatly reduced with the openness of classrooms. Most importantly, no one has to spend more than 75 minutes at a time in the basement.

Changing the Core Curriculum

On most campuses today leading a core curriculum change would likely be the responsibility of an academic vice president/provost. It is also the case that many large campuses have added deans of undergraduate programs/schools/curriculum to work with the college deans in order to have someone, other than the provost, administer the undergraduate core (or general education curriculum) and deal with undergraduate curriculum problems. The magnitude of the responsibility of changing a core curriculum is such that one must be prepared to use all of the skills and tools known to humans in order to be successful. An undergraduate dean with no supervisory authority is going to be greatly disadvantaged. When called upon to complete this task I did have supervisory authority over all of the undergraduate departments on campus, which included nearly all of the faculty members.

The difference between this unexpected agenda item and the unexpected space issue agenda is that in the former I had no choice in the matter. I was basically informed by the president that if I did not successfully complete a major core revision within a relatively short timeframe, my job would be in jeopardy. Several deans before me had been given this charge and all had failed. It had been over 30 years since the curriculum had been significantly changed and the president was willing to do whatever it would take to make something happen. It was, to say the least, a rude introduction to the world of administration.

A detailed layout of strategies, negotiations, bartering, and compromises throughout the process of completing this task would most likely be interesting to some readers, but to save space and avoid the risk of boring others, this discussion will be kept relatively short. There are, however, some recommended steps in this process that might be useful to anyone who might someday have to lead a major curriculum change. The recommended steps should be prefaced by the comment that, as dean, it is useful to have one's own views on what a sound core curriculum contains. How many credits should it be and what should it look like—what types of courses should be included, and so on? It should go without saying that deans should not expect the resultant changes to be exactly as they want them to be, but it is important for the dean to have sketched out a perceived ideal model.

Possible Steps Toward Completing a Core Curriculum Change

1. The first step in the process is to do an in-depth analysis of the existing core curriculum and identify ways it could be improved.
2. Call the faculty together and let the members know that the curriculum is going to be reviewed and most likely significantly changed. Everyone should be asked to cooperate and help with the process.
3. Chairs, as a group, should be emphatically informed that all departments should expect to have to give something up in order to make the curriculum transformation possible, and they should be thinking about what that might be.
4. It is strongly recommended that each chair subsequently be interviewed to determine what problems they are currently having with the existing curriculum, if any. Typically demand for core curriculum change comes from departments that want their students to take more courses within their own majors, so they are pressuring the university to reduce the number of core credits required. This curriculum change project was happening at a time when there was a lot of public pressure being placed on universities to reduce total credit requirements so that students could be graduated within 4 years. So departments that had fat curricula were feeling the pressure. Rather than give up courses of their own it was easier for them to pressure the administration to cut the core.
5. After interviewing the chairs an analysis of the identified problems can be thoroughly conducted and all the possible ways of solving those problems can be investigated.
6. One can now address the question of how one's previously constructed model will address the identified problems and/or what changes need to be made to the model to make it viable.
7. Given that many departmental "problems" are self-inflicted, it is important to review the various program curricula to find situations

where departments can actually solve their own problems by finding areas in which they can reduce the number of required credits for their major. Typically this step also involves reviewing accreditation requirements and guidelines because oversized curricula are typically defended in the name of accreditation requirements. After studying such requirements for various programs one finds that the "requirements" identified by some departments are often really recommendations, and those recommendations, as well as the actual requirements, can be fulfilled in multiple ways—not just by adding new courses.

8. Meet with individual department chairs again. This meeting is to discuss how departments can participate in the core curriculum change process by making changes to their own programs. Some chairs may have anticipated this meeting in response to the original signal that everyone will need to be prepared to give up something. Chairs from oversized departments may have already thought about how certain courses could be combined to reduce the number of required credits while still meeting accreditation standards. There will be various levels of cooperation and resistance on this issue, but ultimately it becomes one of the important cornerstones of a successful core curriculum transformation. Changing the core, or the general education requirements as they are called in some institutions, cannot just be about the core alone. It must include changes to the programs driving the core curriculum change as well.
9. Ultimately, the dean should not single handedly force a department to make specific changes to its curriculum. At the very least it is safe to say that doing so is not good administrative leadership. The curriculum belongs to the faculty. Hence, core curriculum changes should also include university-wide mandated program boundaries relative to the number of credits required. The way this can be done is by including with the core curriculum proposal a requirement that all programs be brought within a certain amount of credits. This leaves oversized programs that do not want to cooperate on their own no choice but to reduce the number of required credits in order to meet the university's maximum program credit requirement.
10. It is wise to be flexible, especially with departments that are willing to make changes. Some programs have become so credit heavy that even combining course content does not bring them to a reasonable number of credits. So deals have to be made in order to bring about the final result. One common deal is to double count specific courses within some programs as meeting both core and program requirements. This is especially easy to do with the arts, but it can also be done with some physical science programs.

In summary, changing a core curriculum is not about slashing the core credits, as has happened in many universities across the United States, but about everyone working together to come up with a creative and meaningful core that serves all students well. Yes, some courses might be eliminated from the core because they are no longer as meaningful as they once were, but it should also be possible to add others that are, indeed, consistent with the needs of a contemporary student body. What clearly should not happen is that core standards become notably different for different departments—some departments having a 55-credit core while others have only a 45-credit core. The core is equally important to all students, and is arguably the most important part of every student's education.

AGENDA OPPORTUNITIES

Along with unexpected agenda items, which may involve activities you would not choose for yourself, there emerges from time to time, a situation that you didn't plan or expect, but which you might want to welcome as part of your agenda—what might be called an agenda opportunity. In an early section of this book there was reference to deaning as activism. If a person doesn't have ideas about how education can and should be improved for all, there is some question as to whether (s)he should be in a leadership position. Strong academic leaders know when to follow the faculty, but they also know when to take action on something that is important to the identity of the college within the broader social network containing that college. In other words, an intentional dean doesn't rely solely on standard agenda items, but recognizes and seizes opportunities to make a positive difference. As stated by Buller, "Negative leaders become fixated on problems; positive leaders are aware of possibilities and can build something useful out of even the worst type of problem" (2013, p. xi). Accordingly, it sometimes occurs that one's broader life agenda can find opportunities for small positive changes in academia. Here are three of those small but meaningful examples.

Dead Cats in the Lab

One of the departments at the private university where I was deaning had a long-standing practice of purchasing, at no small cost, cat bodies for students to dissect. Since the university had two large and successful medical programs, nursing and physician assistant, it was thought essential that students be able to differentiate various muscles and other body parts, even if they were not human. When students came to the dean's office with concerns about having to dissect dead cats, something they thought to be of questionable utility relative to what they needed to know and relative to the cost to the cats, they could have been dismissed, as many deans have most likely done over the years, and told to buck up and do what they had to do. Instead, I studied the situation and discovered that sophisticated electronic labs allowed students opportunities to electronically dissect various types of anatomy, not just cats. As someone who has been concerned about the treatment of other animals (as well as the treatment of humans), and knowing something about the dead cat market, I was happy to have an opportunity to take up this issue.

The students were called back to the dean's office and a discussion commenced on how it might be possible to convert the anatomy lab to an electronic lab. After a number of discussions with the professors and a number of trial experiments with electronic lab software products, the conversion to an electronic lab was finally made. There was some initial set up cost, but in the long run there were considerable savings by not having to continually purchase, store, and dispose of dead cats.

Shortly after I left, the university was given an award by People for the Ethical Treatment of Animals (PETA) for finding a humane way, via the electronic lab, of reducing harm to animals. While PETA may be a controversial organization, it is nonetheless an important international entity that has a great deal of support from within many important circles. It was gratifying to have played a role in making the PETA award happen. It was also rewarding to be able to make change in this way after a lifelong commitment to making the world a better place for all forms of life.

From Dead Cats to Live Rats

When senior faculty members spend their entire careers teaching students how to do research with live rats and new faculty members are hired specifically because that is the type of research they do, it is difficult for an incoming dean to see any possible way of helping the rats. One might ask, "Why should the dean be concerned about rats?" The answer to that question is surprisingly simple. The dean is responsible for the maintenance and care of everything and everybody within the college. It is called stewardship, and stewardship does not stop with humans but extends to equipment and all materials, used within the college. But in this case there did not appear to be sufficient space to create an agenda item to in any way impact on the treatment of the rats. The department had a long and well-recognized history of doing various forms of rat research and to interfere would most likely only serve to alienate the dean's office from that department, one of the largest and most productive in the university, as well as in the college. The chair of the department, having served on the search committee that hired me, knew my position on using animals for research and was somewhat apologetic when (s)he showed me the rat lab, demonstrating, in a careful way, a sentiment that showed a soft commitment to what they were doing with the rats.

But agenda items sometimes appear unexpectedly from around a corner to suddenly demand the dean's attention. Again, the primary required skill of the dean under these circumstances is to recognize the opportunity when it appears: an email—a simple email from the department chair asking for additional funds for . . . more live rats. The department underestimated the number of rats that would be needed for the number of sections they would be teaching and the amount of research that would be conducted, and they were over budget on that item. Could the dean help? The request was accompanied by a comment from the senior faculty member involved with the rat research. The comment said something to the effect that the department hoped to continue to teach these classes and conduct this type of research to preserve its role as one of the few remaining departments in the country engaged in teaching undergraduates with the use of live rats.

Once the opportunity is recognized the next step is to act on it. Typically that is not easy to do, but in this case I was given a little help by the senior faculty member's comment. "One of the few remaining . . ." Hummm . . . why would that be? So, I looked up the ethical standards of the national organization for this particular discipline and discovered why we held the distinction of being one of the few universities in the country continuing to do this type of work. The guidelines for teaching and doing research with live animals were rigorous, and if taken seriously were quite restrictive. I sent the web link of the ethical guidelines to the department chair with a note saying something to the effect that we should not be surprised that we are among the few remaining universities doing this kind of work. It is possible that we were in violation of the national organization's ethical guidelines for the treatment of animals, especially as pertains to teaching.

In response to the chair's request for additional funds I indicated that I would provide the department with what was needed for the current academic year but would not be providing additional funding for this activity in the future. The message was deliberately constructed in a way that indicated my lack of support for that particular component of their teaching and research. That was all that was needed. It is, however, quite likely that the chair played an important role in helping fulfill this unexpected agenda item. Had (s)he reacted defensively the department would have rallied behind her/him and they would most likely still be buying rats. That isn't what happened. Shortly after this event the senior faculty member in charge of the rat lab classes announced her/his retirement. And at about that same time, one of the two new faculty members whose research was based on the use of live rats announced being allergic to rats, established a new research agenda, and began a gradual career shift. The second new faculty member sought and found employment elsewhere. Suddenly there were no more rats in the rat lab. The lab was empty, waiting to be cleaned and converted into a regular classroom.

The department was able to use the vacated positions to support other programs that were in need of additional faculty members. While it was always a pleasure supporting this excellent department, the pleasure increased dramatically after the rats were gone.

Gender Bias in the Catalogue

Earlier, when discussing the undergraduate catalog, a comment was made to the effect that "sometimes good things come out of the tedious and mundane." It was stated that this comment would be revisited, and this small section makes good on that promise. As the sole person in charge of the undergraduate catalog at a relatively small private university, one has a great deal of responsibility, but also a great deal of latitude. During my last year there many catalog adjustments had to be made in order to formalize all of the curriculum changes related to the new core. All eyes were on those changes, which had to be overseen by the dean's office.

For about 2 years efforts had been made to get all of the departments and other university offices to make their catalog language gender neutral. Up to that point there had not been attention given to gender neutral language and, while a few chairs complied with the request, the language throughout most sections of the catalog still included "him" "his" and "freshman"—at a school historically for women. As one sits at her/his desk in the last few weeks of their administration one should think seriously about the good that can be done in those closing moments. There is little to lose and there are decisions that can be made without worrying about negative reactions—decisions worthy of a dean's executive status.

Once all of the other needed catalog changes were made all gender biased language was searched, identified, and neutralized. "Freshman" became "first year student" and all of the gender biased pronouns were changed accordingly as well. Yes, I understood fully all of the arguments against using the term "first year student." But the arguments in favor of doing so were far more compelling.

Shortly before completing this book that same undergraduate catalog was reviewed to see if gender neutrality was maintained. A quick scan of a recent catalog revealed that it has been maintained throughout the discussions of the departmental programs, with the exception of two programs. Gender-biased language (specifically "freshman") was, however, reinstated in the discussion of the general requirements and expectations for first year students—a section that appears at the beginning of the catalog. In situations like this, one needs to focus on the successful part of the action taken and realize that changes of this nature are difficult for many to accept. Three steps forward and one step back are actually more than one should expect when making this kind of change.

One cannot expect to be able to march into a position and necessarily make the above kinds of changes. Sometimes an opportunity must present itself before the dean can act. But it is important for deans to recognize the opportunities that can be acted upon to make a positive difference at the university and/or the outside community. Opportunities do arise, and choosing the right ones to act upon is a critical component of the dean's ever evolving agenda.

Lessons Learned Regarding Unexpected Agenda Opportunities

"Unexpected" agenda opportunities are often challenging in a number of ways. Before embracing an unexpected agenda opportunity deans should ask: How real are these issues? How important are they? Are there potential winners and losers involved and how might that play itself out relative to other important agenda items? Finally, does the dean have a reasonable chance of being successful? A lot of time and energy can go into a cause that produces no notable positive outcome and yet strains relationships with others across the campus.

DEPARTMENTS ARE NOT EASY

It is rarely easy to help academic departments—even with their most serious problems. This is true for a number of reasons. Perhaps most significant among these reasons is that academic departments are mostly accustomed to hearing the response that nothing can be done to help them. So when someone comes along who offers a possible solution to their problem they tend to back up in disbelief. There has to be a catch to it or the "solution" would not exist. This type of suspicion is common in academia and difficult to mitigate.

There are also mini agendas working themselves out within departments. Some might actually be legitimate, such as how a particular faculty member's teaching and/or research might be impacted by a scheduling change, but others are foolish and even petty: whose offices will be next to whose, a classroom needed for offices was attained 30 years ago in some special deal, a faculty member likes being isolated so people don't notice when they are there, another faculty member has so much "litter" in their office that they cannot imagine moving before they die, and so on. It is important to investigate the significance of these latter mini issues and, if necessary, separate them from the serious decision-making process—not unsympathetically, but with reasonable assertiveness. Once the decision is made to embrace an issue as part of a dean's agenda it must be done vigorously and with well thought out plans and backup plans.

A System's Approach

When solving complex difficult problems one must be constantly looking at how the parts of the problem can be resolved in an integrated fashion. For example, when looking at the space that could be built out in the strip mall it was recognized that the department that would be housed there would also be the department that could make the best use of the theater lecture hall, which happened to be just around the corner. They would also be close to the lecture hall that would eventually be built beneath the arena. Prior to the faculty from that department being moved to the strip mall, plans were already made for converting their old office and lab space to modern classrooms so that rooms could be taken on the first floor to convert into offices and labs for the second department that needed to be moved. And, of course, all of this has to be done within the financial constraints of the dean's budget, expected summer school surplus, and other potential sources of funds, most of which usually require lobbying and negotiating. This is sometimes referred to as taking a systems approach, as promoted by Buller (2013):

> . . . adopting a systems approach means looking at each decision as though it were a chess move. A chess player can't think solely in terms of a single piece and a single move but has to consider each piece's relationship to all the others on the board, all the possible moves his or her opponent may make, and all the possible results of each decision ten to fifteen moves further into the game. Positive academic leaders work in this way as well (p. 165).

It is difficult to be an effective intentional dean without being able to conceptually analyze complex multivariate relationships.

CONCLUSION

Indeed, the particular qualifications, strengths, and skills, that a dean brings to a position will determine the dean's agenda for adding value to the college and university overall. The same is true relative to which "unexpected" items the dean decides to add to her/his list.

In addition to heavy dependence on cooperation and support from the faculty, enough cannot be said of the important roles played by administrative assistants, assistants to the dean, and some department chairs in helping the dean with her/his agenda. The normal responsibilities and corresponding activities of the dean are clearly enough to keep the office assistants busy. Each time a new dean comes into that position the staff's workload must shift to accommodate the corresponding new agenda. This can be unsettling as they work to make this adjustment. The extent to which deans depend on their staff and office colleagues for their success overall cannot be overstated.[2]

NOTES

1 Evidence of the importance of a dean's leadership attributes can be seen in the work of Wilkes, Cross, Jackson, and Daly (2015).

2 For a helpful essay on hiring and evaluating staff see Benders (2014).

REFERENCES

Alessio, J.C. (1996). Curriculum transformation through critique. *Transformations: The Journal of Inclusive Scholarship and Pedagogy*, 7 (2), 79–92.

Benders, A. (2014). Effective hiring and evaluation of staff, in L.L. Behling (Ed.). *The resource handbook for academic deans* (pp. 255–259). San Francisco: Jossey-Bass.

Buller, J.L. (2013). *Positive academic leadership: How to stop putting out fires and start making a difference.* San Francisco: Jossey-Bass.

Conboy, K. (2014). Establishing and implementing your vision: Strategic planning in Academic Affairs, in L.L. Behling (Ed.). *The resource handbook for academic deans* (pp. 149–154). San Francisco: Jossey-Bass.

Krahenbuhl, G.S. (2004). *Building the academic deanship: Strategies for success.* Westport: Praeger Publishers.

Santamaría, L.J., Jeffries, J. & Santamaria, A.P. (2016). Unpacking institutional culture to diversify the leadership pipeline, in L.J. Santamaría & A.P. Santamaría (Eds.). *Culturally responsive leadership in higher education: Promoting access, equity, and improvement* (pp. 17–29). New York: Routledge.

Wilkes, L., Cross, W., Jackson, D. & Daly, J. (2015). A repertoire of leadership attributes: An international study of deans of nursing. *Journal of Nursing Management*, 23 (3), 279–286. Retrieved September 11, 2016 from http://eds. a.ebscohost.com.libproxy.stcloudstate.edu/eds/pdfviewer/pdfviewer?vid=3&sid=645c4cd7-2d58-4553-9a7f-4dbb8675ecf2%40sessionmgr4008&hid=4208

Wolfgramm-Foliaki, E. (2016). "Do not assume we know": Perspectives of pacific island first in the family students, in L.J. Santamaría & A.P. Santamaría (Eds.). *Culturally responsive leadership in higher education: Promoting access, equity, and improvement* (pp. 122–135). New York: Routledge.

Chapter 6

Budgeting and Budget-Related Activities

It is best to think of the dean's budget as part of the budget of academic affairs, which hopefully is the largest portion of the university's expenditures. Within this framework, it is safe to say that academic affairs budgets are done differently from institution to institution. Sometimes this difference is a function of the overall budgeting process of the university, and sometimes it is a function of the way in which a particular academic vice president (AVP) chooses to handle the budgeting for academic affairs. There seems to be an increasing tendency for vice presidents for administrative affairs (VPAA) to play an important role in shaping the budgeting process for the institution. This is a role that has gradually transitioned from glorified bookkeeper to significant institutional decision-maker—especially during times of financial shortfalls or other financial exigencies. For the purposes of this discussion, we will focus on the dean's role within different approaches taken by the AVP's office. The reader should be warned that this is pretty boring stuff, but there are some important pieces of information in this chapter that deans should be thinking about.

CENTRALIZED VERSUS DECENTRALIZED BUDGETING PRACTICES

Centralized Budgeting

In some institutions budgeting for all of academic affairs is highly centralized. Under these circumstances deans may have little actual control over most of the money being spent in their college. The dean's office may have a small operating budget with some discretionary money, but the AVP's office controls all of the major expenditures: faculty and staff salaries, faculty and staff hires, new program expenses, money for repairs and renovations that are not covered by the physical plant budget, and even adjunct hires and other forms of part-time hires. A department chair in a medium to large university might be thinking, "wow, I'm doing most of that now as a department chair." That is probably true, but there are dean's positions that have little budgetary control. These kinds of positions, typically associated with smaller private institutions, are most likely decreasing in numbers as the smaller schools try to become more like the bigger schools and try to compete for quality administrators.

If, prior to signing a contract, the AVP is being evasive about letting the offeree see something that looks like a real budget for the dean's office, that probably means the AVP does not want the offeree to know that (s)he will control very little of the financial resources. In my first deaning position, on a day-to-day basis, the dean's office had direct control over less money than many of the departments that were under the dean's administration. The dean did have the ability to electronically shift money from one department to another, but that could only be done under unusual circumstances after serious negotiations with the department about to lose the money.

While this kind of budgeting makes a dean's administrative ability somewhat restricted, it does serve the purpose of affording the higher administrators the ability to keep careful track of how much money they have at all times. This approach may come across as unnecessary or even petty, but for smaller schools that have relatively modest donors and endowments, keeping a clear unflinching eye on the bottom line is important. It is ironic that part of the process of keeping a tight centralized hold on every cent in the institution is a budget building system that is somewhat inductive in nature. Keeping tight control over the money doesn't necessarily mean that the higher administration doesn't care about what the needs actually are in the departmental and college trenches. They want the institution to succeed. So a process has to be in place to make sure that the central administration assigns funds as closely as possible to the actual departmental needs since there are no discretionary funds at the dean's level to make adjustments for possible discrepancies.

"Inductive" Budget Building and Centralized Spending

One method of building a college budget uses a grass roots approach—within predetermined parameters of course. Keep in mind that it is perfectly logical that a budget can be constructed from the bottom up and "spent" from the top down—separate from one's position on the efficacy. From the standpoint of the academic college, this method begins with the AVP receiving from the administrative affairs office the budgets for the current year for all of the units within academic affairs. These budgets are based primarily on the previous year's budgets. This typically happens around late September or early October. The AVP reviews those budgets and writes in recommended amounts for each line that needs to be changed, decreasing some and increasing others. Once that step is completed the budgets are sent back to administrative affairs and processed within the constraints of the overall university budget and corresponding resources in conjunction with the president's oversight. New printouts are created and sent from the president to all of the units throughout the university, including all of the units in academic affairs.

Upon receiving these budget printouts (probably all done electronically now) containing the past, current, and recommended expenditures, the heads of each unit (mainly department chairs) make their budget requests for the coming fiscal year. They are typically given until about the third week in December to return these requests to the dean's office. The dean must then review them, make recommended penciled-in adjustments for each line where deemed necessary, and submit them signed and dated to the AVP by mid-January. The dean should take into consideration whether the money allocated during the previous year was spent as requested and whether requested changes are properly justified with documentation. The dean should also contact chairs as needed to discuss any discrepancies or unclear requests. The AVP reviews the budgets again, and after consulting with the deans about any notable changes, returns all of them to the president.

"Decentralized" Budgeting and Spending

The just described budgeting process is highly structured and precise. Other methods are a variation of the above method with some being rather loose and disorganized. Those campuses that provide a lot of college level autonomy are probably less likely to have a highly structured, and thus highly controlled (by the higher administration), budgeting process. Such budgets might be considered decentralized both in terms of how they are constructed and how they are spent. Budgets may go from year to year with little or no change, since there is not a scheduled systematic annual budget redistribution process up and down the administrative line. An abbreviated version of budgetary oversight might be an annual meeting with an associate provost who will review the college budget with the dean based primarily on what the budget was the year before, incorporating any changes related to new hires or retirements that may have occurred. Decentralized budgeting and spending allows deans to be independently supportive of their faculty and programs as needed. It also promotes innovation, creativity, and relative self-sufficiency.

The drawback of decentralized budgeting as described above, which is probably the norm in higher education, is the possibility of budget stagnation. If resource reallocation does not take place voluntarily, at least within units, it might not happen at all until there is a major economic crisis of some sort. That is why some university systems occasionally feign a budget crisis thereby allowing them, with an eye on collective bargaining agreements especially, to force a major shake-up in the various budgets of the institution. The inability to effectively reallocate resources is viewed by some as a serious problem in academia (Dickeson, 2010).

Decentralized budgeting and budget control as described here is not the same as Responsibility Center Management (RCM), a decentralized budgeting method that is promoted primarily by for-profit privatization advocates. RCM makes lower level academic units responsible, not only for balancing their budget in the usual sense, but in the additional sense of building into one's budget all of the possible short- and long-term costs of any segment of the institution touched by that unit, including the physical plant—analogous to indirect cost recovery from externally funded grants (see Krahenbuhl, 2004: 163). It turns departments and colleges into self-contained islands that either sink or swim on their own. Under these circumstances one can imagine the possible consequences. Departments are motivated to eliminate courses from their programs that are taught by other departments, and the concept of interdisciplinary programming across departments is pretty much unthinkable. Such a disposition toward programming runs counter to current educational trends and counter to a more general movement in society to soften rather than harden organizational unit boundaries (Helgesen, 1999). From the analyses that have been done so far it appears that RCM is not a good fit for the operation of higher educational institutions. It ignores the synergistic nature of universities, which are not just sink or swim cost centers, but interrelated parts that make critical contributions to the whole educational enterprise. And the overall value of these contributions and their cost are not necessarily correlated (Dubeck, 1997).

BUDGETARY "PLAY"

A key question guiding university budgeting processes is, "how much play do I want my budgeting system to have?" If administrators want colleges and departments to be innovative with some ability to be creative, exploratory, entrepreneurial, and supportive of those who excel within their units, they should want a university budget system that is sufficiently decentralized that there are pockets of money spread throughout the various levels and units of academic affairs. However, the more the funds of academic affairs are spread out, the more difficult it is to track those funds, and the more play that budgeting system will have.

What does it mean to have "play" in the budgeting system? Not all money that is budgeted is spent. And not all money that is budgeted is spent when, or even where, it is supposed to be spent. Faculty members get sick, overly stressed, or become disillusioned, and go on leave. Frequently, position searches are failed for various reasons. When adjunct faculty members are hired to replace fulltime faculty members, costs are reduced considerably. The same might be true of other types of positions, but there are many faculty positions at a university, and faculty salaries make up the most costly budget item overall for the institution.

What happens when the salaries of fulltime faculty members do not have to be paid for some period of time, and when this sort of payment deferral, for one salary or another (possibly many), is occurring in an ongoing manner? When this occurs, as it is certainly bound to do in large academic budgets, one is faced with fairly large amounts of budgetary play? Budgetary play also occurs within smaller budget lines when a new printer costs less than expected, or the faculty member who proposed to order new lab equipment decides (s)he won't be able to use that equipment, so the order is canceled. But the play that continuously occurs due to an ongoing relatively stable number of faculty positions remaining unfilled is substantial, and represents an amount of money that is tempting to use in a variety of productive ways.

Depending on the size of the institution, there could be millions of dollars "floating" in the budget of academic affairs . . . possibly hundreds of thousands within a particular college. Play within an academic affairs budget is highly predictable within certain margins of error—albeit the exact magnitude of that margin of error generally remains unknown. Without knowing the exact margin of error, one can still arrive at a number representing a conservative estimate of the amount of play within a budget. This number can be determined through trial and error over a period of a few years. If, for example, the amount of play has not gone below one million dollars in an academic affairs budget over the last 3 years, then one might make spending decisions based on that amount or some monetary figure close to that amount. The same is true of college budgets, but on a much smaller scale.

In other words, an administrator can behave as if (s)he has an additional one million dollars, or three quarters of a million dollars, in their budget that they in actuality don't have. This means that if a provost wants to do so, (s)he can give a dean permission to hire a faculty member for which there are no budgeted funds. Of course, if that position costs the institution $100,000 a year then that means that the $750,000 spendable (to be relatively safe) out of the expected approximately $1,000,000 of annual play is now reduced, theoretically, to $650,000 for subsequent years. How many provosts actually keep careful track of the exact amount of spendable money they have from play is uncertain . . . probably not many—although in recent years provosts have learned to be more careful than in the past and have associate provosts in place for that purpose.

Indeed, committing funds out of budgetary play for long-term annual expenditures can become risky. This is true for deans as well as provosts—albeit deans do not typically have the large margins of flexibility that provosts have, and as mentioned earlier, some institutions budget in a way that provides deans with little budgeting flexibility. Assuming a dean does have control over a significant budget, (s)he might give a department $45,000 from anticipated unspent budgeted funds to set up a new lab as a one-time expenditure. This would be a reasonably safe use of funds from budgetary play. It is something completely different, however, for that dean to give a department $45,000 to create a permanent position to hire someone to manage that lab. This latter expenditure represents a long-term annual commitment over an indefinite period of time, so the dean would have to subtract that amount from all future budgetary play that might occur; and, of course, the assumption is that the budgetary play will always be over the $45,000 dollar long-term commitment.

Use of budgetary play is curbed somewhat by institutional or system restrictions on what budget lines can be crossed. For example, personnel funds typically cannot be used for other purposes—albeit they can be moved among personnel lines. There is, however, enough flexibility among many of the non-personnel budget lines that money can often be transferred from one line to another.[1] It is also possible in some instances to transfer money from other lines into personnel lines. These comments continue to be prefaced with the understanding that there are different forms of budgeting and different budgeting rules across institutions.

Risks of Spending from Budgetary Play

The obvious risk of allocating money from budgetary play for long-term commitments is that it is possible that during a particular year the amount of play in the budget could drop dramatically and one might not have enough funds to cover all of the unbudgeted long-term commitments that have been made. This could happen under normal circumstances, but there are extenuating circumstances that can dramatically increase the odds of this happening. One such extenuating circumstance is when a new president wants to have more funds under her/his control for certain projects (s)he has in mind . . . new stadium, new dorm, new classroom building, and so on. So, the president hires a new VPAA whose responsibility is to make those projects possible. The first task of that new vice president is to eliminate the play in the budgeting process and collect all the available "loose change" for the president. Discretionary money will be reduced and all unspent budgeted funds will be tracked and returned to the general fund. What now happens to the "permanent" positions that were filled using budgetary play? How will they be funded in the future?

Equally problematic, if not more so, is the circumstance of a budgetary crisis, such as the crisis state university systems experienced following the 2008 national financial recession. Under these conditions, university colleges are asked to cut their budgets by a certain amount of money or by a certain percentage. If a dean of a college was so "lucky" as to have been given positions funded from expected budgetary play, that dean could be in for a big surprise. The provost who assigned those funds will no longer have them for future years, and of course will not want to admit to anyone that (s)he committed unbudgeted funds indefinitely by assigning them to faculty positions. Hence, the funding for those positions is now being funneled back into the general budget. The play is gone. The dean is now in a position of being accused of annually spending $350,000 over her/his approved budget. What does (s)he have to say about that? Is (s)he going to attribute blame to her/his boss and say these positions were in place before (s)he arrived and (s)he had nothing to do with the over-expenditures? Is the dean going to tell the faculty members involved, "sorry, you were hired without proper funding and I now must let you go"?

The answers to the above questions are generally: "no" and "no." No one will believe the dean's whistle-blowing approach because no one of decision-making importance will want to believe it. And, of course, there is tenure, collective bargaining agreements, and due process that prevent the dean from simply eliminating the faculty positions that were not properly funded, positions added unwisely before the dean arrived. The dean cannot simply let the involved faculty members go.

More importantly, the dean may not even know what the source of the gross over-expenditure is when the budget shortfall is first brought to her/his attention. (S)he may have to spend time with her/his staff unraveling the mystery. But whether the dean figures it out satisfactorily or not, (s)he is faced with having to add the $350,000 to the amount (s)he is otherwise expected to cut from her/his budget due to the, by now, publically declared institutional (in some instances state) financial crisis.

The actual process of cutting budgets will be discussed later, but for now it is important to realize the dangers of using budgetary play too casually. Being in a situation that allows one to have a lot of budget play does not necessarily mean that it is a good idea to use it. It is best to monitor one's college's expenses carefully as best one can and anticipate unspent budgeted funds that can be moved around toward the end of the fiscal year. Taking this approach still allows one to spend some of the "left over" funds for important one time expenditures . . . building out a new office complex for a department, renovating classrooms and offices, upgrading classroom and laboratory hardware/software, and so on. If the provost should offer a dean tenure track positions for which the dean does not have funds, which the provost might do in order to support a new program (s)he wants to champion, the dean will be wise to decline—unless (s)he is certain those funds are coming specifically from some other part of the provost's existing budget. Keep in mind one important simple truth: for a college to receive a new faculty line that increases a dean's overall budget, someone else in the university has to give up a similar position, or the university has to have received new money from somewhere. New money for tenure track positions cannot be one-time money. It has to be money added to the budget permanently, so that it is available every year indefinitely. An alternative to declining the provost's position offer altogether would be to accept the funds for fixed-term positions (typically 3–5 years max) in hopes that retirements or other departures in the university will eventually allow the positions to be converted to tenure track.

TWO ADDITIONAL USEFUL CONCEPTS

Non-Discretionary Funding

Sometime during the fall, in some institutions, the dean will ask the chairs for non-discretionary funding requests. These requests will be due approximately a month later. This is a call for chairs to identify financial needs that are not covered by their budget, but which are clearly necessary to run a program or maintain an accreditation, run a new lab and so on. For example, a new sports physiology program might discover it needs a certain piece of equipment if it is going to be competitive and if it expects to attain accreditation. The importance of this expenditure makes it a non-discretionary extra-budgetary item. Non-discretionary funds may also include items determined essential for future budgets but which are currently not in the existing budget. In the case of the need for a particular piece of equipment, this will not be an ongoing part of that department's budget. It is a one-time non-discretionary expenditure. New accreditation fees, however, will eventually have to become part of the department's long-term budget, and that money will have to come from some specific location in the overall budget of academic affairs.

Pro Forma

Where does the money for new program expenditures, such as accreditation costs, come from? New programs are approved with a pro forma, which is a financial (input/outcomes) projection for the new program if approved. A pro forma usually covers a period of about 3 to 5 years. It shows projected costs and projected income for the new program. The new income projection is based primarily on the number of new students the program is expected to draw to the campus. Hence, a pro forma may include requests for new faculty lines, as well as other related expenses. Sometimes funding the identified pro forma personnel positions is contingent upon the new program generating a certain amount of new funds or new students within a designated time period. Yes, there is a "catch 22" of sorts associated with this process. How does a program generate students before it has the faculty members to sufficiently offer the program? The answer to this question unravels one of the great publically unknown truths about academia: much of the work of creative entrepreneurial faculty members comes out of faculty hide.

Anyone who has been a faculty member and developed new programs will fully understand the "out of hide" phenomenon. In most universities across the United States, if a department wants a new program it must develop and teach the new courses first and then hope new students will be followed by new faculty positions. Only in rare situations where it is clear that a new very promising program does not have someone with a specific required credential, or if there is an existing accreditation at stake, will an administration approve a pro forma that involves an immediate new hire. The pro forma is less a mechanism for putting in place what is needed to actually run a new program as it is a means by which departments, after a certain period of time, can say they have done their part, and now it is time for the administration to do theirs. The faculty has a right to expect the agreed upon positions required to bring a reasonable workload and the appropriately specialized personnel to the over-stretched department.

In some instances the pro forma becomes a tool for stopping programs that an administrator does not like for some particular reason other than its curricular value or student drawing potential. Sometimes deans or higher officials do not like the faculty of a particular department because they are not cooperative or they require a great deal of administrative intervention of some sort or another. Administrators might also be opposed to a new program on ideological grounds. None of these reasons are acceptable, in themselves, for determining the fate of a newly proposed program—just as they are not acceptable for determining the fate of an existing program. If the curriculum is sound and there is student demand for the program it should be approved and supported. Curriculum decisions and personnel decisions should be kept separate to whatever extent possible. Too often they are not, causing students, potential students and the university overall to suffer more rather than less. With that said, however, administrators are charged with protecting the mission and corresponding objectives of the university. If a program would somehow work against the mission of the institution it should be questioned and possibly not supported. Institutional missions too often get lost in the scramble for students and funding.

Zero Cost Pro Forma

When a newly proposed program is not in high favor with the administration the faculty members proposing the program have no choice but to request zero new funds on the pro forma, which means zero new positions. While not normally a reasonable expectation of faculty, it does happen. I once initiated and co-developed an unusual interdisciplinary graduate program, and suspecting the dean would not want to approve it, no new funds were requested. The entire program was to be done out of hide. The concept of "out of hide" is sometimes a little misleading since those involved in projects like this often receive a lot of professional satisfaction when they are successful.

In this case, even with a pro forma zero budget, the dean refused to support the proposed program. Yet, this was a program that clearly addressed the mission of the university and college. It promised to bring diversity to the curriculum and bring diversity to the student body, which were identified as university objectives and were supposedly highly valued by the institution. The student demand for the program was well documented, and still the dean refused to sign off on the program. During a meeting with the provost present the dean gave as her/his reason that the program was too radical. The proposal had to be resubmitted to the curriculum process through a different college that had a more forward looking dean. The program was eventually approved by the university and the state and it became one of the most successful graduate programs on campus in every important respect.

The curriculum "belongs" to the faculty, but it is the dean's responsibility to protect the institution's resources and the institution's mission and manage the programs of the college. A dean's influence through control of the purse should bring the curriculum closer to respective institutional missions by simply following due process and established decision-making criteria. Under those circumstances, if the missions are consistent with broad-based values and global social and environmental needs, deans can be comfortable that they are, indeed, bringing about positive social change and thus making the world a better place. Simply stated, good programs, within the above context, should be approved and supported with adequate levels of resources identified on the pro forma—resources commensurate with the program's potential drawing power from outside communities.

The Imperative of New Students for a Healthy Budget

When there are additional position lines conditionally "approved" for a new program via a pro forma, for those positions to eventually actually exist within a department, new students, and thus new money, must come to campus. If that does not occur as projected in the pro forma (or some formal document representing a pro forma), there will not be a basis for the administration to assign new funds to the program. This is a much clearer and cleaner reality in the private systems than it is in the state systems, since the relationship between students and money is relatively clear in the private world and much less so in the public world.

Some state systems have funding policies that are awkward, and they are difficult for many within the system to appreciate and/or understand. All income is sent to a central system office that then redistributes the money to the campuses according to a formula (variable by systems) designed to, in effect, keep all the campuses operating smoothly. Highly successful campuses are then sometimes subsidizing the less successful and smaller campuses. This means that some campuses are funded at a higher rate per student than others and that it is quite possible, if not likely, that the most successful campus will receive the lowest per student funding from the central office. Typically an important contribution of the distribution formula is controlling for what is called "economy of scale," which is based on the belief that it takes a certain baseline amount of money to run a campus regardless of its size. Hence, smaller campuses, theoretically, must be assured of having the same stable infrastructure as the larger campuses. While this is certainly true to some extent, it is difficult to know exactly how much the smaller campuses should be subsidized. Redistributing funds in a manner that over-subsidizes the smaller campuses poses a danger of creating a disincentive for larger campuses to change and grow. The relationship between creative entrepreneurial program development, corresponding student recruitment, and funding should be protected, but sometimes it isn't.

This problem tends not to be an issue in the private universities, but it can be if a private university has multiple campuses. Increasing numbers of private schools have multiple campuses today since, given the availability of online programs, it has become fashionable and almost necessary to bring education to the student rather than the other way around. The matter is complicated further by state universities being more heavily supported by the state than the private universities. That may seem like a truism and thus a goofy thing to say, but the notion that private universities are not supported by the state is clearly a myth. Indeed, in some states the difference might not be great.

Likewise, the notion that state universities are completely funded by the state is equally a myth. Today, if a "state" university receives 40 percent of their needed funds from the state, it is doing pretty well. There are "state" universities that receive less than 30 percent of their needed operating funds from the state. Whatever the funding sources and the corresponding distribution formula, state universities, like private universities, must find a way to effectively predict and measure the student and/or credit dollars that new programs bring to a campus, and this information needs to be used when evaluating new programs for approval and resource allocation, whether this takes place through a pro forma or some other similar cost benefit analysis.

Controlling Enrollments

Some universities and university systems have imposed enrollment caps on campuses. Under these circumstances, new programs serve a slightly different role. All institutions want to be at the cutting edge of curricular innovation and future program demand, particularly as relate to the university's mission. Institutions that have enrollment caps support new programming almost exclusively for that purpose. The difference between capped enrollment campuses and uncapped campuses is that for the latter new student markets are also targeted for enrollment growth purposes. Whether capped or not, cutting edge programming protects future enrollments and allows institutions to continue to selectively draw high-level students, which tends to enhance the vitality of a university in a variety of ways.

When enrollment growth is not considered desirable, program resource requests become somewhat complicated. A faculty cannot grow if the student body remains stable, or unless new money is brought into the university from some other source. Hence, for new programs (or significantly altered programs) to develop in a stable university environment there must be ways of moving faculty members and faculty lines from program to program. If a new program requires four faculty positions and only two of those can be moved into the new program from an existing related program within that department, there needs to be a reallocation of two positions from somewhere else in the university. For the most part, new programs in universities with capped populations require moving both students and faculty positions into the new programs from somewhere else within those same universities. This doesn't mean literally moving existing students, but shifting recruitment and enrollment targets.

Sometimes departments that are understaffed develop new programs as a way of being able to argue for additional staffing. This is generally not a good idea without a corresponding strongly supported pro forma, since doing so will add more stress to an already overworked faculty. The bottom line is that universities do not typically commit to full staffing for new programs upfront. There is often an expectation of some personnel shifting (positions or parts of positions) to accommodate new programs. This, of course, is the purpose of the pro forma whereby in an honest system staffing additions are committed around student enrollment targets. In a dishonest system vague promises are made that may or may not ever be fulfilled. Even the pro forma is no guarantee of exactly what will happen, but at least there is something on paper for a faculty to turn to when it finds itself short staffed. Administrators don't get paid to hire faculty without sufficient justification, and bringing new students, or a new market of students, to the university are the strongest reasons available.

If a department is losing enrollments while maintaining a stable number of faculty members, it behooves that department to consider designing a new program that might be consistent with current student markets. This could be a program staffed with existing faculty members, some of whom might gradually retool to meet the specific needs of the program. Under these circumstances, a zero-cost pro forma might be justifiable.

POLITICS AND UNIVERSITY FUNDS

Enrollment Issues and Politics

As deans struggle with the complexities of maintaining a strong college budget they need to realize there are forces outside of the university that are difficult, if not impossible, to reconcile. For example, some enrollment caps and enrollment reductions are part of a bigger picture that extends far beyond the local college or university budget. Some politicians, representing the interests of venture capitalists and financial investors, would like to convert public education funds into private investment funds. Of course, the best way to make this happen is to argue that public education is ineffective, inefficient, and wasteful and that the solution is to transition public educational into for-profit private education.

Private for-profit institutions should not be confused with private non-profit institutions. Once one leaves the upper echelons of higher educational institutions that have the capacity for large endowments and large research grants, the private non-profit universities are constantly struggling to maintain the budget necessary to provide the staffing required to deliver a well-rounded quality education to all of their students. Key market areas are typically targeted, resources are concentrated in those areas, and the quality of many other programs sometimes suffers. It takes exceptional skill and understanding of interdisciplinary curricula to be able to provide a quality education to all of the students drawn to a private non-profit campus.

Among religious orders that operate non-profit universities, for example, the Immaculate Heart of Mary Sisters are probably among the most skilled at knowing how to minimize damage while cutting corners. But make no mistake about it, there is a prominent goal of cutting corners and it doesn't always work—either in terms of providing high quality education or in terms of keeping the books balanced. Many private schools close due to financial problems. In the United States there has been an average of five non-profit private college/university closures per year over the 10-year period between roughly 2004 and 2013 (Lyken-Segosebe & Shepherd, 2013: 1). More than fifty non-profit private schools have closed in only 10 years—a considerable number.

Public degree granting colleges and universities, on the other hand, rarely close, even though they do sometimes falter. In part that is because they have the support of local politicians representing the district where the campus is located. State level political bargaining forces funding formulas to be created that assure the preservation of failing public institutions. Public institutions with declining enrollments are subsidized by the more successful institutions with the state acting as the mediating redistributor of the incoming funds.

While reasonable sounding arguments can be made for closing failing campuses during difficult financial times, doing so is a complicated matter. Both private non-profit and state university campuses are important parts of the social, economic, and cultural life of many of the more remote parts of some states. When schools close, not only are present students affected, but so are the alums, all of the employees of the school, and the surrounding community. Revenue flow of a small community can be dramatically impacted by the lost jobs and lost income previously provided by a local campus.

In the process of protecting public higher education campuses the state also protects a more well-rounded educational delivery than one finds in the private sector. Private schools are known for smaller classes and more individualized attention, but the public schools have more faculty members and more classes from which to choose for a particular course. The point is that both private non-profit and public colleges/universities have something special to offer the public. The average amount of state support for "public" campuses in the United States is now only 24.4 percent of total campus revenue (Snyder & Dillow, 2013: 315). Even with that remarkable statistic, because of ongoing political support, public higher education represents a more stable environment for deans and faculty members alike than either the private non-profit schools or the private for-profit schools.

For-Profit Privatization Movement

Increasingly university systems are hiring university presidents and chancellors with the long-term goal of privatizing education altogether. That is, there are serious efforts to create a for-profit educational "system" nation-wide out of the current public system. This is different than simply weakening state support to create another non-profit secular education system, as some have thought was the trend (NEA, 2004). The for-profit movement is far more consequential than that. For-profit privatization is based foremost on profit maximization. The expectation that quality will follow is unrealistic since the drive to increase profits never ends. Ultimately, everything is expendable for the sake of increased shareholder and CEO wealth. The downward spiral of quality and upward spiral of customer cost has been shown to be true with the privatization of other public services (Prentis, 2014; Buchheit, 2013). Profit maximization in higher education means greater reliance on adjunct faculty members who typically cannot spend much time with students and who do not always have the credentials and corresponding depth of education to provide high quality instruction and advising to their students.

Recent to writing this book a great deal of turmoil occurred over a university presidential search in Florida whereby the Florida State University (FSU) board, against the wishes of the faculty and students, appointed a state legislator with little experience in higher education. This new president—within a state system—is a strong advocate of privatizing higher education. This is clearly a "fox guarding the hen house" approach to public education leadership. There are indications of similar board appointments in other states as well. Boards are appointed by governors who have political agendas. With board appointments consistently of a particular political orientation a board can take on an agenda commensurate with the agenda of the governor who appointed them. The governor's agenda could in turn be the agenda of the people who financed the governor's election.

The influence of private money on public universities and their curricula is a growing phenomenon. For example, the above mentioned appointment of the FSU president was likely to have been influenced by the donations of the wealthy Koch brothers who have not only donated to FSU but have offered FSU a 1.5-million-dollar contract in support of the school's economics department, stipulating that the Koch brothers can appoint an advisory committee that oversees the hiring and evaluation of faculty members brought to campus with "their" money. The Koch brothers are buying influence on numerous campuses, including George Mason University where Charles Koch chairs the board of one program to which he donates, and he sits on the board of another (Levinthal, 2014).

If the public campus or system for which a dean works is being downsized (s)he may want to determine whether the enrollment changes are due to state economic factors, population shifts, decreased demand for higher education in that state, or a broader plan to channel public funds into private for-profit pockets. A dean most likely does not want to stay in a system or on a campus where the latter option is the reality. If a dean is in such an environment, (s)he might be in charge of downsizing her/his college which means reducing their budget and laying off faculty members. Deans in such environments may also be responsible for increased fundraising and more careful "monitoring" of the curricula.

Discretionary Spending and Politics

It is important to understand that the political pressures relating to how to spend the college funds do not always come from outside the campus. The AVP (provost) and the VPAA of a dean's campus are going to be aware of how college money is spent. If a dean has budgetary discretion (s)he will need to monitor that discretion carefully. Discretionary money is not always as discretionary as one might hope, and thus a dean's discretion, or lack thereof, could lead to broader consequences: budgetary practices being changed, particular sources of funds (like summer school funds) being intercepted, or simply questions being asked at the dean's next private session with the provost. Deans might know where their provost stands on academic philosophical political issues, and they might assume they can act accordingly. But the provost must operate within a small cluster of vice presidents and the president—the president's inner cabinet. If a dean does something that embarrasses the provost in the president's cabinet, especially if it is something that (s)he is unaware of before going into the meeting, the dean's next conversation with the provost will be difficult and memorable. If the issue relates to how money is being spent in the college, one's discretionary funds could be in jeopardy.

The message is that deans want to be careful with what is done with discretionary college funds. Being careful should not be interpreted to mean being watchful for certain political or philosophical ideologies. Academic freedom should never be compromised. It doesn't matter if the people brought to campus are radical left or radical right, it is important that the dean establish a good track record of supporting quality guest speakers and programs.

To whatever extent possible, deans want to fund interesting and informative programs and let the faculty members in charge take responsibility for running those programs. Most of the time that approach works fine, but not always. One problematic guest speaker, that costs the college more than expected, can cast a long shadow over ten excellent speakers. This kind of mishap can add fuel to the higher administration's interest in taking greater control of college generated summer money, which is often the primary source of college discretionary funds. When efforts are made by the VPAA to reduce college discretionary funds the deans might have to organize to defend their lifeline to supporting creativity, entrepreneurialism, and critical thinking within their colleges. It is not possible to be an effective intentional dean without discretionary funds. Deans must be vigilant on this issue if they hope to be successful. The university is primarily the faculty and the students—not the president's office, not the provost's office, and not the dean's office. But the dean's office is the mechanism by which support is brought directly to the faculty and the students, and the dean knows how and where to place that support to maximize desirable outcomes. Financially starving the dean's office is denying the dean the ability to help faculty, students, and the college in general, as needed. An intentional dean cannot honorably serve as a functionary robot.

NOTE

1 For a useful discussion of this issue and other important budgeting issues, see Buller (2007). As do I, Buller strongly advocates for watching your budget carefully, but it is unclear whether he is saying to do it yourself or make sure one of your staff members does it. I advocate for the former.

REFERENCES

Buchheit, P. (2013). 8 ways privatization has failed America. *Common Dreams*, (August). Retrieved September 25, 2016 from www.commondreams.org/views/2013/08/05/8-ways-privatization-has-failed-america

Buller, J.L. (2007). *The essential academic dean*. San Francisco: Jossey-Bass.

Dickeson, R.C. (2010). *Prioritizing academic programs and services: Reallocating resources to achieve strategic balance*. San Francisco: Jossey-Bass.

Dubeck, L.W. (1997). Beware higher ed's newest budget twist. *Thought & Action* (Spring). Retrieved February 25, 2016 from www.nea.org/assets/img/PubThoughtAndAction/TAA_97Spr_07.pdf

Helgesen, S. (1999). Dissolving boundaries in the era of knowledge and custom work, in F. Hesselbein, M. Goldsmith & I. Somerville (Eds.). *Leading beyond the walls*. (pp. 49–55). San Francisco: Jossey-Bass.

Krahenbuhl, G.S. (2004). *Building the academic deanship: Strategies for success*. Westport: Praeger Publishers.

Levinthal, D. (2014). Inside the Koch brothers' campus crusade. *Politics* (Center for Public Integrity). Retrieved January 6, 2015 from www.publicintegrity.org/(2014)/03/27/14497/inside-koch-brothers-campus-crusade

Lyken-Segosebe, D. & Shepherd, J.C. (2013). *Learning from closed institutions: Indicators of risk for small private colleges and universities.* Retrieved January 6, 2015 from www.ticua.org/public_policy/sm_files/Learning%20from%20Closed%20Institutions.pdf

NEA (National Education Association Higher Education Research Center). (2004). Higher education and privatization. *Update*, 10(2), 1–6. Retrieved September 25, 2016 from www.nea.org/assets/docs/ HE/vol10no2.pdf

Prentis, E.L. (2014). Has privatization failed Texas utility customers? *Electric Light & Power*, (October). Retrieved September 25, 2016 from www.elp.com/articles/2014/10/has-privatization-failed-texas-utility-customers.html

Snyder, T.D. & Dillow, S.A. (2013). *Digest of education statistics 2012*. (NECES-U.S. Department of Education). Retrieved January 6, 2015 from http://nces.ed.gov/pubs(2014)/(2014)015.pdf

Chapter 7

Personnel Requests

PRELIMINARY ISSUES IN PREPARING A PERSONNEL REQUEST

The request for new positions, especially faculty tenure track lines, is typically the largest budget issue a dean faces, other than budget cuts due to a financial emergency. The process of making such requests varies from campus to campus.[1] Even the timing of such requests varies. Deans should continually strive to have the position approval process as early as possible so as to allow departments more time to fill their positions. Some higher administrators prefer to have this process take place later than sooner because there are always budget uncertainties that emerge, and sometimes new positions require board or system office confirmation that the money for a position will actually be there. Ideally the approval process for new positions begins two springs before a faculty position is filled. That is, if a position is to be filled in the fall of 2018, the approval process should begin in the spring of 2017. If faculty lines are approved two springs before positions are filled, the departments have a full year to run their searches. The intent is not to give the department faculty time to have a leisurely search.

Early Pools Are the Strongest Pools

The intent of early approvals is to give the faculty an opportunity to run the search as early as possible to make sure it has a chance to hire the best candidates available that season. Arguably, the richest candidate pools, those with the greatest number of highly qualified candidates, are the early ones. That doesn't mean that there are not good people available later in the academic year. It simply means there are more good candidates clustered in the early part of the season when a critical mass of finishing students begins applying. These are the people scheduled to finish their doctoral programs sometime during the academic year in which they decide to enter the job market. The decision to enter the job market will probably be made by the prospective candidates in the spring or summer and they will begin applying early in the fall.

Hence, ideally departments should have their position announcements ready to post sometime in early September and, if funded, they should run a short search so as to be sure to be able to make an offer to the best candidates in the best pool—the autumn pool. Not all possible positions can be cleared that early, so by having some searches approved early an additional approval process may have to take place for the remaining positions. The approval process itself can sometimes be stressful for all involved—particularly if some departments are losing positions and others are gaining.

From Where Does the Money Come?

A simple truth that is sometimes difficult for faculty members and some deans to accept is that if there is no new money coming from somewhere, a dean's personnel funds for next year are the same as this year. The question every dean must ask their provost, and this should be cautiously done before accepting a dean's position, is whether the provost is willing to move personnel funds from one college to another—and if so, under what circumstances. If the provost is not willing to reallocate resources based on need and/or merit, then the dean's request for positions is going to be strictly confined to a relatively static budget. Deans may have college policies in place that allow them to move positions within their own college, but one typically cannot anticipate additional positions beyond what one already has.

Retirements

Exceptions arise when there are retirements whereby the vacated positions have nearly twice the salary funding that it would cost for a single replacement. Under these circumstances deans should be able to create new positions by splitting the salary of the vacated position in two. But not so fast . . . don't get too excited. Some institutions do not operate that way. Some higher administrators (presidents, vice presidents for administrative affairs, and provosts) consider money from retirements their money, and require that it either goes back into the general fund or goes into the redistribution plan of the provost. Yes, you read that right. Be careful what you wish for. If the provost does redistribute money across colleges it might be based on a policy of collecting retirement funds and reallocating the "excess" to other colleges. If a college has a lot of retirements on the horizon such a policy could be the basis for that college losing substantial resources that could be used to fund additional faculty positions.

Just as the provost might use retirement salaries to take resources from one college to give to another, deans may be in a position to do the same thing. If the higher administration does not claim the salary left over from retirements, then the dean will want to develop a college policy regarding such monies. Salaries from retirements are the most reasonable and defensible way to move resources around within a college. Some departments will try to claim that the money from their faculty retirements belongs to them, just as a dean might make that claim for their college when the provost starts threatening to pull that money into their coffer. Allowing those departmental claims to prevail would be a disaster for the effective management and progress of a college. Large departments would be allowed to grow larger regardless of need, and high student growth departments would remain understaffed. The most effective manner in which retirement money should be redistributed is within colleges (across departments)—not across colleges or within departments.

With the possible exception of very small institutions, provosts and other higher administrators do not have as clear an understanding of ongoing resource needs at the departmental and program levels as do deans. And there is usually enough need within colleges to warrant allowing colleges to keep the money they have. There might be exceptions to this rule in cases where colleges themselves are particularly small or when there is considerable and thus notable imbalance within academic affairs overall. Under these circumstances provosts should intervene strictly as an exception to the rule, with the understanding that it is being done on a one time emergency basis only.

College Criteria for Re-Distributing Personnel Funds

If colleges do have the opportunity to keep their personnel funds from retirements and vacancies that occur for other reasons, such as someone leaving for another position, or administrative non-retention, the college should have a policy that identifies a set of criteria that will be used to systematically determine which positions should be funded. As stated by Dickeson, "The inescapable truth is that not all programs are equal. Some are more efficient. Some are more effective. Some are more central to the mission of the institution" (2010: 23). The difficult part is arriving at a set of criteria that allows the dean, working with the chairs, to differentiate department position requests from one another based on the success and quality of the departmental programs.

Upon arriving at my second dean's position I felt fortunate to learn that the college already had a set of criteria for determining which position requests should have the highest priority. With only slight modifications I was able to continue with that set of criteria, which were introduced by the simple statement, "when a line becomes vacant, it will be allocated as needed in the college on the basis of the following criteria . . ."

CHECKLIST:

1. The top priorities will be replacement of probationary faculty who were not renewed and the re-authorization of unsuccessful probationary searches.
2. A second criterion will be balancing student-faculty ratios in the majors across the college.
3. A third criterion will be balancing overall faculty responsibilities (reflected in Gen. Ed. credits and/or service courses, student faculty ratio, advising loads, internships, etc.) across the college.
4. A fourth criterion will be the centrality of the position to the departmental/programmatic mission and goals.
5. A fifth criterion will be the potential contributions the position can make to the college mission and goals, especially to potential contributions to enhance cultural diversity efforts in the college.
6. A final criterion will be the potential for program expansion based on previous or predicted success as reflected in increasing student demand, job opportunities in the field, quality and reputation of the program, and other indicators of success.

Two of the six criteria refer to missions and goals. Departmental goals are typically expected to be compatible with the college goals—albeit not exactly the same. Consistency with the mission and goals of the college should be considered extremely important. Oftentimes missions and goals are not used in the important decision-making processes of colleges. They clearly should be.

THE PERSONNEL REQUEST PROCESS

Once the criteria are established the next step is to effectively implement those criteria in a way that the faculty will have ownership of the results. Toward that objective, department chairs are asked to first provide a written position request document that identifies the positions they need and why. They are then asked to circulate their document to all of the other chairs as well as to the dean's office. Each chair is asked to rank all of the requests based on the provided rationales, which should relate to the six just mentioned criteria. There is undoubtedly some behind the scenes lobbying and deal making that takes place, and while discouraged, it obviously cannot be prevented. It is for this reason, possible collusion, which could cause departments with less politically minded chairs to be disadvantaged, that the dean should reserve the right to make position assignment request decisions not completely in accord with the outcome of the composite chair rankings. But to whatever extent possible the dean should try to respect the outcome of the department chair rankings.

In those areas where the two rankings, the chairs' and the dean's, are not the same, the dean should provide a rationale for not acting in accordance with the composite chair rankings. In the interest of maximizing transparency, both sets of rankings can be provided for the chairs to take back to their departments. Discrepancies and disagreements can then be brought back to the table of the dean's regularly scheduled meeting with the chairs. Deans should be able to demonstrate that they have well thought out reasons for the decisions they make.

Once the main personnel request process begins, which, unfortunately, is usually not until the early fall, the provost will ask for position requests from the deans and a decision will be made as to when these requests will be brought to the provost's council of deans meeting. A hard copy report as well as an oral/visual presentation to the entire council will likely be expected. To prepare for that event the deans ask the chairs to have their departmental requests to the dean's office 2 to 3 weeks in advance. These requests could be for any departmental positions, including office staff positions. Departments might request something as unusual as having vacated faculty lines converted to "permanent" graduate assistantships.

No Automatic Replacements

From a provost's perspective, there is no assumption of an automatic replacement for a vacated position, and there isn't necessarily such an assumption from a dean's perspective either. Position requests are serious decisions and must be made after analyzing all of the variables carefully. There is a clear and predictable reason that the above replacement criteria place a high priority on refilling positions vacated through non-retention decisions and failed searches. This priority is important to the faculty because it provides some assurance that non-retention decisions will not result in position losses. Looking at the issue from the administration's standpoint, it is often difficult to get department faculty to address the promotion and tenure process as rigorously as they should. Any sign of departmental costs for doing so would kill faculty participation in the P&T process. Thus, when such a possible outcome is considered, this priority is important to the dean as well. Deans want departments to take their personnel evaluation responsibilities seriously. It makes the dean's job easier and her/his working relationship with departments stronger.

Once the deans have made their position requests to the provost on behalf of their departments, there is nothing left to do but wait until one receives a response that can then be passed on to the department chairs. This response might take a while if the provost is uncertain about university finances during a particular year or if (s)he doesn't have a strong position relative to the vice president for administrative affairs (VPAA). The provost should not ordinarily need clearance from the VPAA in order to approve personnel decisions in academic affairs, but sometimes such clearance is expected. This is where provosts need to earn their title. The provost label is typically given to the vice president of academic affairs because it is this position that runs the core of the university's activities: academic programs. Short of a financial crisis, the provost should not have to answer to the VPAA, and it is the president's job to make sure such is the case—albeit that may not be the inclination of many presidents who are perpetually in search of funds for the general budget.

No Surprises

Provosts should know enough about the existing budgets that they should not have to hesitate in making their personnel decisions once they have the deans' personnel requests. And there should be no surprises if the deans have kept their requests within their existing budgetary limits. The decisions based on existing funds can be made as soon as the provost evaluates the position requests. If new personnel money is expected to be coming into academic affairs then that is another matter. Positions beyond existing budgetary parameters would most likely have been worked out in advance of the deans' presentations.

At some institutions, especially smaller private institutions, personnel requests are approved by a board of trustees. Under those circumstances the approval process might even take longer, sometimes delaying the position announcements until well into the spring semester for searches expected to take place that same semester. In some instances it is only the new positions associated with the approval of new programs that require board of trustee approval.

For reasons discussed earlier regarding maximizing pool quality, the timing of the provost's announcement regarding position requests is extremely important. Provosts and higher administrators are nervous about conducting the personnel request process early because of possible unexpected budget problems.

OVERSEEING THE SEARCH PROCESS

Once the positions have been announced to the departments they should immediately begin the search process. Presumably the departments have already worked out a position description that can be easily converted into a position announcement and have selected a departmental search committee. Human resource departments typically have a specific hiring process that search committee chairs need to follow. It will vary slightly from campus to campus. Your responsibility as dean is to make sure that the process, whatever it may be, is rigorously followed by the search committee chairs. There are typically steps that need approval before search chairs can move to the next step and so on. Once those steps have been completed the search committee should then run their advertisements in their discipline's respective employment outlets. The dean should make sure that the ads contain language that is consistent with university policy and with the mission, goals, and objectives of the college and the university. Basic items to look for in a search ad might be:

CHECKLIST:

1. Sufficient reference to, and description of, the university
2. Type of university it is, for example, comprehensive undergraduate, undergraduate and master's level degree granting, and so on
3. Public, private, private religious, and so on
4. Whether the position is tenure track or not
5. At what rank the hire will be made
6. When the position starts
7. Degree requirements to apply
8. Required and preferred areas of specialization
9. Preference for someone who brings diversity to university and programs, if that is a college/university goal
10. Provide the website for additional information
11. Application deadline
12. Application materials required (e.g., CV, cover letter, teaching philosophy, research agenda etc.)

A prioritized list of the desired qualities of the successful candidate might also be established (Buller, 2015).

Working with the Committee

It is important for the dean to meet with the search committees and make sure the members understand the institutional hiring guidelines. Such a meeting usually takes place initially with the human resources director and/or the diversity director. The dean may have to stay in close contact with some departments and committees to make sure the searches are being run according to all applicable guidelines (Bright & Richards, 2001). This can be a time consuming task and could be delegated to a due process oriented assistant or associate dean. Committee members must be made aware of the serious legal and ethical issues related to conducting a fair and accurate search. Some of the key issues are: the approval (by HR) and careful following of a screening form that accurately measures the items in the position announcement; the approval of interview questions that correspond with the screening form; committee members removing themselves from decisions involving applicants that are friends/relatives; and having a predetermined timeline and sticking to that schedule.

Making sure search committees follow their timelines carefully is extremely important for two reasons. (1) When an ad is placed the corresponding pool is defined by the timeline that has been set. The more a committee deviates from that timeline the more applicants will be lost from the pool, especially if the search goes well beyond the expected final decision date. (2) Sometimes committees that have a preferred candidate from the beginning will stall a search to deliberately "lose" the best candidates in the pool, since the best candidates are the most likely to get early offers from other places. Then their candidate emerges as the best one left in the pool.

In specialty areas where there are few qualified candidates available it is common to specify that the search will remain open until the position is filled. In all other cases the benefit of maintaining a strictly enforced relatively narrow timeline most likely far outweighs any possible benefit of being able to wait for more applicants.

Assuring an Honest Search

There are primary and secondary characteristics to consider in a search. It is important to make sure those characteristics are delineated carefully and pursued accordingly. For example, is diversity sufficiently important for a department that it should be a requirement among the qualifications or should it simply be a preferred characteristic? The same question could pertain to a number of characteristics. Departments that are in the greatest need of diversification are the ones typically the hardest to deal with on that issue. A department at one university where I served as a dean was assigned a new position before I arrived. The department had fourteen tenure track positions and only one woman. Yet, they resisted including anything in their position announcements that would attract women. In fact, they did everything possible to avoid the potential of considering a woman. When the search committee was confronted on this issue they responded that less than 5 percent of doctoral graduates in that discipline were women. When researched, the actual graduation data showed that women represented 28 percent of the doctoral graduates in that field, and an investigation of the department's candidate pools actually reflected that number.

"High Market" and Application Numbers

The same above mentioned department represented a field identified as "high market," meaning that doctoral graduates from that discipline were supposed to be in higher demand than those of most other fields of study, and therefore they would have fewer candidates from which to choose. This, also, seemed to be a false reality that had been successfully created over time, and is a reality that has apparently been shared across many universities. Their position announcements consistently drew well over 100 applications and the number of women in those pools was consistent with the number of female graduates in that discipline. How did they get around these simple facts? They made their screening job easier and at the same time made their pool look representative of the high market field they claimed by eliminating anyone who did not have a doctoral degree in hand at the time of application.

Their position announcements stated they would only consider people with their doctorates in hand, but most people familiar with the hiring process in academia know that "having a completed doctorate" usually means by the time of hire. Furthermore, most departments are willing, and some prefer, to hire people who are ABD if they can get verification from the candidate's dissertation chair that they will be finished by a certain date. By not allowing for this kind of flexibility departments are not only eliminating a large portion of their natural pool, but are also most likely losing proportionately the best part of that pool. This makes their search easier to manage and gives the appearance of having fewer qualified applicants. By advertising that ABD candidates will be considered, which is what many departments do, and which is what truly high market disciplines must do, departments are likely to receive even more applications than the 100 plus received by the department mentioned above.

Intervention Is Sometimes Needed

It would be very easy for a dean to look the other way and let the false reality described above continue to be served without question. That is not, however, the inclination or tendency of an intentional dean. When departments play what appear to be deceptive games as described above, deans must invest time and energy to correct the situation. Searches should be failed and eventually positions removed until departments are willing to recognize the importance of gender equity and balance among their faculty. This strategy generally works. Keeping departmental searches fair, honest, and on track is an ongoing challenge of the dean's office. It is an extremely important responsibility and yet one that can be quite draining. One quickly learns to choose one's battles carefully—just from the standpoint of maintaining sanity and enough time to take care of other duties. Based on my observations, however, technical/procedural and substantive violations related to searches are common serious problems in academia, and are not just occurring at the departmental level, but at all levels.

Once finalists are selected, the committee chair should seek approval from the dean to interview the chosen candidates. Universities typically bring in two finalists for departmental positions, but more are allowed under certain circumstances—especially if there are candidates representing diverse backgrounds, or if there are local candidates that allow travel reimbursements to remain relatively low. All original applications for the position should be delivered to the dean's office, or at least available for the dean's review, prior to the candidates being contacted for an interview. The committee interviews the candidates brought to campus and the dean interviews them as well. At smaller campuses the academic vice president may wish to interview the candidates, since the campus community is small and each hire has a significant presence on the campus at large.

Who Decides?

The actual decision of which finalist to hire is a little tricky. Typically the committee has a preference and may let the dean know which candidate that is—even though the procedure usually requires the committee to present a document identifying only strengths and weaknesses of the finalists—not a ranking. The choice is supposed to be the dean's, but it is the department that knows their field the best and should know who is most qualified. On the other hand every dean should know that departmental preferences are sometimes influenced by criteria that do not serve the best long-term interests of the department or the institution. Potential friendships are sometimes considered—having children the same age—having common interests outside of the professional sphere. And if you can believe it, yes, people still consider looks and even potential for intimacy. Things have not changed in this regard as much as one might think. Unfortunately, sometimes still, "boys will be boys" even if they hold a terminal degree and claim to be enlightened. And as women have increasingly attained their rightful place in academia they have, unfortunately in many ways, come to behave like the "good old boys" their second wave feminist predecessors worked so hard to break through.

It is the dean's responsibility to protect candidates and the search process from the various forms of discrimination and bias that can take place in a variety of ways—in addition to discrimination related to gender as in the above. As a faculty member I witnessed, and reported, frequent and blatant search violations. I could literally make a list. As a dean I was determined to guard against that kind of behavior. It is an important and difficult responsibility.

Yes, You Can Reject a Department's Recommendation

For the above reasons and more, it is important that the dean reserve the right to override the recommendation of the search committee. This must be done carefully, sparingly, and only when the dean is quite certain that the right person for the job, based on all the criteria publically advanced, is someone other than the person the committee wants to hire. Sometimes there are dissenting voices on the committee to which the dean may want to listen. And it is a good idea to pay careful attention to minority reports that are submitted with the final report. Going against committee recommendations is sometimes a necessity—albeit it is not a practice that a dean would want to carry out frivolously. This responsibility should be taken seriously since it could save the dean, the college, and even the institution from a lot of problems. A useful practice is to have the search committee deliver their final report to the dean in person as an entire committee so that an open discussion can be held regarding any concerns anyone might have about the prospective hire. I also had individual committee members come to my office with legitimate and verifiable concerns that resulted in my office taking greater control of the hiring decision. Intentional deans, trying to build the strongest departments possible, will accept this responsibility and the pushback that sometimes comes with the corresponding actions.

PHILOSOPHY OF HIRING AND NEGOTIATING A CONTRACT

Once a decision is made the dean contacts the chosen candidate to determine if (s)he is still interested in the position and, if so, to extend an offer. University criteria for determining salaries usually result in a salary range with which the dean can work. This will especially be the case when working within a collective bargaining environment where there is actually a salary table that determines raises and promotion increases. New hires have to land somewhere on that grid and it cannot be too far from where existing faculty with similar credentials are already located. In some special circumstances it is possible to get permission to go beyond the range provided by the human resources office. This is true in situations where the candidate has experience that the dean or the department considers relevant, but which does not register on the HR list of criteria.

Is tutoring math for a mathematics department considered official teaching experience? Probably not, but you might think the candidate deserves some credit for that activity—especially given the high reviews of their work. Perhaps more importantly, does this person have credentials that are hard to find given the demand for those credentials? Some fields of study, like social work, because of the relatively few doctoral programs in social work, have a high university demand for their doctoral graduates. Yet, because of their unjustified relatively low status in academia (in comparison with business and some areas of science), they are not typically considered a high market field. Some social work searches might yield less than fifteen candidates, with only two or three being highly qualified. Under these circumstances a dean can request special permission for a salary above the HR range, providing data related to the demand in this field and the number of qualified candidates.

At this juncture one needs to think about their philosophy of hiring. Deans vary considerably on this issue. Different philosophies can result in some notable differences in the hiring processes that take place across deans over time—sometimes within the same college. One deaning approach is to set as the highest priority getting the most highly qualified people available to come to the college. When a dean decides that a candidate will make a strong contribution to a department (s)he wants to do everything possible to make that person want to accept an offer, and that includes finding more money if doing so will make a difference. Even more importantly, a dean should want the faculty of the college to be happy, or at least as happy as work-related circumstances will allow. This means accommodating as many requests from an incoming faculty member as possible.

Dealing with Pay Inequity, a Personal Example

Differences in decanal hiring philosophies within colleges over time can present some challenges. The college of one of my dean's positions had pockets of dissatisfaction due to faculty members, mostly women, being hired by former deans at notably low salaries. When I interviewed for the position I was quizzed by some of those unhappy people about what I would do to correct their low pay. Having a lot of experience on that issue (Alessio, 2007, 1999), I knew what the available options were for a dean in that system. I said I would hire new people at competitive salaries so that existing low salaries would appear even lower. The resulting notable difference would allow equity adjustments to be made during the promotion process and possibly force other general equity adjustments in the system as well. The collective bargaining contract, which I knew quite well, allowed for this window of opportunity.

I learned later that my candidacy was not supported by those disgruntled about their pay. They did not like my interview response. Perhaps I should have said I would lead a sit-in of the president's office or start a letter writing campaign. While my own record demonstrates I am not beyond working outside the system to create change, as a dean who works at the pleasure of the president such behavior would be foolish on a number of levels.

In a collective bargaining environment both sides of the workforce are equally bound by the specified rules, and the administration should actually be even more tightly bound to those rules than the faculty. A candidate for a dean's position could say they are going to do a lot of things during their interview, but in reality they can only do what the contract allows. Once hired I did exactly what I promised and some of those unhappy folks benefitted greatly when they came up for promotion. They not only received their promotion steps but received significant equity adjustments as well. It made a big difference in their professional lives. They finally felt validated and became interested in becoming more involved in the college and on the campus in general. Many campuses today, unionized or not, have some way of correcting for salary inequities.

A Philosophy of Saving Money

Some deans see saving the institution money as a primary goal in the hiring process, and they feel good about getting a candidate to accept a position for notably low pay. This approach often times does not save the institution money in the long run. Competitive pay draws high quality faculty members and helps to keep them happy. High quality faculty members are what make high quality programs, and high quality programs, along with the individual reputations of the professors, are what draw students to the campus. Hiring faculty members at the lowest possible salary is a long-term ticket to low morale and eventual enrollment problems. Support for the faculty is support for the students and the health of the college. Few faculty members, especially at comprehensive universities, are overpaid by any defensible metric.

Don't Forget the Candidate

When the search has been completed, all applications and search materials should be sent to the human resources office. That is not the final act, however. Everything possible should be done to make the newly hired faculty member feel welcome. A department mentor might be assigned and there should be a steady flow of communication with this person to help them with their move and corresponding adjustments. The extent of the dean's involvement in these latter steps varies with the size of the college and the nature of the hiring department. Notwithstanding, the dean needs to make sure that a welcoming and mentoring system is in place. There is a lot more that could be said about department searches, but it is important to move on since there are still many topics to cover about effective deaning.

NOTE

1 For an excellent example of a step by step guideline for a college faculty personnel process, see the online document put together by Murphy and Davis (2012). Krahenbuhl (2004) also provides some useful information regarding this issue.

REFERENCES

Alessio, J.C. (2007). Increasing stratification by gender: The results of a gender equity adjustment, in R.M. Martin (Ed.). *Transforming the academy: Struggles and strategies for women in higher education, Volume II* (pp. 39–51). Tehachapi, CA: GrayMill Publications.

Alessio, J.C. (1999). Using discriminant analysis to predict professorial rank by gender. *Journal of Applied Sociology*, 16 (1), pp. 123–143.

Bright, D.F. & Richards, M.P. (2001). *The academic deanship: Individual careers and institutional roles.* San Francisco: Jossey-Bass.

Buller, J.L. (2015). *The essential academic dean or provost.* San Francisco: Jossey-Bass.

Dickeson, R.C. (2010). *Prioritizing academic programs and services: Reallocating resources to achieve strategic balance.* San Francisco: Jossey-Bass.

Krahenbuhl, G.S. (2004). *Building the academic deanship: Strategies for success*. Westport: Praeger Publishers.

Murphy, J. & Davis, R.H. (2012). *Recruiting and hiring process for tenure line faculty*. Retrieved February 28, 2016 from www.colorado.edu/engineering/sites/default/files/tt-recruitment-process-11-15-12.pdf

Chapter 8

Promotion and Tenure

THE IMPORTANCE OF PROMOTION AND TENURE

Sometime in the early fall all promotion and tenure (P&T) application documents are supposed to be in the dean's office. The process and corresponding timelines will vary from institution to institution—timelines set typically by the provost/ vice president for academic affairs. Sometimes those timelines are set in consultation with the deans, and sometimes they are not. It is also possible that the timelines may be governed to some extent by a collective bargaining agreement. Collective bargaining can impact on the P&T process in some important ways. Keep in mind that all processes discussed in the collective bargaining agreement are part of a legal document protected by state law and subject to legal scrutiny within the relevant state statutes. The collective bargaining agreement, however, is only as powerful as the language used therein and the enforcers of the agreement. Enforcement often means protecting "your side's" interpretation of the language. "Should," "must," and "normally" are all carefully negotiated terms that can greatly impact on the enforceability of a particular interpretation.

"Guidelines" Carry Legal Weight

Most universities that do not have collective bargaining also provide clearly stated guidelines for the P&T process, and documents containing these guidelines can sometimes be treated as the bases for legal challenges by faculty members denied promotion and/or tenure. They do not normally have the same strength as a carefully guarded collective bargaining contract, but they are sometimes successfully used to challenge administrative decisions, especially when discrimination claims are involved (Bombardieri, 2014). It is also the case that there have been recent challenges by parent groups to the notion of tenure. While occurring primarily in the K-12 public systems (Baker, 2014), if successful, the challenges will most likely move into higher education.

File Size?

There are normally fairly strict guidelines available in contracts and/or faculty manuals that tell faculty members when they are eligible to apply. Forms must be filled out by both the faculty member and dean. Faculty members address their accomplishments relative to the corresponding qualifying criteria, and they must provide supporting documentation which can include actual publications. Hence, the P&T files can become quite bulky. As a dean, one might consider attaching some constraints to the P&T files, otherwise there can be an escalation toward greater size and weight (Bright & Edwards, 2001). This can be done in a soft way because faculty members just need to know that file size and weight are not, in themselves, going to make a positive difference. For example, a dean might encourage faculty members to keep their files to no more than one 5 inch binder with first and last pages of articles and first and last chapters of books. Full-sized documents should then be made available through the department's central office, or they can be kept separately in the dean's office for ready access.

Qualifying Criteria

The qualifying criteria are outlined in the collective bargaining contract or the faculty manual, depending on the institution. There are usually slightly different requirements for promotion than for tenure. There are also slightly different requirements for promotion to each rank. The dean normally receives a recommendation from the department's personnel committee and a separate recommendation from the department chair. Sometimes there is also a separate college level and/or university level P&T committee.[1] College level P&T committees might send their recommendations to the dean while university P&T committees may be expected to make a recommendation directly to the academic vice president. Of course, all recommendations from departments and committees should be taken seriously by the dean and followed to whatever extent possible. But as anyone who has spent time in academia should know, there are often politics within departments and colleges that interfere with objective faculty P&T evaluations. Amity and enmity sometimes take the place of careful honest judgment and an important part of the dean's job in this process is to be prepared to serve as a check for such behavior.

The dean usually has until sometime in late October or early November to complete the reviews and recommendations relative to P&T requests. On some campuses a draft of the recommendation is sent to the faculty members for review before it goes to the AVP. The faculty members can then meet with the dean and/or write a response. They can also request language changes in the dean's written recommendation. Normally it is only the negative recommendations that trigger a response from the respective faculty members, but occasionally even the strongest positive recommendation will elicit a request for some sort of change in the wording of the dean's statement. The dean's recommendations then go directly to the provost/AVP.

P&T AND PERSONNEL FILES

In a strictly enforced collective bargaining environment, if both the contract and its enforcement provide maximum protection for the faculty, there can only be one legitimate personnel file for each faculty member and that file is housed in the human resources office where all official faculty documents eventually land. Other files can be maintained for record keeping purposes, but those files are not considered official files from which important decisions are made. Everything in an official file can only be there as a result of the faculty member, colleagues, and administrators following due process related to the designated responsibilities of the faculty member—responsibilities that should be specified either in the collective bargaining agreement, or the faculty manual in the case of a non-collective bargaining environment. During the P&T process, which is quite protracted, the faculty member's P&T file technically serves as an extension of the official file that is housed in the human resources office. This is generally true in collective bargaining environments and should be assumed to be true in non-collective bargaining environments as well.

Keeping Disciplinary Issues Separate from the P&T Process

As stated above, two of the most important issues related to the P&T process, especially within a collective bargaining system, are what can be placed in the faculty member's file, and when it can be placed there. An important corollary to these issues is what information can be considered within the P&T process: both in terms of the information already in the faculty member's personnel file and even more importantly, information that is not in the file.

What then may be considered when making P&T recommendations and decisions? The first mentioned issues of "what and when" should be pretty straightforward. "When" is normally agreed upon by faculty and administration prior to the P&T process beginning. Timelines, however, are sometimes extended by mutual agreement between the faculty member and the administration or the faculty union/organization and the administration. There are also typically provisions in the process regulating timelines that allows the faculty member to update the P&T file after it has been submitted—such as when a paper is accepted for publication shortly after the P&T review process has begun.

What Should Be Considered?

Of the two issues, what and when, the question of what can be placed in the personnel file is typically far more important than when it can be placed there. Keep in mind that the P&T file is an extension of the personnel file, and materials can be put into the personnel file within contexts other than the P&T process. For example, it is possible that someone might have a letter of reprimand in their file from some previous behavioral disciplinary action. Can that information be used in the P&T recommendation? Many administrators will be inclined to say that it can, and they will probably be incorrect. Behavioral issues are not normally part of the P&T criteria identified in the P&T documents. Let us look at the P&T language from a collective bargaining contract:

> Subd. 1. Tenure. The decision to award tenure shall normally be based on the work of the faculty member during his/her probationary period. A faculty member's work at the university prior to the commencement of the probationary period, if any, may be considered. To be awarded tenure, the faculty member must demonstrate a record of positive performance and professionally competent achievement over the duration of the probationary period that is consistent with the goals and objectives of the university /college/department/program and with the goals of the process outlined in Article 22. The faculty member's record will be evaluated based on all the criteria outlined in Article 22. Completion of the probationary period alone does not mean the standards of tenure have been met (IFO/MnSCU, 2013, p. 93).
>
> Subd. 2. Promotion. The decision to promote shall be based on the cumulative work record of the faculty member since his/her last promotion or since the date of hire as applicable. To earn promotion, the faculty member must demonstrate a cumulative record of professional performance and high achievement appropriate to the relevant rank and consistent with the goals and objectives of the university/college/department/program. The faculty member's record will be evaluated based on all the criteria outlined in Article 22 (IFO/MnSCU, 2013, p. 93).

P&T Evaluation Language Excludes Behavioral Issues

As one can readily see, there are not references to behavioral issues in the P&T language of this particular collective bargaining agreement. This careful separation is relatively standard, whether the P&T process is part of a collective bargaining agreement or not. So what is contained in Article 22, referenced in the above statements, which serves as the basis for both the P&T decisions? Can one find any reference to behavioral problems in that document? No, one cannot. Here is the language as taken directly from the contract's Article 22 (IFO/MnSCU, 2013, p. 83).

> Section A. Purpose. The purpose of professional development is to provide for continuing improvement in teaching, in other student interactions, in the quality of scholarly activity and other service to the university and community. The purpose of evaluation is to provide faculty with information which will contribute to their professional development. The evaluation processes are intended to be supportive of a faculty member's desire for continuing professional growth and academic excellence. This process contributes to various personnel activities and supports the interest of each faculty member to achieve continuing professional growth and to pursue the highest possible level of academic excellence.
>
> Section B. Criteria. The criteria shall include:
>
> 1. Demonstrated ability to teach effectively and/or perform effectively in other current assignments.
> 2. Scholarly or creative achievement or research.
> 3. Evidence of continuing preparation and study.
> 4. Contribution to student growth and development.
> 5. Service to the university and community.
>
> Appendix G provides guidance regarding some of the types of evidence that may be considered appropriate for addressing each category.

"Not Here Either"

Appendix G contains a long list of examples representing the five criteria identified above and none of them resemble anything related to evidence of good behavior. So what is fair game for consideration in the P&T process? As a grievance officer and president of the faculty union I confronted this question many times. Frequently, faculty evaluators will want to bring in information that they "know" from "experience" or from what someone told them. And administrators may want to include information that is from the faculty member's personnel file that does not relate to the criteria within the agreed upon P&T process. Yes, the P&T file is an extension of the personnel file, but only documents related to the P&T process, which includes annual progress reports, may be used in the decision-making related to P&T. Chief labor relations officers for the administration, especially at the system level, are likely to disagree with this position. Some unions, likewise, have yielded to the erroneous administrative interpretation.

Deans in collective bargaining systems sometimes seek advice on this matter from one another. They are typically considering a faculty member who has been a "behavioral problem" and who most everyone else wants to get rid of, but who also has a solid record as a teacher and a scholar. It is the perfect opportunity—right? After all, there is a behavioral warning letter in her/his file and denying tenure to this person will possibly save a lot of people a huge amount of grief. There are good reasons for protecting due process in higher education, and this situation serves as an important example of those reasons. Due process will not be served by using the P&T process to get rid of a behavioral problem, and expediency is not a sufficient reason for violating that principle. An actual example will be discussed in Chapter 9.

ANNUAL EVALUATIONS AND PROGRESS REPORTS

P&T decisions at most universities today do not just happen out of the blue. From the moment that a faculty member is hired they are typically put on a regular review schedule to make sure they are keeping up with the expectations specified in their contract. Borrowing from the previously cited contract again, one can see that there is a process in place that, if carried out with due diligence, should leave no surprises by the time the P&T process is underway.

> Section C. Schedule and Frequency.
>
> Subd. 1. Frequency. Faculty shall be evaluated and shall submit progress reports according to the schedule set forth in this section. Faculty members who are scheduled for evaluation less frequently than every year may request more frequent evaluation. With the agreement of the Dean/designee, faculty who are not required to submit professional development plans may do so in order to receive feedback (IFO/MnSCU, 2013, p. 83).

As indicated in the above quote from a collective bargaining contract, faculty members are expected to develop plans and then later submit a report corresponding with those plans. Ordinarily untenured faculty members must do this annually, with tenured faculty members submitting reports less frequently and according to rank. But today even full professors are required to submit periodic progress reports to the dean for evaluation. Post-tenure review is important as a motivator for faculty members to keep improving even after they are relatively secure in their position. More importantly, albeit seldom viewed this way, post-tenure review is important to make sure that faculty members are performing at least the minimum of what is expected of them as employees of the university.

Enforcement of Workload Responsibilities

Collective bargaining contracts and faculty manuals sometimes identify, in addition to the specified requirements for P&T, workload responsibilities. For example, in the collective bargaining contract cited earlier there is a separate article on workload which outlines what faculty members are expected to do once they are hired. This is a sorely underutilized article in the system that uses this contract, and it is likely that workload expectations for tenured faculty members are not enforced in most universities. "Workload" is an article that identifies the minimum/maximum activities a faculty member must/can perform in order to achieve and maintain their status as a faculty member—separate from attaining tenure and promotion. It might also identify what constitutes extra-workload activities and how they will be compensated, such as directorships and other quasi-administrative activities.

Establishing a consistent record of workload negligence might take a while, but if a faculty member fails to perform their minimum responsibilities over an extended period there should be some consequences for that faculty member. To make this happen deans have to be prepared to identify this shortcoming in the work of tenured professors, and cite the activities identified in the workload article, or its equivalent, in the post-tenure review process. When this is done in a clear and straightforward manner the faculty members recognize what is happening and often decide to change or retire. Deans should not be eager to provoke or fire anyone, but if faculty members are not doing their job it makes more work for everyone else, which is neither fair nor good for faculty morale. Additionally, there are eager and excellent hard working potential faculty members waiting for positions who would do an excellent job if only they had the opportunity.

Self-Evaluations

All faculty members who are to be evaluated during a particular year, tenured and non-tenured, are notified of this expectation by the dean's office sometime in the spring. They may be sent a general guiding survey form, like the one that follows, which covers the criteria for evaluation. Alternatively, they may simply be given the list of evaluation criteria taken from the collective bargaining agreement or faculty manual and told to list their corresponding accomplishments. In both approaches a self-report process is being used, but it is also the case that the faculty member is expected to provide documentation of their accomplishments to whatever extent possible. In this manner, the junior faculty member is essentially building their P&T folder 1 year at a time.

Faculty Self-Evaluation

Academic Year XXXX

Please list responsibilities as requested, provide your reflections on this academic year, and consider your plans for next year.

1. How would you assess your teaching in relation to the philosophy and goals of XXXX University?
2. How would you assess your work with students in class, in academic advising, and in other types of activities?
3. Teaching responsibilities (fall and spring).
4. Departmental activities (fall and spring).
5. College-wide activities including committee membership.
6. Professional association memberships and activities.
7. Describe faculty development activities in which you have been engaged. Include additional degrees, research, publications, honors, and other professional contributions.
8. How have you made use of various assessment and feedback methods by students, peers, chair, college assessments?
9. Discuss your strengths and weaknesses as a faculty member.
10. Discuss what you would like to accomplish/improve/develop as a faculty member at XXXX University in the next academic year.

Faculty Signature Date

The degree to which chairs and departments are involved in the self-evaluation process varies. That issue notwithstanding, the dean must write a response to the self-evaluation that will be sent to the faculty member. The dean's response is based on the department/chair feedback, if there is any, as well as the submitted self-report itself.

It is important that the dean's response to the self-evaluations be clearly differentiated from the dean's response to the faculty activity reports since they are separate documents with separate purposes. The faculty activity report (to be discussed later) is generally an acknowledgment of accomplishments, sometimes used for determining merit pay, and the self-evaluation is an assessment of the faculty member's performance during that year(s) relative to an eventual P&T decision or post-tenure retention evaluation. It is quite possible that a faculty member may have many accomplishments that result in significant praise and merit pay, but may not be performing sufficiently well in a critical area to attain tenure and/or promotion.

Usefulness of Chair's Response to Self-Evaluations

In reviewing the chair's response letter the dean must consider that some chairs will never say anything about a faculty member that might be construed as negative. Deans must recognize this pattern and learn to consider the chair's comments accordingly. The chair is actually not helping their colleague by failing to point out shortcomings in the faculty member's activities, since the dean must ultimately make a P&T recommendation based on the available evidence relative to the university P&T criteria. In fact, the chair may be giving the faculty member a false impression of success that will only elevate the faculty member's disappointment if tenure and/or promotion are denied. In general, the dean needs to look for patterns of both positive and negative bias in each chair's responses to faculty self-evaluations in order to determine how helpful they will be to the dean when writing the response. After the faculty members receive their response from the dean they are then asked to meet with the dean to review their evaluation and are also able to write a response to the dean if they choose to do so.

This Is Important!

The dean's response to the annual evaluation of untenured faculty members is one of their most important responsibilities. If done correctly this process serves two important functions: (1) it helps the new faculty member develop professionally within the framework of the university's expectations; and (2) it allows the dean to identify patterns of shortcomings over a period of time that, if not attended to, could be the basis for considering a non-tenure recommendation to the higher administration. One bad year is not a basis for a non-tenure decision, but 3 or 4 in a row is a serious flag. If a faculty member is unable or unwilling to improve their teaching, submit some scholarly papers for review, or become involved in the life of the community, college, and/or university over the years leading to the tenure application, it is not likely they will ever do so. These are all important responsibilities for faculty members.

Non-Tenure Decisions Should Be Rare

The current pre-tenure review process adopted by many universities today is designed so that non-tenure recommendations should be quite rare. If faculty members follow the dean's advice each year, assuming the dean is taking her/his responsibility seriously, they should have no problem attaining tenure. Following the dean's recommendations in most instances might simply mean continuing to do what they are already doing. In a relatively healthy college most annual evaluation response letters will be filled primarily with acknowledgments of accomplishments and a general statement to keep up the good work. On the other hand, there will always be some that need some specific advice and guidance, and most faculty members will accept the dean's advice with gratitude. Unfortunately, there are also typically a couple that do not, and it is for those isolated individuals that the entire process must be completed with absolute due diligence.

Giving tenure to a poorly performing faculty member has long-term negative consequences for a college and the university. The college and corresponding department could be stuck with this faculty member for the next 30+ years, and the students and productive faculty members will suffer because of it. Departmental reputations can hang on a single faculty member who teaches critical courses for the department's degree programs. That reputation can actually deter students from coming to the university or staying there.

Example of a Chair's Positive Bias in a P&T Review

Not all chairs are the same, but some do not feel comfortable participating in the process in a manner that is helpful to either the administration or the untenured faculty member. For example, a department chair, year after year, wrote only positive comments in her/his evaluation responses. (S)he thought (s)he was helping the faculty member get tenure but in actuality gave the faculty member false hope instead of needed direction and motivation to improve. The faculty member was having serious problems with both scholarship and teaching responsibilities and these problems were carefully documented by the dean year after year. The department chair assured the faculty member that tenure would not be a problem, and had this individual doing much of the busy work for the department instead of urging her/him to do more scholarly work and improve her/his teaching. When the time came there was no choice left but to recommend non-tenure. It was a clear-cut case since the shortcomings of the faculty member's professional activities had been well documented with quotes from the dean's responses to the annual reviews. The department chair was outraged, and the recommendation, backed by the provost, was appealed to the president. In this example, the president apparently granted some time concessions, but the faculty member in question is no longer at the university.

There are actually three valuable lessons for a prospective dean to learn from this example: (1) take the annual professional development evaluations seriously and document everything to the greatest detail; (2) carefully assess the integrity and usefulness of chair responses; and (3) learn to ignore what happens after the dean's part of the job is done. Deans have no control over the provosts and presidents. If they are good at their respective jobs, they will make the right decisions, as they ultimately did in this example.

KEEPING UNIVERSITY/COLLEGE BUDGET ISSUES OUT OF THE P&T PROCESS

Anyone who has been in academia for a while knows that university budget crises do sometimes occur. Funding sources are cut or threatened to be cut and campuses must make adjustments accordingly. The causes of the budgetary "crisis" are sometimes real and sometimes dishonestly contrived by management or the state in order to be able to redistribute resources. Agreements between the faculty and the administration typically have provisions for dealing with financial exigencies, allowing administrators to make budgetary reductions accordingly. If the financial problem is serious the administration may have to eliminate faculty positions as a way to effectively meet targeted goals. (The process of carrying out such reductions is discussed in Chapter 11.) There is normally a special section of the faculty-administration agreement that specifies the circumstances under which such reductions can be made and how those reductions should be carried out relative to the order in which positions should be targeted: part-time positions first, fixed-term positions second, untenured next, and so on. This section of the agreement is typically titled "retrenchment" or "layoffs."

It is important to recognize and emphasize that, as with disciplinary cases, retrenchment/layoff cases are not to be confused with P&T decisions. That is why they are typically discussed in completely separate sections (articles) of faculty-administration agreements. P&T decisions are about individual faculty members. Retrenchment decisions are about positions, costs, and in some instances, programs. As with disciplinary cases, it may be tempting for administrators to try to solve budgetary problems, at least in part, through the P&T process. Such a deviation from due process is a serious abrogation of management responsibilities and a corresponding violation of faculty rights. It must be understood that violations of faculty rights do not just have implications for the faculty members involved in a particular decision, but they also have long-term implications for academic freedom, faculty morale, and institutional stability—all of which impact on the search for truth, program diversity, service to students and the community, and thus the ability of a university to perform its legitimate function within the broader spectrum of academia and the world in general.

A university that fails to protect faculty rights jeopardizes the integrity and professional futures of the deans who are called upon to participate in the unethical and possibly illegal management behaviors—behaviors that will surely put faculty morale and productivity into a downward spin.

Oh What a Tangled Web We Weave . . .

It was under the previously discussed circumstances that a faculty member from a small campus sought advice on her/his termination case relative to possible legal recourse. The case had already gone completely through the grievance and arbitration processes so all of the relevant documents representing both sides were readily available.

During a state-wide financial crisis beginning in 2009 all campuses in the state system were asked to make fairly deep budgetary reductions. Some campuses did it right away and did it well, while others dragged their feet and fumbled around until the system crisis was basically over. The small campus in question falls into the latter category of failing to properly respond to the state-wide problem in a timely fashion and benefitting from the reductions made by the larger campuses. Once the crisis was over the administration used the "crisis" that no longer existed as an excuse for eliminating faculty members. If that isn't bad enough, after falsely claiming the existence of a financial crisis they employed the P&T article of their collective bargaining contract to actually carry out the faculty eliminations. So they denied tenure to faculty members as a means of retrenching them without ever invoking retrenchment.

Sadly, and somewhat inexplicably, the union that was supposed to be protecting the collective bargaining contract, and thereby protecting faculty rights, missed this serious abrogation of due process entirely. They grieved on the basis of a number of violations far less defensible and having nothing to do with the most serious issue, which is the issue of misapplying the P&T article for the purpose of making what were claimed to be financial decisions. In their testimonies under oath, the administrators openly stated that the performance of the terminated faculty member was not an issue. Indeed, this person had consistently received glowing evaluations from the dean and was a well-liked hard working faculty member. At no time throughout the entire grievance/arbitration process was the misuse of the P&T article even mentioned—by anyone. While this example primarily addresses one case, other faculty members were also terminated in this manner.

Implications of Wrong Article Usage

Aside from the illegal termination itself, employing the wrong article for termination had other serious implications for the people being terminated. Under the layoff article the faculty members had certain layoff rights that they didn't have under the P&T article. There were also quite different timelines that had to be followed under each article. The layoff notification deadlines had already been missed by the administration, which should have guaranteed the faculty members in question a legitimate tenure review. Having a legitimate tenure review would have guaranteed the faculty members at least one more year of employment as a contractual condition of a non-tenure decision. However, it would have been difficult to deny them tenure through a legitimate process since they met all of the qualifications.

If financial exigencies actually did exist the administration could have met the layoff deadline for the following year and actually conducted a legal layoff. But misusing the P&T article to conduct retrenchment is an unfortunate miscarriage of due process—not to mention justice.

This tangled web of deception and incompetence should be quite glaring to anyone who understands the importance of maintaining a clear separation between position terminations for financial reasons and P&T terminations for performance reasons. Anyone who doubts the importance of the separation of those processes should be aware that some of the faculty members who were illegally terminated in this case had been previously called into the president's office and informed that they were to stop teaching about certain issues, a clear violation of academic freedom. The president was at least smart enough to know that (s)he could not claim teaching content as a basis for the terminations, even though course content probably did play a major role in the termination decision. This violation of academic freedom was never mentioned during the hearings by either the president or the attorney representing the union.

Had the careful separation of P&T and layoff articles been respected the terminations could not have occurred. The records of the faculty members were excellent, so the only negative issue the president could raise about their performance was that they didn't like what the faculty members were teaching. That would have been an obvious violation of academic freedom so it couldn't be stated as part of the record. The president chose instead to claim financial reasons for the terminations, even though there was no longer a financial crisis for the campus. Furthermore, the P&T article was used instead of the appropriate layoff article to execute the terminations.

Consequences?

Once arbitration is completed there is little that can be done short of hiring a personal attorney and taking both the state and the union to court. While it is easy to give advice to someone, an unemployed faculty member who has just filed for bankruptcy does not have the resources to hire an attorney. Even the step of filing the case with the courts involved costs this faculty member could not afford. After months of unsuccessfully trying to attain attorney representation on contingency, the deadline for filing passed and this person dropped their legal case altogether. Attorneys that were approached identified the case as strong but because it meant taking on both the state and the union nobody wanted to take the case. The dean involved in this case was ultimately fired, but apparently not for her/his contributions to the just described contract violations.

It is doubtful whether this serious miscarriage of due process and justice will ever be corrected. The negative consequences of this action will live on long into the future. Once a precedent is set it is difficult to restore the correct interpretation of the contract. The door has now been left open for future violations of academic freedom and violations of other faculty rights. The faculty members on this particular campus now live in fear and it is with considerable reluctance that they even talk to someone about their situation—even those who are tenured.

Some administrators might view this as a good thing, claiming that their management prerogatives have been rightfully restored. This is the thinking of a weak-minded insecure person who should not be in management. If the current processes are insufficient for a person to do their job they need to work to change them. Violating existing agreements, especially legally sanctioned collective bargaining agreements, is nothing short of vigilante behavior and should not be condoned by anyone. Intentional deans aspire to protecting faculty rights and due process. They will, therefore, avoid crossing the due process lines as described above, and they will advise others to do the same. Taking this high road approach to fulfilling one's responsibilities is not an act of weakness, but an act of strength.

Proper P&T Actions During Budget Reductions

There is often confusion about what is proper P&T due process during budget reductions. Should the application of a person targeted for retrenchment be continued through the entire P&T processes? If they are allowed to continue through the P&T processes should they be awarded tenure and/or promotion at the same time they are being terminated for financial reasons? The answer to both of those questions is a resounding "YES." Nothing should change internally relative to due process as a result of a financially required retrenchment. Retrenchment applies to everyone, including tenured faculty members. The fact that a person receives tenure does not protect them from being terminated through the agreed upon retrenchment process. Indeed, the least a university can do for a person who faces retrenchment is give them their full rights under the P&T process. Hopefully they will be approved for tenure and/or promotion and that will help this person find another job more easily. Being able to demonstrate that one has already been tenured through a rigorous review process is one of the strongest recommendations a person can take into their job search.

The Importance of Positive Comments

After the above rather dismal, and perhaps somewhat depressing, section relating P&T with budget reductions, it is important to find something more upbeat to say about P&T decisions. And there are, of course, many positive comments that can be made. For instance, it is important that all promotion and tenure decisions contain the rich praise that a faculty member deserves. A negative promotion decision does not mean that a person has not done good work for which they can be praised. It typically means that they have not quite reached the performance level expected for a promotion in that particular college, and it might be in just one important area of their responsibilities. The faculty member should be informed of what they can do to meet that level of expectation before they apply again.

Even a negative tenure decision response should identify the positive contributions of the faculty member. A faculty member denied tenure or promotion has likely made positive contributions worthy of praise. Contrary to what some advisors might say, it is not legally necessary to leave deserved praise out of the decision letter. Some of the best teachers are not effective researchers and some of the best researchers are too busy to do university and community service. It is, of course, important to be careful how non-tenure and negative promotion decision letters are worded. There are sometimes collective bargaining constraints on how much a dean can say. It is probably the case, however, that more can be said than the higher administration, the human resources office, or the State Attorney General's office would like the dean to say. It is important to choose one's words carefully, but it is equally important to do right by the faculty of the college. Including the positive contributions in a non-tenure or negative promotion decision letter reduces rather than increases the likelihood that a grievance will be filed.

CELEBRATE!

Finally, and of high importance, the P&T successes should be celebrated in as big a way as modest budgets will allow. There should be a dinner or luncheon showcasing the major accomplishments of each person tenured and/or promoted, and there should be symbolic gifts appropriate for welcoming the person into their new status. There are too few opportunities for celebrating the hard work of faculty members. Each of those opportunities should be actualized to the fullest extent possible.

NOTE

1 Buller (2015: 359) seems to suggest that P&T decisions at most institutions are more so in the hands of committees and department chairs than deans. While committees and chairs are typically involved, normally their input is advisory to the dean and/or provost. The dean, or designated associate dean, should always assume responsibility for the careful evaluation of P&T files, since it is likely (and appropriately so) her/his recommendation will carry the most weight with the higher administration.

REFERENCES

Baker, A. (2014). Lawsuit challenges New York's teacher tenure laws. *New York Times*. Retrieved February 28, 2016 from www.nytimes.com/(2014)/07/04/nyregion/lawsuit-contests-new-yorks-teacher-tenure-law

Bombardieri, M. (2014). Harvard professor challenges school's denial of tenure. *Boston Globe*. Retrieved February 28, 2016 from www.bostonglobe.com/metro/(2014)/06/12/harvard-professor-challenges-tenure-denial/E64ruokHoD1WpokjwsbR3M/story.html

Bright, D.F. & Richards, M.P. (2001). *The academic deanship: Individual careers and institutional roles*. San Francisco: Jossey-Bass.

Buller, J.L. (2015). *The essential academic dean or provost*. San Francisco: Jossey-Bass.

IFO/MnSCU. (2013). *IFO/MnSCU master agreement*. Retrieved February 29, 2016 from http://ifo.org/contract-benefits/contract/.

Chapter 9

Disciplinary Actions

In Chapter 8 an important point was made regarding keeping disciplinary issues out of the P&T process. This chapter begins by taking up that issue again to look at the reasons in greater detail. The chapter then moves on to discuss other concerns related to taking disciplinary actions. Some examples involve faculty members; others involve students; and some involve both students and faculty members. Unlike issues where the information is public, the issue of discipline involves personnel files that are to be kept private. Hence, information that might reveal a person's identity to others is avoided. Most behavioral details will also be avoided for the same reason and because they are not necessary to make the essential point.

TENURE IS NOT THE ENEMY

Faculty leaders can grow quite tired of hearing administrators blame tenure for not being able to fire people. Public officials outside of the university and political leaders listen to these whining excuses and start trying to figure out how they can get rid of tenure in the schools and universities. Universities (and probably schools in general) do not exist, unionized or non-unionized, without carefully laid out rules of conduct and work responsibilities. The basic productivity and behavior rules are the same for tenured and untenured members of the faculty and should be applied in the same manner to all. When basic productivity and behavioral rules are not being met faculty members should be called in and advised accordingly. If change does not occur, disciplinary action can and should be taken. Tenure is critical for protecting academic freedom and should not be used by administrators as a scapegoat when behavioral problems continue. Administrators should expect to be continually challenged to take their personnel responsibilities seriously if they are to keep the educational system running in a relatively healthy and productive manner.

Obligation and Merit

There is often confusion between basic productivity and productivity that is meritorious. Promotions and merit pay are based on meritorious productivity. Retaining one's position at the university is based on general expectations laid out in other sections of the faculty/administration agreement—what might be called basic or minimal productivity. This distinction should be particularly clear in agreements involving collective bargaining, but faculty manuals typically also make this distinction clear. Unfortunately, it is a distinction often lost to confusion and neglect. Highly productive faculty members often burn themselves out compensating for the lack of basic productivity from their colleagues. These problems occur far more often than they should and deans should be prepared to handle them appropriately, which means paying careful attention to corresponding documents and due process.

Crossing Performance and Behavior Evaluation Lines: Weaving the Web of Deception

Some deans are unclear about the importance of maintaining clear separation between performance evaluations and behavioral evaluations that could lead to disciplinary action. Other deans know they are supposed to keep the boundaries separate but find it difficult to avoid the temptation of trying to take what they think is the easy way out: crossing the performance and behavioral evaluation lines. There are two common ways of making the mistake of trying to surreptitiously combine disciplinary action with P&T. One approach is to deny tenure based on behavioral issues by indicating that the tenure denial is based on the faculty member's inability to contribute to a positive work environment. Now this reason could be legitimate if there is language in the P&T process documents that allow such behavior (or lack thereof) to be considered in the P&T process. Under these circumstances the faculty member should have been talked to about the behavioral problems and warned about possible consequences during each year of the professional development evaluation process. That is not usually what occurs since this kind of behavioral language is not normally included in the professional development evaluation criteria (as noted in Chapter 8). Furthermore, departments and deans often times do not have the foresight to document behavioral problems systematically and consistently (which is why they end up trying to terminate faculty members through a tenure decision rather than a disciplinary decision). Openly denying tenure based on behavioral issues gives the faculty member a viable grievance and legal case against the university. They were denied tenure using criteria that are not part of the P&T evaluation process.

Raising the Performance Bar to Avoid a Positive Tenure Decision

The second approach that is frequently taken when illicitly using the tenure evaluation process to deal with behavioral problems is to try to make the faculty member's job performance record appear to be insufficient even though the record is strong. This technique has two possible detrimental effects. One is similar to the effect mentioned previously where the faculty member has a legitimate basis for suing the university. However, in this instance the faculty member will be able to show data from other tenured or promoted faculty members who have done less and thus will be able to build a legal case around those comparative data. The second detriment is that playing with the faculty data in relation to the evaluation criteria has a destabilizing effect. Faculty members who are not aware of the alleged disciplinary problems of faculty member X become somewhat anomic when they find out that someone with six publications was denied tenure and here they are with only three. There is enough confusion about what the criteria are for P&T; it is a disservice to play with those criteria in a way that makes the confusion even worse. Administrators have a responsibility to be clear and consistent, knowing, of course, that they cannot always make perfect judgments. Imperfections notwithstanding, deans should always strive for accuracy within the process language provided. To do anything else not only creates the risk of other problems and greater harm, but it is also dishonest and unprofessional. In effect, deans then become the behavioral problem by not following due process with utmost care. Deans have peoples' professional lives in their hands. Deans owe it to their faculty to be honest, forthright, and transparent.

Saved By a Second Reality—A Case in Point

There was a case where I was investigating student complaints of a faculty member's behaviors in class and during office hours. This faculty member looked like (s)he was in a reasonably good position to be tenured with good course evaluations, publications, and important leadership positions on campus. Hence, her/his annual evaluations from the dean had been fairly strong, both from me and my predecessor. As the investigation continued, however, and I began to see how serious the behavioral problems were, I began to understand how tempting it would be to simply take care of the problems through the tenure process. I resisted doing that, however, and continued with the behavioral investigation as a completely separate matter, which it was.

As it turned out, there were also serious problems with the faculty member's tenure application and file. Publications were claimed as being refereed when they actually were not, and other areas of questionable honesty/quality were also revealed through a careful review of the faculty member's documents. These problems were not only identified by me, but to some extent also by the University Promotion and Tenure Review Committee. The problems that were discovered in the tenure review were not identifiable in the annual review process because the data were not presented in the same manner and the full documents were not made available to the extent that they were in the tenure application. The negative tenure decision was honest and straightforward. The behavioral investigation, which continued until the faculty member left, was nearly complete and would have quite likely led to disciplinary action, if not dismissal.

Of course, a non-tenure decision is typically quicker and cleaner than taking the disciplinary route, but that should not tempt the dean to violate the important distinction between the performance and behavioral processes. And the "quicker and cleaner" only happens if the decision is not legally challenged. Had the faculty member been tenured and disciplinary action taken in the form of a letter of reprimand for example, it is likely that it would not be long before other complaints against this person would arise and dismissal would be justified. Meanwhile, however, the university has to give this person a chance to change and allow due process to work. Following due process carefully assures that all faculty members are treated equally and fairly. It is critical, however, that administrators not avoid taking the disciplinary route and that they are not afraid to carry it through to its legal and logical conclusion.

AVERSION TO DISCIPLINARY ACTION

It has been my observation that the failure to separate behavioral problems from the evaluation of faculty members' professional activities is one of the most serious and entrenched personnel problems university administrators face. There are mechanisms for not retaining faculty members under conditions of unacceptable behavior. The tenure review process also allows for the discontinuation of a faculty member but for inadequate performance reasons that frequently have little to do with unprofessional/unacceptable conduct. Hence, the disciplinary process should not be used to fire a weak academic, and the tenure evaluation process should not be used to fire someone who behaves poorly as a human being.

A significant part of this entangled problem is that administrators, like most professionals, are busy most of the time. Following up on what appears to be a minor behavioral issue seems unnecessary and possibly somewhat distasteful. However, if there is a "minor" complaint about a faculty member on a dean's desk, there is a good to excellent chance that it is not the first time this behavior has occurred and it is highly likely that it will not be the last.

Disciplinary processes in higher education are almost always progressive in nature: warnings lead to reprimands which lead to suspensions which lead to dismissals. Not following up on a behavioral complaint systematically in accordance with the disciplinary process outlined in the university faculty manual or contract will mean that a dean will have only a portion of the needed evidence to take action the next time the problem occurs. Realizing this, one might think there is no point to following up on the problem the second time there is a complaint because (s)he has already lost data and it will take a lot of data to make something serious happen regarding the future of this faculty member—especially before the person is tenured. So, one might think, quite erroneously, that it will be best to simply deal with the problem in the tenure process.

Most disciplinary problems are long-term problems and administrators should not feel they have to solve them before the faculty member is tenured or within any other timeframe. Tenure does not protect a person from disciplinary issues. As stated by Buller,

> Despite popular beliefs to the contrary, tenure does not offer faculty members lifetime job security. Tenured faculty members need to fulfill their contract terms, demonstrate that they remain competent in their disciplines, and refrain from violating any of the standards that would make them liable to dismissal for good cause (2007: 291).

If the disciplinary process is followed systematically and the behaviors are sufficiently serious, the dean must eventually make a disciplinary recommendation to the higher administration. Being human, higher administrators often struggle with these decisions, and deans should not be surprised if their recommendation is not followed—even though in some instances the evidence screams "fire me!!" Perhaps because the higher administrators have not been involved in the data collection process over an extended period of time and have not actually taken the testimony from the students and other faculty members, they cannot fully appreciate the seriousness of the situation. There are most likely many other possible reasons for the system to fail at this point, including that a higher administrator may know someone who displayed similar behaviors at some point in her/his career, the faculty member might be a friend of a friend, or the administrator simply doesn't have the courage, or possibly the heart, to make this kind of decision. It isn't, and actually should not be, easy. Nevertheless, a good administrative team should be prepared to make such decisions when they are needed.

Anecdote: The Wizard of Oz in the Provost's Office

I recall a provost for whom I worked whose mere appearance in a room struck fear into the hearts of faculty and deans alike (for convenience I will call this provost, OZ). I presented OZ with a disciplinary case and, being astute about such matters and protective of the students, OZ recognized that my recommendation to fire the faculty member was valid. I had done an extensive investigation following some quite serious complaints. When we met with the faculty member to convey the results of our investigation provost OZ, after some questioning and discussion, began to become noticeably upset about the prospect of actually carrying out the termination. The faculty member was sent out of the office momentarily so the provost could be reassured that we were doing the right thing. To OZ's credit, composure was recovered and the difficult task of firing the faculty member was carried out. We both knew we were doing the right thing, and yet it was still unpleasant and distasteful for both of us. It was also an experience that made our working relationship stronger. I didn't think less of the provost for feeling badly about having to make this decision. To the contrary, I respected OZ more for it. I saw OZ's humanity–something that had been carefully hidden until that moment. Likewise, OZ saw in me someone committed to due process, fairness, and the wellbeing of our students.

Regardless of how recommendations are handled, it is important to feel good about doing one's job as it is supposed to be done. In those instances where disciplinary action is taken it is ignoble to revel in the outcome. The goal is never to punish someone, but to protect those who, without action, would continue to suffer. It is sad when people cannot control themselves sufficiently to behave toward others in an acceptable manner, but it is often sadder for their victims.

It Doesn't Always Turn Out That Way

In another case, with similar kinds of complaints and problems, the outcome was not the same. A series of relatively minor complaints resulted in issuing warnings to a faculty member, and then an incident occurred that resulted in my submitting a letter of expectation to that same individual. Shortly thereafter another quite serious complaint against the same faculty member emerged. I conducted a preliminary investigation and found sufficient evidence to bring the case to the Affirmative Action Officer (AAO) with the data. Based on the information I had collected, coupled with previous complaints, a full investigation was completed. The findings were turned over to a trained decision-maker, who found the evidence serious enough to recommend dismissal. I was consulted and, after examining the full report, firmly concurred with the decision-maker's recommendation.

It is uncertain who made the decision to ignore the dean's and the decision-maker's recommendations. I did not have access to that information. Somebody probably flinched in the line of duty and it is likely that many more students paid for that mistake. It is important for deans to do their job and not be discouraged by the actions of others—actions not within the dean's control.

The reader will note that this example involved the AAO and an independent decision-maker. In most universities today sexual harassment and discrimination complaints are supposed to be handled by an AAO whose job it is to handle such cases. It is also possible that there will be within the institution trained decision-makers who have the responsibility to evaluate collected and synthesized data and make a judgment about what should be done. Technically, as I understand it, the decision-maker's judgment is supposed to be respected and followed, making the outcome of the above case still more questionable. Not all universities have the same structure and deans have to be prepared to accept more or less of the responsibility for investigations and decisions, depending on the structure within which they are working. Most important of all, however, a dean does not want to let complaints go unattended, and (s)he wants to make sure due process is followed at all times.

INVESTIGATING COMPLAINTS

Not all deans have the skills needed to cover every aspect of a complaint investigation as well as carry out a decision and remedy. This is why more complex systems have been created over the years to cover important aspects of the process when needed. In some instances, such as in sexual assault cases, invoking a process external to the dean's office is mandatory. That point notwithstanding, deans need to be able to effectively deal with complaints.

The first step is to listen and take notes. Whether one has an assistant present or not, taking one's own notes assures that key statements are documented. While listening, one can ask oneself, and possibly the complainant, basic questions about logic, contradictions, conflicts of interest, and overall validity. The ultimate question is whether the complaint is serious enough to pursue further. It does sometimes happen that misunderstandings are involved and those misunderstandings can be sorted out during the interview with the complainant, allowing her/him to leave your office feeling reasonably confident about how to deal with the concern—mentally and/or behaviorally.

The Source Matters

Related to the issue of validity, is who brings the complaint to the dean's office. If the complaint is brought by the complainant it should be viewed differently than if brought by a third party faculty member or a department chair. It is often the case that faculty members have grudges against one another and chairs have department members who give them a difficult time in a variety of ways. Under these circumstances one wants to be careful about rushing into something that might be based on a personal conflict where the person delivering the complaint might be using a student or a junior faculty member to get at someone they dislike. It is always important to speak directly to the complainant alone and not simply take the word of a third party before deciding on whether to pursue the matter further.

Once a decision has been made that there could possibly be a serious problem that needs attention, the dean should continue with the investigation: calling in witnesses identified by the complainant and any other witnesses that might be relevant to the case. Always taking careful notes, the dean should constantly be cross-checking information to determine if there are patterns that will either corroborate the complaint or show sufficient contradictions that would make pursuing the case further an unproductive use of the dean's time.

As an investigation continues, the dean must, on an ongoing basis, assess whether the issue should continue to be handled inside the dean's office or involve an outside office, such as the affirmative action office or the human resources office. Depending on the nature of the case the dean may want to consult with one of those offices for guidance. Consulting with the provost is also an option, but effective provosts like to have their deans run their own shops and prefer that they handle the problems of their colleges. Consulting with the provost may also run the risk of contaminating the appeal process, should the faculty member decide to submit an appeal.

Continuing with Interviews

If a dean decides to handle the complaint her/himself, the next step is to interview the person or persons allegedly responsible for the complaint. They may have a perfectly good explanation of what happened that might be consistent with part of what was found in the preliminary investigation. So again, there may be a misunderstanding that needs to be cleared up—this time much further into the investigation, but nevertheless, the complaint might still be resolved without having to take disciplinary action. It is, however, tempting to reduce the complaint to a misunderstanding when such is not the case. It would be nice if the complaint simply went away so the dean can "continue with her/his job." However, personnel issues are an important part of the dean's job as well, and the dean has a responsibility to resolve them whenever possible. Misunderstandings among otherwise reasonable people are, indeed, generally a relief for the dean and easily resolved. It is a matter of calling the parties in together or going to them individually and clarifying what happened to all concerned in such a way as to set everyone's mind at ease and allow them to go on with their jobs.

Unfortunately, not all people are reasonable and not all people are honest. Some complaints cannot be resolved as misunderstandings but must be resolved by either dismissing the complaint as having insufficient verifiable evidence or by disciplining the alleged perpetrator(s). Discipline may involve issuing an oral warning or, depending on the seriousness of the case and how many other complaints a person has generated, the discipline could be more serious: oral reprimand, written reprimand, suspension, or dismissal.

Anecdote: The Importance of a Preliminary Investigation: an Example

I recall a case brought to my attention by a chair. I was suspicious of the complaint because I knew the chair had other problems with this faculty member unrelated to the complaint. But the complaint was serious enough that I felt obligated to follow up on it. So I cautiously pursued the matter as described previously. When I called the faculty member in I advised bringing a grievance officer, which (s)he did. Under these circumstances the dean should also have someone with her/him serving as a witness.

Neither the faculty member nor the grievance officer realized that I had already conducted a preliminary investigation up to that point. The typical approach when a complaint is registered is to call the faculty member in to discuss the matter. There are situations where doing that is useful for simply establishing a record of the occurrence. But there is little to be gained otherwise from doing that before doing some preliminary investigative work since the faculty member can deny the action and the dean is sitting there with no evidence to the contrary. It is simply one person's word against another's. Of course the investigation can be conducted *after* talking to the faculty member, but that sometimes drags things out longer than necessary. Sometimes a preliminary investigation will reveal that the complaint is unfounded and thus the faculty member should best not be bothered at all. That doesn't happen as often as one might think, but it does happen.

When I asked the faculty member mentioned above about the action of which (s)he was accused, the immediate response was a flat out denial. I believe the words used were, "That never happened. I never said anything like that." Looking at my notes I was able to confidently tell the faculty member that the denial was not true. I informed her/him that I had interviewed two people who, unbeknownst to the faculty member, happened to be within hearing distance at the time of the incident. They were students who had no connection with the people involved in the complaint. It seemed that both the perpetrator and the grievance officer were quite surprised and no objections were raised whatsoever when I gave the faculty member a clear warning to not let it happen again. As it turned out this faculty member was in my office responding to complaints again, and eventually for some quite serious accusations. I cannot write what happened in this case without risking revealing the identity of the faculty member involved. But I can say that my persistent and thorough investigations eventually benefitted the students of the college.

When a complaint surfaces it almost always occurs at a bad time, but in the life of an intentional dean there actually is no good time. It is important to follow up and document everything that happens. The problem a dean ignores today will surely come back to bite her/him tomorrow—or the next day—or next year. One can count on it. As stated by Tucker, "Don't just let things slide; hold people accountable for following established guidelines. Any time you can be proactive in preventing a crisis, you minimize unnecessary overreactions and having to clean up a bigger mess later" (2014: 301).

SERVING AS A DECISION-MAKER

If special training is available to allow deans to become decision-makers at an institution where you are deaning it is advisable to attend such sessions since they help one to better understand some of the institutional documents governing behavior within that system. Once one has completed the training (s)he can be called upon to review data in investigated complaint cases and arrive at a conclusion about what should be done to resolve the matter justly. This experience helps one deal more effectively with complaints within one's own college. Once through such training, one can be asked to be a decision-maker in cases involving students, faculty members, or a combination of students and faculty members.

SEXUAL ASSAULT AND THE UNIVERSITY

While sexual harassment continues to be a problem on college campuses (Washington et al. 2015), a 2015 East Coast campus study produced evidence that rape is possibly at epidemic proportions on university campuses. Hence, there is considerable concern among students and the general public at large that university administrators are possibly sweeping rape cases under the rug (De La Hoz, 2016). The failure of campuses to prevent rape has been a concern for a long time (Streng & Kamimura, 2015; Hollis, 2006). My own experience as a decision-maker evaluating alleged rape cases supports the cited literature. It is not possible for me to discuss the details of these cases, not only because of the confidentiality involved but also because of the incredibly violent and heinous nature of the alleged actions. The classic behavior patterns emerged: laced drinks, black outs, a key perpetrator with other possible men involved, and a very sad ending corroborated by witnesses.

The first such case I handled was, in my mind, an open and shut case with multiple witnesses. My decision was to expel the accused student immediately and not allow him to return to the campus or any of the other system campuses. My write up brought an immediate reaction from key people in the university, expressing surprise at my decision, stating that the university had never had a decision quite like it before. My response was that perhaps it was about time that such a decision be made to send an appropriate signal to others who might behave in this way. I never formally heard from anyone about what was actually done—whether my decision was upheld or not—but I have reason to believe that my decision was upheld completely.

Somebody Is Watching

Then there was a second case. I don't remember the details of this case as clearly as the first (and I wish I couldn't remember any of the details), but it was also quite gruesome. I wrote up my decision and didn't hear anything about it until, as I recall, I received a communication from an external office stating that the wording of one of my sentences would have to be changed. I responded that making such a change would allow the perpetrator to escape responsibility for his actions and that I, therefore, could not change it. It wasn't long after that I received another visit from an important university spokesperson who explained that a call was received from that same outside office, and that if I did not change my wording as advised, they would no longer provide their services to the university. I made it clear that I did not feel I could change the language in my letter because doing so would be a *de facto* change of my decision, but I did agree to let someone else redo the decision-making case. I don't know who that was, but I suspect that a milder decision was attained.

The experience with the mentioned outside legal office reveals how complicated these matters can be. Here was an administrator (me) at a university willing to actually do something about rape on campus and it was, in effect, taken out of the university's control by an external office. Whether there was genuine fear of being successfully sued, or whether there were other even more problematic explanations of their behavior, I will most likely never know. Many highly educated people still do not understand what rape is and are thus inclined to blame the victim or minimize the damage done to the victim. That still happens, including at the university and in related external offices, including the criminal courts (Tribune News Services, 2016). My advice to deans who might find themselves handling such cases is to stand their ground. Call rape what it is and take life changing action against perpetrators. It may be our only hope for eliminating, or even significantly decreasing, sexual assault at the university.

Whose Findings Are Correct?

A third significant decision-making case involved a faculty member and a student. As I recall the case, a rising star faculty member with important publications and some external funding was accused of sex discrimination by a female graduate student. While it was clear from the evidence that sexist behavior toward this woman had occurred in a variety of ways, a careful and thorough reading of the communications and documents unraveled something quite different. As it turned out, the graduate student, a star in her own right, had worked closely with the faculty member, assisting him in his research. For her thesis she decided to replicate the work of her mentor, adding some pieces to make it her own. In the student's replication of the research, the findings of her mentor did not hold. She was so shaken by this result that she redid the entire study over. The findings were the same the second time. She wrote it up and submitted it to her committee, chaired by her mentor.

Responses from her mentor were negative and took a long time in coming. Various changes were recommended when a response did arrive. The student made them promptly and with due diligence. Of course rewrites are to be expected when a thesis is involved, but this thesis was highly quantitative and thus, by design, a relatively short document. At the time of the complaint being filed the thesis had been revised sixteen times. The student complied with everything she was asked to do, and still received no valid reasons for her thesis continuing to be rejected. A near straight "A" student (one "B" grade), she had good job prospects but could not follow through with those opportunities because of the absence of her degree.

An Unethical Demand

Following the initial submission of her thesis, months passed and eventually turned into a period exceeding a year. In desperation the student tried to get one of the other committee members to intervene on her behalf. Finally, her mentor agreed to accept her thesis if she would change her hypothesis to fit the results. In other words, if she would predict an outcome different than the claimed outcome of the mentor's research (being circulated for publication at the time) he would accept her thesis. Recognizing that it would be unethical to change her hypothesis after the data were collected and analyzed, she refused to do so and filed a complaint.

Having taught quantitative research methods for many years I was appalled when I read this case. The evidence was clear that the mentor was protecting his interests at the student's expense and at the expense of an honest scientific search for the truth. Whether his findings were accurate or whether hers' were accurate doesn't matter. A student was being prevented from obtaining her degree so that the faculty member's reputation would not be in jeopardy. He was asking his student to fake her predictions after the fact. It doesn't get much more dishonest than that when it comes to experimental research that is supposed to be following a deductive process—a process implied by asserting hypotheses at the onset of the research. Negative findings are a fact of life in the research enterprise and they should be reported and valued as boldly as positive findings. This professor failed to use the student's findings as a teaching and learning moment for his student and himself. Instead of moving on to find out why the findings were actually different (assuming the mentor presented his findings honestly) he became threatened and punished his once star student for daring to report findings different than his own.

The right decision seemed clear. The student was to be cleared for graduation and the faculty member was to be given a reprimand for his mistreatment of the student and also for his numerous sexist comments and behaviors that surfaced through the course of the investigation. As previously stated, a decision-maker typically doesn't know whether her/his "decision" is actualized, but I'm quite certain the student received her degree, and that was what was most important.

A HOUSE DIVIDED

It is an unfortunate fact of academia that many—far too many—departments are torn apart internally. Typically it is an "us" and "them" arrangement, but often times it is even more complicated with multiple factions. Many years ago I was hired as an assistant professor into a department of fifteen faculty positions. I was, so to speak, the swing vote in a completely and evenly divided department. There was so much venom released daily that the department corridors were slick with it. One had to be ever on guard to avoid being pulled into a hate conversation about someone else. Department meetings were amazing. I recall one meeting where one person from each faction stood up and read a hate letter to specific people of the other faction. In retrospect it could be somewhat humorous, but at the time I was terrified. I had just moved my family halfway across the country and found myself faced daily with a group of quite crazed and scary people. I would listen in disbelief as one faction openly referred to the chair of our department as a pizza man, spaghetti bender, and mafioso. The chair was short, dark, and obviously of Italian descent—more so than myself. But being of Italian heritage I was dismayed and quite shocked. By the end of the first year I was elected director of the sociology program. Being new I was the only person either side would trust. As a result of term limits being put in place there was a chair election that same year and both sides had "their" candidate. The person for whom I voted (neither candidate was qualified in my opinion) was unable to do the job, so I ended up doing much of the chair's work, including attending the dean's council meetings. I was an untenured assistant professor and my research was suffering, so after 2 years I resigned my position as program director.

Where Is the Dean?

Before I resigned as program director I tried to bring the sociologists together around the idea of a graduate program, and it worked to some extent. It was the first of two such programs I organized for the department. The first program was not approved by the state but the second program was approved. I also became heavily involved in faculty leadership on campus and eventually began serving as a grievance officer. It was in this capacity that I came to realize that my department was not the only department divided against itself. As the campus grievance officer, I found myself going to meeting after meeting to try to help departments resolve their internal differences so they could function as a whole unit. I had no actual authority to do anything—albeit I was able to help in some instances. What was missing in every case was leadership from those who actually did have institutional authority. There was no evidence of the deans spending sufficient time on these problems, which were often serious.

A Promise to Do Better

When I became a dean I vowed to be aggressively intentional about resolving departmental splits and fights. In both of my deanships I was fortunate to not have nearly as many problems as existed at the institution of my professorship, but there were some. My approach was to call the departments together and listen to their grievances against each other. I did not hesitate to give my viewpoint and offer ways of resolving the problem, and in some instances I gave specific instructions to particular individuals. I also went over possible future scenarios if they did not follow my suggestions/instructions: Law suits could be filed, people's careers could be ruined, and departmental resources could be lost. The key was to avoid emotional involvement, remain factual, and lay everything out in a planned systematic fashion. I wasn't always successful, and one is never completely successful in these situations, since it is not possible to make people like each other. But I was most often successful enough that departments were subsequently able to function as units. And while it is not possible to make people like each other, in a couple of cases I was able to get two factions to appreciate what each brought to the department and thus got them to stay together in a relatively peaceful manner.

Letters of Expectation

The above discussion sets the stage for a case where I could not resolve the differences—largely because of the presence of two faculty members whose personalities were such that they created problems in what seemed to be an unconscious manner. The departmental split became much more complicated with new hires. I met with the department and specific individuals more than once and went over the possible future negative scenarios if the problems were not resolved, but it made no difference. The problems continued and culminated in a particular event that was handled poorly by everyone in the department—not just the usual instigators. In fact, an individual who had worked hard to stay neutral in the department got pulled into the riff in a rather strange and uncharacteristic manner. My knowledge about all of the players made me aware that the situation was much more complicated than anyone involved or any onlooker might suspect.

After interviewing all of the parties involved in the culminating incident, I removed two of the newer faculty members from administrative control of the department. They could still teach the courses they were hired to teach, but they would no longer have to worry about being evaluated by a dysfunctional department. The department would lose the credits that were produced by the two removed faculty members and essentially lose those positions. I had warned the department that this might happen when they were in the process of completing their searches for those positions.

Perhaps the most significant action I took was to invoke a seldom used administrative option that I believe to be useful. I wrote letters of expectation to everyone involved. The letters detailed what behaviors were in violation of university and state rules and warned against future violations. The letters were individualized according to the specific actions each person had taken. Letters of expectation turned out to be quite effective in bringing about a reasonable state of calm. There were, however, adjustments to be made, especially for the people moved to other departments. Some individual problems continued and were handled through the progressive disciplinary process, but the department (what was left of it) seemed to be stabilized until after my retirement.

While letters of expectation are not meant to be used frivolously—any more than letters of reprimand are meant to be frequently used—they can be a useful tool when all else fails. It is useful for academics to have a document in their hand that they can read multiple times that lets them know exactly what their responsibility is and what might happen if that responsibility is not fulfilled. Under these circumstances no one can say they didn't know or that they had not been warned.

Letters of Expectation and Decision-Makers

As a decision-maker I was able to use a letter of expectation written by the provost to strengthen my recommendation of disciplinary action in a decision-making case where a faculty member in another college continued problematic behavioral patterns. The evidence for the case was sufficient to force the conclusion to which I came, but given that the faculty member had clearly been warned and specifically instructed on how to correct the problem in a letter of expectation, the case that I presented for disciplinary action was much stronger. Again, the evidence was clear. The faculty member had been warned and had not changed behaviors commensurate with those warnings. Letters of expectation, provided they are carefully worded to be in compliance with the institutional documents governing what constitutes appropriate behavior, can be an important asset to the disciplinary process.

WHEN BASIC PRODUCTIVITY AND APPROPRIATE BEHAVIOR SLIP

At the onset of my first deaning position I discovered a file about 5 inches thick that was completely filled with complaints about one faculty member. My administrative assistant informed me that the previous deans as far back as when she started working there had all tried to deal with this individual but soon gave up. For the purpose of discussion I will call this person Chris. I called Chris to my office and holding up the file informed the individual that I had carefully read all of the institutional documents related to acceptable behavior and corresponding complaints. I talked about what the appropriate administrative course of action would be if the complaints continued and informed Chris with certainty that I would be following due process accordingly if the complaints continued. This was all said in a calm, gentle, and relaxed manner. I then put the file down and said, "Chris, you could not possibly be enjoying your work here while generating so many complaints. Is there anything that brings joy into your life? I'm not seeing any joy in what you are doing here." Chris, who had been casually eating an apple up to that point, sat silent for what seemed like a rather long time with jaw open quite wide. After determining that I was sincere in my inquiry, the seemingly surprised faculty member proceeded to tell me about an important spare time activity that was fulfilling, meaningful, and joyful—an activity on which Chris would enjoy spending more time.

The complaints stopped, and 2 years later Chris retired to spend more time on the activity that was discussed in that first meeting we had together. Teaching had become a paycheck and an ongoing battle: with students, other faculty members, and, of course, administrators. I received an email from Chris indicating that I should be the first to know about the retirement, an apparent expression of gratitude for taking the time to inquire about and listen to personal interests.

Deans and Perpetrators Both Have Options

A great deal was learned from the experience with Chris. First, it is important for faculty members to know that the dean does, indeed, have options that will work and that can be used should a tenured faculty member not behave appropriately. Second, faculty members must also be clear that the dean intends to exercise those options in an effective and legal manner. And finally, the experience with Chris made it clear that faculty members who have reached a point where they are just collecting a paycheck sometimes need some encouragement to explore other life circumstances for themselves. When a faculty member is working past typical retirement age without enjoyment and to the detriment of the students it is not a good situation for anyone. A quote from Buller is once again helpful:

> Now that mandatory retirement ages are forbidden, institutions are often compelled to initiate agonizing and often unsettling processes to revoke the tenure of senior faculty members who are no longer performing their responsibilities at an acceptable level. The implementation of post-tenure review procedures at many institutions has helped make evaluating tenured faculty members somewhat more equitable (2007: 291).[1]

Because of the abolition of mandatory retirement, it is generally not acceptable to even suggest to a faculty member that they consider retirement. In fact, human resource guidelines and collective bargaining agreements might outright forbid such administrative behavior. I do not support mandatory retirement. There are many highly productive people working well past 66 years old. There are, however, no rules against having a conversation about what makes a person happy and about how that person might best achieve that happiness, as long as the discussion is genuinely about the faculty member in question and not simply a ploy to remove this person.

When Performance and Behavioral Issues Become One

The dean sometimes has the awkward responsibility of letting senior unproductive faculty members know that they are expected to fulfill their contractual obligations to the same extent as others. That means they are supposed to be active scholars, community servants, and good teachers through their last days on the job. Anything short of that contractual expectation needs to be addressed. When performance evaluation reaches a point of assessing whether someone is actually fulfilling the minimum expectations of her/his post-tenure contract, a dean could be forced to leave the realm of performance evaluation and move into the behavioral area where discipline may eventually need to be considered. This is true of the performance of faculty members at any post-tenure career stage, but the challenge is greatest when dealing with tenured full professors.

By consistently responding to faculty activity reports in an honest and responsible manner the dean can encourage lagging senior faculty members to improve their contribution to the college. Those who prefer not to change their behaviors will most likely feel some embarrassment since typically the department chair and department also have a chance to respond to those reports. What sometimes happens is that the senior faculty members quit filing their reports since they are, at some universities, not required to file every year and thus are not as easily tracked. This is where a good administrative assistant is important since they have to keep track of when all of the reports are due. Overworked administrative assistants, in looking for areas where they can cut corners, will sometimes become less rigorous about tracking the tenured full professors since it is assumed (often by the dean as well) that nothing can be done about them anyway. This assumption is false and should be continuously challenged. Tenure is a vitally important tool for protecting academic freedom, but it is not a tool to protect people who consistently fail to fulfill their minimum employment responsibilities.

I did not have the benefit of reading Buller before completing my deanships, but his claim regarding responses to post-tenure reviews is substantiated by my experience. He states, "Some tenured faculty members see the handwriting on the wall when they receive an unsatisfactory post-tenure review and volunteer to retire" (2007: 291). Or, as Benders writes, "In some cases, faculty members will realize that their performance in teaching, scholarship, or service is not meeting the expectations of their college or university, and will actively seek employment elsewhere" (2014: 310–311). Indeed, once word got out that I was actually making suggestions for work performance improvement in the reports of the senior faculty members as well as the junior faculty members, some senior faculty members worked up to the due date of their next report and then announced their retirement. Other senior faculty members actually accepted my advice and began doing things that they probably would not have done before. Those who took the latter route typically enjoyed their newly productive state and were more vital members of their departments, their college, and the university community. Most people who continue working want to have a sense of success and usefulness. They sometimes simply need some encouragement and additional support.

When Is Low Productivity a Disciplinary Issue?

Low productivity is not a basis for disciplinary action unless a faculty member who has been sufficiently warned continues to refuse to perform the basic contractual requirements for employment as stated in the relevant institutional documents. Once this occurs, the failure to perform according to minimum required standards, as well as the failure to meet the dean's stated expectations, become a behavioral issue and must be treated accordingly in the post-tenure case. It can also happen in a pre-tenure case where from the onset it is clear that a faculty member is not doing their job and must be fired before the tenure decision occurs. But this kind of case is relatively rare since fulfilling basic responsibility is seldom an issue with new faculty members. Since new faculty members generally deserve some startup latitude, by the time basic responsibility neglect can be verified departments and deans are ready to employ the tenure review. I came close to letting a faculty member go in her/his third year based on basic performance issues and consistent corresponding warnings, but a slight improvement gave me enough hope to see her/him to the tenure decision.

Warnings of inadequate work performance being ignored over a period of time represent the only place where performance evaluation and behavioral evaluation legitimately come together. It is important to let faculty members, who are not doing their job, know that a disciplinary action is possible and that it will be exercised if necessary. As discussed above, while this is true of both tenured and non-tenured faculty members, it is primarily an issue for tenured faculty members.

Keep in mind that what is being discussed here is completely separate from the tenure review process which solves the problem of inadequate productivity through a negative tenure decision. Negative tenure decisions typically only occur after the faculty member has been consistently warned about the weaknesses in their performance—assuming the faculty member has been honest about their progress and corresponding documents in their annual reports. Fortunately, I never had to take performance-based disciplinary action in the colleges I administered because the lagging senior faculty members with whom I had to work either retired before it was necessary to discipline them, or changed their professional disposition once they saw where my letters were heading.

Challenging Basic Work Performance as a Decision-Maker

As a decision-maker for a case in another college, however, I invoked a rarely used article of the collective bargaining agreement to direct performance-based disciplinary action toward a tenured faculty member. As previously stated, all faculty administrative agreements have a clause/article defining what the minimum workload expectation is for each faculty member. In the collective bargaining unit with which I worked the just mentioned article was Article 10 (IFO/MnSCU, 2013). Hence, when writing up a case where a tenured faculty member had been neglectful of their duties, I cited Article 10 as follows:

> In other words, the general behavior pattern described in the documentation associated with this decision case is a violation of the basic responsibilities identified in Article 10, Section A of the [institutional name] contract, which all faculty members are expected to know and follow.

And then again later in the decision document I wrote, "Professor [name] has been accused of not responding to students in a timely fashion, and in some instances not responding at all. This accusation relates to Article 10, Section A, and specifically pertains to 'student advising' and 'contributing to student growth and development.'"These contract citations take the mystery out of the decision-making and put the responsibility squarely where it belongs: on the faculty member who is not performing according to the institutional-faculty agreement. Rather than just saying a person is not doing what (s)he is supposed to do and describing those behavioral issues, the behavioral issues are grounded in the documents that govern them.

While this case did not result in dismissal, I am quite certain that serious disciplinary action was taken—probably in the form of a letter of reprimand or possibly a suspension. I gave the administrator in charge some latitude when crafting my decision. Suppose that dismissal was recommended, as in other cases for which I had responsibility, how should that dismissal be executed? Benders (2014) gives a quite useful description of how the letter should be written and who should be involved. Some of the process will vary from institution to institution. The dean is not likely to be the one writing the dismissal letter, but the dean will in many cases be the primary impetus behind the dismissal. It is important that the dean work closely with the human resource director to make certain everything is done according to due process.

Option to Resign

An issue that is somewhat controversial is whether the person being fired should be given the option to resign. Benders (2014) maintains that they should be given that option. The reasons, while not specified by Benders, are institutionally sound: If the person resigns the process ends and everyone can go home. There is no battle to be fought as when the faculty member decides to challenge the decision, and there will be no lawsuit. On the other hand, however, if a tenured faculty member has done something sufficiently wrong to be fired the question of whether they should be offered the option to resign becomes an ethical one. Too many faculty members who do significant damage to students and the institution are then hired by other universities to effectively do the same thing all over again. I believe we have a moral responsibility to call the situation the way it actually unfolds. Certainly if a person decides to resign before they are dismissed that is their option and no one can stop them. But we should not seek ways to protect ourselves or the accused at the expense of students at other institutions. Offering someone the option to resign rather than simply giving them the dismissal letter is not being a good team player in the broadest sense of the word "team." As educators we are all in the same game and thus should support each other.

Deference to Senior Faculty

On the one hand it may seem that we owe our senior faculty members some latitude since they have been serving the institution for a long time. On the other hand, some senior faculty members may have been allowed to slide by when they were junior faculty members and simply kept up the same pattern. Others may have gotten tired and allowed their productivity to drop in later years. Either way, it is important that everyone does their share. Certainly some latitude can be granted for how one fulfills her/his obligations as a career unfolds, but the work has to be done. We are not talking about digging ditches or foundry work. Yes, mental work and working with students everyday can be difficult, but such activities are not so difficult that age alone should affect one's ability to carry out the related necessary tasks. It has been my observation that the most productive junior faculty members tend to continue to be productive in their later years as well—often in different ways than when they started out, but still productive.

WHO IS SUFFERING?

Several years ago my wife attended a weekend Bodhisattva Peace Training, and was so impressed that she encouraged me to attend one as well. Bodhisattva Peace Trainings are typically 2- or 3-day programs designed, in part, to help individuals see the harm they do to themselves by harming others and the world around them—primarily through their attachments and aversions. The teachings are based on some of the fundamental principles of Buddhism, but are not directly intended to convert people to Buddhism.[2]

Some of the practices taught during the peace trainings are invaluable to becoming a successful intentional dean. There is not enough space in this book to go into the numerous useful principles attainable through the peace trainings, but I would be remiss if I did not encourage those aspiring to a deanship, as well as those already deaning, to attend a Bodhisattva Peace Training.[3] The usefulness of the trainings becomes particularly apparent when dealing with difficult disciplinary issues. Problems related to inappropriate faculty or student behavior should not be turned into personal crusades to get the "bad guys" or vendettas against "enemies." The goal is never to make someone suffer, regardless of what they have done. The goal is always to help people correct their harmful behavior, and when that fails the goal is to protect those who could be affected by the perpetrator's harmful behavior in the future.

When deans, or any administrators, choose to make someone else suffer they also are foremost choosing to make themselves suffer. Resentments and hostilities toward others are poisons that diminish and disrupt our own personal and professional lives. Make this fundamental Buddhist principle your own and your deaning experience will be far more fulfilling and enjoyable than it would be otherwise, especially when dealing with difficult disciplinary issues.

NOTES

1 For another useful discussion of Post-Tenure Review see Krahenbuhl (2004: 108–110).
2 For a related discussion see Gandhi (1999).
3 See, *Change of Heart* by Lama Shenpen Drolma (2003) for more information about the principles.

REFERENCES

Benders, A. (2014). Difficult disciplinary decisions, in L.L. Behling (Ed.). *The resource handbook for academic deans* (pp. 309–313). San Francisco: Jossey-Bass.

Buller, J.L. (2007). *The essential academic dean*. San Francisco: Jossey-Bass.

De La Hoz, F. (2016). *A conversation with the hunting ground's Kirby Dick*. Retrieved September 2, 2016 from http://observer.com/2016/04/a-conversation-with-the-hunting-grounds-kirby-dick/

Drolma, S. (2003). *Change of heart: The bodhisattva peace training of Chagdud Tulku*. Junction City: Padma Publishing.

Gandhi, A. (1999). The four cardinal principles of leadership, in F. Hesselbein, M. Goldsmith & L. Somerville (Eds.). *Leading beyond the walls* (pp. 217–224). San Francisco: Jossey-Bass.

Hollis, M.J. (2006). Predators on campus: examining the alarming rate of sexual assaults on U.S. College and University campuses and why prevention communication messages are failing. Online MLA Thesis, Saint Edward's University. Retrieved September 2, 2016 from http://eric.ed.gov/?id=ED511503

IFO/MnSCU. (2013). *IFO/MnSCU master agreement*. Retrieved February 29, 2016 from http://ifo.org/contract-benefits/contract/.

Krahenbuhl, G.S. (2004). *Building the academic deanship: Strategies for success*. Westport: Praeger Publishers.

Streng, T.K. & Kamimura, A. (2015). Sexual assault prevention and reporting on college campuses in the US: A review of policies and recommendations. *Journal of Education and Practice*, 6 (3), 65–71. Retrieved September 2, 2016 from www.iiste.org/Journals/index.php/JEP/article/view/19426

Tribune News Services. (2016). Judge in Stanford rape case to stop hearing criminal cases. *The Chicago Tribune*. Retrieved August 27, 2016 from www.chicagotribune.com/news/nationworld/ct-judge-aaron-persky-stanford-rape-case-20160825-story.html

Tucker, D. (2014). The responsibility of leadership in dealing with difficult people, in L.L. Behling (Ed.). *The resource handbook for academic deans* (pp. 299–304). San Francisco: Jossey-Bass.

Washington, F., Kahla, M.C. & Crocker, R.M. (2015). Sexual harassment on campus: "He's just a pervert and everybody knows it!". *Journal of the International Academy for Case Studies*, 21 (5), 333–337.

Chapter 10

Merit Pay

MERIT PAY EVALUATION

If a university distributes all or part of their pay increases according to merit, then all faculty members must submit evaluation documents for each year pay increases are considered, which could be every year. The evaluation process for merit increases could actually be a separate process from the professional development evaluation process and might require an entirely different set of documents—albeit it is basically the same information put into a slightly different form. Approximately 34 percent of university administrations use some form of merit pay (Euben, 2003). Yet, it remains, for the most part, a contentious and legally difficult issue, especially as pertains to measurement, distribution formulas, and who actually makes the award determinations (Euben, 2003; Guess, 2008). What is the goal of the intentional dean under these circumstances? One option is to try to convince the higher administration to eliminate merit pay increases and use only an across-the-board pay increase approach. This option is probably not very realistic. The faculty would have a better chance of making this happen than the deans would. A second option is to design a system of merit distribution that is fair and reliable—albeit this is not an easy goal to accomplish. What follows is an example and explication of the second just mentioned option.

Faculty Activity Reports

Sometime in the late fall the academic vice president/provost or dean will send out a reminder to all faculty members that they are to write and submit a faculty activity report (FAR). This is a report on all of the faculty member's professional accomplishments during the spring semester of the previous academic year through the fall semester of the current academic year. "These reviews typically start with the submission by faculty of materials to update their academic record. This information helps reviewers understand the nature of the faculty member's workload and the quality and volume of the academic work completed during the review period" (Krahenbuhl, 2004: 103). The dean should then send a reminder to the faculty members of any special issues that might need to be addressed.

The dean's responsibility relative to these reports is to evaluate them carefully and provide every faculty member an opportunity to meet with the dean in order to discuss the reports. The dean then uses these reports as the basis for making "variability" recommendations to the provost. Variability, which might otherwise be thought of as merit pay, is a small amount of money, or a percentage of the person's salary, that is added to the across-the-board pay increases (if there are any) of the most productive faculty members. Merit pay can be an annual award that is given separate from one's salary, or it can be given as a percentage of one's salary that is permanently added onto the salary. Generally, it is expected that somewhere around 50 percent of the faculty will receive a variability adjustment when there is also an across the board adjustment. If there is no across the board adjustment the number of faculty members receiving merit pay increases should be higher, and there should also be more levels of adjustment.

Two Guiding Factors

There are two guiding factors behind the number of merit awardees: (1) how much money is available for salary increases, and (2) faculty morale. If less than 50 percent of the faculty receives merit increases the level of faculty dissatisfaction with merit pay rises significantly. It is also important that it is not always exactly the same group of people receiving variability each year. There will probably be a few people that will receive variability every year and a few that will rarely receive variability, but the merit pay group should otherwise be a constantly shifting demographic so that most faculty members receive some additional reward some of the time. If this does not occur morale may suffer and faculty cooperation may suffer along with it.

Standard Criteria Are Essential

Making sure that the merit pay group varies over time is not easy. There are two variables that can be manipulated to achieve this purpose. One variable is the standards by which merit pay is assigned, and the other is the number of faculty members actually receiving merit pay. If one wants to be systematic about assigning merit pay and maintain a constant set of criteria for evaluating the FAR, which is what should be done ethically, the first of the two variables essentially disappears.

Clear standards should be set, thereby making it as difficult as possible for you, the dean, to pick and choose recipients.[1] By making it difficult for you to pick and choose recipients you are actually making your job easier because you are avoiding much of the distrust and complaining that frequently accompanies merit pay decisions. Deans want to be able to effectively demonstrate that a neutral unbiased system is in place that minimizes the importance of the dean's personal preferences. Under these circumstances, if the dean wants to include more recipients, (s)he ends up relying heavily on her/his ability to change the percentage of people actually receiving a merit increase. Of course this must mean decreasing, as well as increasing, that percentage from year to year, otherwise the number of merit recipients would eventually approach 100 percent. There is also a certain amount of change in the merit pay group that occurs simply by some people having exceptionally good or bad years in terms of their productivity.

It Multiplies

While a small amount of money for an individual during any one particular year, merit pay salary increases can add up to a great deal of money over the span of a person's career. The amount that is added onto one's salary each year becomes part of the new salary base upon which future percentage increases will occur. So there is a multiplicative, as well as additive, effect over time. At universities where merit pay is given each year there can be significant pay differences between faculty members in the same department with the same number of years of experience—and possibly even with the same rank. While it may well be justifiable based on who works the hardest, administrators, including deans, need to assess whether this kind of disparity is healthy or unhealthy for a university (or college) in the long run.

MERIT PAY IS NOT A WEAPON

Some deans recommend merit pay for few faculty members and some recommend merit pay for as many as they can. In assigning merit pay one must keep in mind the overall objective: increasing productivity and/or improving work quality. Productivity and work quality do not increase within a faculty where there is a general state of anomie about what the normative expectations are for attaining merit pay, and thus where there is low morale and constant back biting over who deserves more or less. Some administrators fall into the trap of assigning merit pay to those faculty members they like and denying merit pay to those they don't like—for whatever reason the liking and disliking might occur. This is a serious mistake and one of the best ways to turn merit pay into the antithesis of its intended purpose. Deans should not use merit pay as a weapon to carry out personal wars and celebrations. It is tempting to do that since there will always be faculty members, some of whom are quite productive, who seem to work at making life difficult for the dean. When deans experience mistreatment from faculty members, they should look in the mirror and repeat ten times: "Merit pay is not a weapon."

Faculty unions tend to be somewhat inherently antagonistic toward merit pay. But the faculty of one unionized system left merit awards in the contract for a few years, and then negotiated it out. It became clear that some of the deans were simply using merit pay to reward their friends without any notable attempt to determine who the meritorious faculty members actually were within their colleges. Colleagues would sometimes be shocked at some of the people who received, and who didn't receive, merit pay. The complaints rolled in and merit pay rolled out. It was eliminated completely. Decades later merit pay was reintroduced in the form of an award each year to the top four or five scholars on each campus.[2]

Measurement: What and by Whom?

Merit pay policies that contain some amount of measurement are usually created and administered by departments. Measurement in these instances is most often very general, based on a relatively subjective scoring of how a faculty member does on the university's existing standard (P&T) three to five evaluation criteria, with a single score being assigned to each of those criteria: typically research, service, and teaching.

Research on schools/colleges of business, which tend to have the faculty most likely to embrace merit pay, show moderate levels of satisfaction with the results and many negative comments expressing concern about the process, excessive discretion afforded the dean or department head, and the possible politics associated with their favor or disfavor toward someone (Prewitt & Phillips, 1991). More recent findings on merit pay in business colleges show a relationship between merit pay and research productivity but not teaching quality, leading to speculation that merit pay may be simply reinforcing the research that is taking place rather than actually incentivizing additional research. It is also speculated that merit pay may actually be detracting from attention to teaching (Lindsay, Campbell, & Tan, 2012; Campbell, Lindsay, Garner, & Tan, 2010).

Overreliance on Departments

What one finds at the universities represented by the above citations and other universities as well, is that the burden of evaluation for merit pay is most often delegated to (or one might say, foisted upon) the departments. This is typically done in the name of being democratic and under the rubric of empowering departments to be in control of their own professional lives and decision-making. But it is more likely the case that the higher administration simply does not want to have the treacherous burden of doing the merit pay evaluations themselves. They know how difficult it is to do this task fairly and how many landmines there can be along the way. Departments do the best they can with this activity, but measurement is typically crude and the methodologies vary considerably from one department to another—even within the same colleges (e.g., College of Arts & Sciences:

Lamar University (2006)). And many departments have internal conflicts and biases that make doing this job in an unbiased manner almost impossible.

Faculty Confidence in Merit Pay?

A most interesting website is that of Missouri State University, where the faculty members responded to a questionnaire about their merit pay experience and wrote comments relating to each question (Faculty Senate of Missouri State University, 2008). The comments appear to be quite candid. They are also quite variable in terms of their levels of satisfaction and dissatisfaction. Here again one can see that departments are ground zero for merit pay evaluations, but what also comes through rather clearly is that there is recognized pressure, if not interference, from the dean to assign certain weights. Apparently, at Missouri State University, faculty members are to assign, and/or negotiate with their department head, how much they want certain evaluation criteria weighted. Of course, the deans know where the college weaknesses are and want to correct for those weaknesses, but at the same time want to keep a healthy distance from the actual evaluations. The other problem the dean faces in this situation is trying to somehow distribute the funds across the entire college when receiving quite different data sets from the various departments. The results look like two completely different plans working against each other.

Conflicting Interests

So there is evidence that some chairs are trying to abide by due process and let faculty members participate as much as possible, and at the same time trying to do the bidding of the dean, who has the bigger problems of rewarding what "needs" to be rewarded and spreading the funds around the entire college. A shortened version of an appropriate expression might simply be, "that you cannot fool all of the faculty members all of the time." In fact, it is highly unlikely that you can fool all of the faculty members anytime. As stated by one faculty member from Missouri State University, "The departmental plan operated smoothly and properly in all respects until the dean meddled arbitrarily" (Faculty Senate of Missouri State University, 2008: 13).

The many comments written by the faculty of this university seem to cry out for some sort of college-wide standardization for evaluation. In fact, there are comments to that effect in the Missouri State data. One faculty member states, "My own view is that until department plans are actually comparable across the college there will be confusion about what one may expect for a compensation rating" (Faculty Senate of Missouri State University, 2008: 8).

Assigning merit pay isn't fun and isn't easy. If not done correctly it can be a disaster. The intent is not to pick on Missouri State University. They just happened to have the courage to post the faculty reactions to their merit pay system. There were some reasonably positive comments, but the vast majority of them were quite negative and many spoke to the confusion and low morale that the merit pay system had produced.

DO YOUR JOB

The job of evaluating faculty ultimately belongs to the administration. To whatever extent the department chair or head is part of the administration they too should be prepared to play a role if called upon to do so. If department chairs/heads are responsible for merit pay recommendations, they could use the same method recommended herein for deans. It is, however, the deans who must have the courage to do their job without bias and without concern for their own popularity. It might be argued that in doing one's job honestly and fairly deans maximize the likelihood of ultimately winning the support of the majority of the faculty members within the college they administer.

Deans should strive to develop a system for evaluating faculty members that involves defensible, reliable data. All methodologists know that no created data set about human behavior will be perfect, but the more one strives for a clean fair transparent system the fewer complaints one will have. The method described herein is certainly not the only one possible, but it is offered as an example of how merit pay can be done using a systematic data collection and analysis process.

Tools Can Help Make Work Easier

Making merit recommendations to the provost is difficult to do without having faculty accusations of unfairness—even when the dean makes every possible effort to be accurate and fair. Having a clear method can reduce the arbitrariness that so often plagues a merit system. A method that can produce a great deal of satisfaction among the faculty involves the construction of an instrument that is essentially a coding sheet covering all of the faculty's possible professional activities. Department chairs should be invited to meet with the dean to review the list, offer additions, and discuss how each item should be weighted. In this manner an instrument containing thirty-four items was created. This instrument is first used as a worksheet by the faculty members and then as a measurement tool by the dean.

A copy of the instrument as a worksheet is sent to the faculty members with the dean's memo requesting submission of the FAR. The worksheet copy that is sent to the faculty members does not have the various weight values for each item included, but that information is made available to the faculty through their chairs. The faculty members are asked to arrange their report according to the identified thirty-four items to make it more convenient to evaluate, and to help the faculty members recall relevant activities that they otherwise might have overlooked. A copy of the instrument with the weight values and corresponding formulas is provided below. However, acronym and code interpretations are not included.

FAR EVALUATION ITEMS (MAX POSSIBLE = 8 POINTS PER ITEM, MOST ITEMS = 3 POINTS MAX)

1. # of students taught (less than 60=0, 60=1, 90=2, 120+=3, 200+=5).....
....
2. Quality of teaching (student eval. Mean is 4+ = 4, 4.5+ = 6) ....
....
3. # of advisees (any=1, 10–19 = 2, 20–29 = 3, 30+=4)...........................
4. # of independent studies (0,1,2,3+) ....
5. # thesis supervision type activities (0,1,2,3+)..
6. Other student involvement (qualitative assessment = 3 max)...................
7. New course development (2,3+points)..
8. New program development (0,3+points)..
9. # of preps/year (3=0, 4=1, 5=2, 6=3,7+=4)..
10. # of new preps (0,1,2,3+=3) ....
11. Innovations (0,1,2,3+=3) ....
12. # of professional conferences attended (0,1,2,3+=3).............................
....
13. # of local conference presentations or accepted (state or smaller) (0,1,2,3+=3) ....
14. # of regional conference presentations or accepted (0,1,2,3+=3)............
....
15. # of national/international conference presentations/accepted 0,1,2,3 . . .) × (1.5)(max=8) ....
16. # of refereed (masked) article pubs (0,1,2,3 . . .) × (2.5)(max=8)..........
....
17. # of non-refereed article pubs (0,1,2,3 . . .) × (1.5)(max=7) ....
....
18. # of book pubs (0,5.25each)(3 each if edited)(max=8).........................
....

19. # of applied projects (including artistic presentations)(0,1,2,3 . . .)(×2 if art)(max=8) ....
20. Works in progress (0,1,2,3+) × (.5) ....
21. Grants funded (0,3 per external . . .) × (1.5 × if over $25,000)(max=8) ....
22. Grants not funded (0,1,2,3+=3) ....
23. Service to profession (committees, offices etc.)(0,1,2,3 . . .) × (1.5 if natl)(max=8) ....
24. Community service: boards, committees etc. (0,1,2,3+=3) ....
25. Community service: other (0,1,2,3+=3) ....
26. Dept. service (0,1,2,3+=3) ....
27. Admin. work (0,1,2,3+=3) ....
28. Extent of additional edu. (wkshp,class,degr)(0,1,2,3 . . .) × (CE=1,classes =2,degree=4)(max=8) ....
29. # campus committees (0,1,2,3+=3) × (1.5) for R&T,CC,SN-EXC,NG,P&O, FD,SRCH, H&H(max=8) ....
30. # campus committee chaired (0,1,2,3+=3) × (1.5) or × (2, if one of above)(max=8) ....
31. Other extraordinary campus service (0,1,2,3+=3) ....
32. Other direct contribution to mission and goals of university (0,1,2,3+=3)
33. Honors and awards (0,1,2,3 . . .)(max=5) ....
34. Core values indicators (1,2,3 . . .)(max=5) ....

Methodology

The methodology for implementing this instrument is to conduct a content analysis of each FAR, assigning a numerical value for each of the thirty-four items for each faculty member. The sum of those numerical values is the score that the faculty member receives on the FAR. The values for every faculty member are entered into a data analysis spreadsheet, such as Excel or SPSS, for easy generation of summary scores and rankings. Recommendations for merit pay are given to the AVP based on the resulting rankings. An assistant or associate dean could be trained to perform the content analysis in accordance with the dean's set of rules. Since I did not have the support of either an associate or an actual assistant dean in this deanship, I did the entire analysis myself.

Self-Report as the Starting Point

The process starts with what is essentially a self-report document whereby the faculty members identify all of their accomplishments for the year. Of course they are asked to provide documentation where possible, and documentation is more essential in some areas, such as teaching performance and scholarship, than it is in others. As in any form of social science self-report methodology (e.g., surveys), the information is only as good as the integrity and/or perceptions of the individual faculty member writing the FAR. Hence, this method clearly disadvantages people who tend to be modest about their accomplishments, and this tendency may even have a cultural and/or gendered twist to it, that is, people from some cultures, and possibly women, may be less inclined to engage in self-aggrandizement than people from other cultures or men in general. One can try to adjust for such differences when coding the items based on what one "knows" about the author of the FAR, but this introduces another subjective variable that is difficult to systematize, and calls into question the validity of the data from yet another angle. Calling individuals for clarification can be done, but selectively and seldom (if for no other reason than the amount of time required to do it).

Coding and Scoring

As noted on the worksheet, the method is based on a three-point maximum per item backbone. This was arrived at by observing that three seemed to be the maximum norm for a lot of activities: three presentations; three publications; three independent studies; three committees; three community service activities or organizations; and so on. As the instrument evolved numerous exceptions to the three-point backbone evolved along with it, resulting in the need to allow some individual items to have a maximum number of points beyond three. Part of that evolution also involved the instrument being reviewed by the department chairs who recommended some items being weighted more heavily than others.

It is important to set a maximum number of points for each item so that there is actually a maximum number of points derivable from the instrument overall—even though, with thirty-four items, the maximum score for the instrument would be a number that was unattainable. What makes this method work reasonably well is that there are limits to how much credit a person can get for any one contribution. There are some people who do a great deal in one particular area, such as exceptional teaching or a lot of publications. There are other people who are not exceptional at one activity but make contributions to many activities across the range of possible responsibilities. Allowing some areas to have higher maximum values than the others lets faculty members know that those items represent institutional priorities.

Item Caps Serve a Purpose

Setting a cap on the magnitude of items assures the university that all members of the faculty will participate in the full range of responsibilities that represent their job if they want to receive a merit adjustment. So people who are exceptional in some highly valued areas can benefit disproportionately from those successes in comparison with focused successes in the other areas, but they cannot be assured of receiving a merit increase based on high value items alone. While some groups of items have higher point possibilities than other groups of items, the cap on each item assures that a fairly broad range of activities is needed to attain variability. Given that the university where this instrument was used was a comprehensive university, rewarding a broad range of activities was considered appropriate and quite consistent with the established culture and expectations. Other types of universities might want to weight items differently depending on what the expectations are for the faculty of that university.

Idiosyncrasies and Notations

Knowing exactly how the method is executed might prove to be helpful. It is within that spirit that the following additional details are offered.

One will note that there are imbedded pluses and minuses on the form. A number with a plus (+) after it means that any activities beyond that value do not increase the number of points above the designated value appearing in front of the plus (+) sign. This is true of the items that have representative numerical values as well as the items that have actual numerical values. For example, Item #4 ends with a '3+=3.' This means that if a person has completed three independent studies with students they receive three points. However, if they completed four independent studies with students, they still only receive three points, and the same is true for any number of independent studies after four as well.

Some items require subjective interpretation, such as Item #6. A faculty member may describe an informal project that they worked on with a student, or a tendency that the faculty member has toward working with students—spending extra time advising them informally—writing numerous letters of recommendation—checking up on students to find out why they have not been to class—helping students identify and apply for graduate school and so on. Hence, Item #6 is a catch basin for student related activities that do not fit anywhere else.

Items like #7 and #8 are scored in such a way that if one has any activity (s)he receives a minimum of two points (#7) or a minimum of three points (#8). Item #7 allows for credit up to a maximum of two newly developed courses, which is more than one would expect in an academic year independent of developing a new program. Item #8 covers the development of a new program, which is an all or nothing activity worth three points. Three points is perhaps a small amount given the magnitude of what one has accomplished. However, Item #8 is also an example of an item that crosses over into other areas of the evaluations. If one has developed a new program one has also made a huge contribution to one's department (#26), and most likely did this as part of a committee serving the department (#29). They get credit for the new courses in #7, and if they actually taught the new courses they developed for the new program they get points in # 10 as well. There are other items that have this kind of dispersion and multiplier effect, but Item #8 is one of the better examples. One could take the position that one is going to keep all of the items and corresponding points completely separate, but that is a pipe dream at best. It is better to simply keep all of the points at a reasonable level and allow for the possibility that a faculty member can theoretically max out on every activity—albeit the probability of that happening is pretty close to zero.

SCORES AS DECISION-MAKERS

If there is one thing that a faculty member does not trust it is a score that represents their performance. Faculty members know enough about measurement to know they should be suspicious when it is applied to their own behavior. This is somewhat ironic since a large portion of a university faculty, many physical and social scientists, spend much of their time trying to measure such phenomena as: the weight of invisible gases, the distance between stars, compatibility between plants, pain, emotional attraction between humans, love, cohesion between institutions, and so on. But somehow the application of measurement to them personally just doesn't seem right; and for the most part it isn't. There is always much that is left unmeasured in performance evaluations.

Unfortunately, there is no quick fix for measurement error except to inspire everyone to be honest and thorough about what they report as their accomplishments. Assuming reasonably accurate information, one can then set up a systematic measurement methodology that has the same sources of error for everyone. Therein lays the difference between a measurement of performance and a totally subjective evaluation of performance. The latter is inevitably based, at least in part, on the subjective feelings the dean has toward the faculty member, and those subjective feelings are not likely to be entirely based on performance criteria related to that faculty member's employment activities. This is not a new dilemma. Social scientists have debated the pros and cons of quantitative and qualitative methodologies for over 100 years, and that debate is clearly not over. The most legitimate question today, however, is not: Which approach is true and which approach is false? The relevant question today is: Which approach is best for the situation at hand? Which approach will most likely yield the most accurate and useful results in measuring a particular phenomenon?

Maintaining Neutrality Is the Key

Deans and faculty members are humans, and deaning is challenging work. There will be faculty members who don't like the dean and the dean might not even know why. The dean's subjective opinion of such faculty members might be difficult to suppress. Under these circumstances deans do not want to legitimate a faculty member's suspicions of them and taint their own accomplishments by taking what might be construed as retaliatory actions. Deans want to make absolutely sure they evaluate those who dislike them the same way as they evaluate others.

It is difficult to supervise 130 faculty members, or even 50, and not have subjective feelings that fall outside of the evaluation criteria, and it is success on the evaluation criteria that is supposed to be rewarded with merit pay. It is important to always remember that if there are behavioral problems associated with a faculty member that fall outside of the performance evaluation criteria there are institutional means available for dealing with those problems via other channels, and it is the dean's responsibility to use those channels. A dean does not, however, want to try to punish someone using illegitimate means. It is for this reason that creating a systematic quantitative methodology, rather than relying on a general qualitative approach (possibly peppered with some quantitative "evidence" for justification), is the best methodology to use in this particular situation. No matter how hard a dean tries, (s)he cannot mentally organize and keep track of all of the faculty members' FAR accomplishments in a purely qualitative way that is sufficiently defensible for making comparative merit pay adjustments.

If the above suggested methodology is followed there may be moments when one will have regrets. Someone who is well liked and has tried very hard will not make the cut. Or, someone who has been a royal pain in the gluteous maximus gets a higher pay increase than others who have been supportive. Those occurrences notwithstanding, the results will be far more accurate than any known alternative outcomes, especially the alternative of a department making a recommendation to a dean who then waves a magic wand to make the final decisions. Deans are advised to complete a systematic content analysis of the FAR and let the numbers fall where they may. The coding and weighting factors can always be revisited if concerns emerge, as long as the faculty is involved and informed through its departmental chairs.

Drawing the Line

Once the dean has a set of scores representing faculty performance for the year, (s)he will most likely be expected to make a recommendation to the provost. That action requires drawing a line under someone's score/name. This can be an uncomfortable and challenging activity as well. Given how clean the process has been up to this point, most likely few people would blame the dean for moving the line a little to the north if it meant cutting out someone who has given her/him nothing but grief for the entire year, or possibly even longer. That temptation notwithstanding, deans are encouraged to look south—not north. The provost might say (s)he will only fund merit increases for a maximum of 50 percent of the faculty. If someone is just below that 50 percent line who is working hard but was not quite as productive as needed to make the 50 percent cut, the dean might consider drawing the line under that person's name. The results can be submitted to the provost with an explanatory note. This way someone who has tried hard to be productive will be motivated to keep trying and will most likely be more productive in subsequent years. On the other hand, trying to cut out the faculty member who is difficult yields no predicable positive results in the long run, and rewarding a meritorious faculty member who has not supported you increases the legitimacy of your process. And that is what best serves your interests as dean in this situation: a legitimate process.

DANGERS OF USING A MERIT SYSTEM

The obvious danger of using a merit pay system, aside from its probable misapplication, is that it can discourage those who have a couple bad years and cause them to quit trying. That is, of course, the opposite of what the dean is trying to make happen; so the lower the dean is able to draw that cutoff line the better off the college will be in the long run. If a merit pay system is in place there are probably levels of merit increases—most likely two or three. This makes sense given that there is typically a small group of faculty members who somehow manage to do everything expected of them with the highest imaginable level of success. These people deserve special recognition. After all, they have most likely sacrificed their sleep and personal relationships to complete the outcomes they have submitted. General good judgment for promoting a happy well rounded life is most likely not one of the performance indicators being measured, so why shouldn't those faculty members, who make sacrifices, be more highly recognized for their professional accomplishments? The same strategy discussed above can be used for drawing all of the merit category lines. It behooves deans to be as inclusive as they dare to be within the constraints of the provost's purse. It will only bring positive results and make it easier for deans to address other items on their agenda.

Complaints Might Still Occur

Using a systematic methodology will, in the long run, save the dean from many complaints, and perhaps some sleepless nights. In the 3 years that this methodology was used only one known complaint occurred. It was from a faculty member who was militantly opposed to the merit pay concept and who had a history of harassing the administration about this and other issues. One complaint in 3 years of merit awards is probably a pretty unusual record. It is likely that problems are common in merit pay decisions because it is difficult to convince the faculty that it has been executed in an unbiased manner. If merit pay distributions are done fairly they can make a positive contribution to the college and university. Deans that must work with merit pay are best served if they embrace the task and approach it as systematically as they can. Depending on the departments to do what the dean is paid to do is a mistake. Face the task straight on and do it right.

NOTES

1 Yes, it is sometimes in everyone's best interest to invent ways of protecting ourselves from our own potential biases.
2 This information is based on the author's direct knowledge of one particular university system.

REFERENCES

Campbell, A., Lindsay, D.H., Garner, D.E. & Tan, K.B. (2010). The impact of merit pay on research outcomes for accounting professors. *Contemporary Issues in Education Research*, 3 (4), 55–62.

College of Arts & Sciences: Lamar University. (2006). *Faculty salary merit plans*. Retrieved February 28, 2016 from http://facultystaff.lamar.edu/_files/documents/academic-affairs/policies/FacSal MeritPlans.pdf.

Euben, D.R., AAUP Counsel. (2003). *Compensation and workloads (2003)*. Meetings of the legal issues in higher education 13th annual conference. Retrieved September 16, 2016 from www.aaup.org/ issues/faculty-compensation/compensation-and-work loads-2003

Faculty Senate of Missouri State University. (2008). Qualitative comments across the university. *Faculty Senate Report*. Retrieved February 28, 2016 from www.missouri state.edu/assets/facultysenate/final_merit_report_ for_web.pdf

Guess, A. (2008). Debating the merits of merit pay. *Inside Higher Ed.*, (October 10). Retrieved September 16, 2016 from www.insidehighered.com/news/2008/10/ 10/merit

Krahenbuhl, G.S. (2004). *Building the academic deanship: Strategies for success*. Westport: Praeger Publishers.

Lindsay, D.H., Campbell, A. & Tan, K.B. (2012). The impact of merit pay on teaching and research outcomes of accounting programs. *American Journal of Business Education*, 5 (3), 331–338.

Prewitt, L.B. & Phillips, J.D. (1991). Merit pay in academia: Perceptions from the school of business. *Public Personnel Management*, 20 (4). Retrieved September 16, 2016 from http://eds.a.ebscohost. com.libproxy.stcloudstate. edu/eds/detail/detail?vid=1&sid=f783a443-23ba-42c1-8cf3-b32cbc66bd2a@sessionmgr4007&hid=4108&bdata=JnNpdGU9ZWRzLWxpdmUmc2NvcGU9c2l0ZQ==#AN=9604260543&db=keh

Chapter 11

Austerity and Academia

THE POLITICS OF BUDGETARY SHORTFALLS

From time to time, and most likely more often than truly necessary, university presidents and/or system chancellors will declare the need to reduce budgets in order to avoid a financial crisis. The bottom line imperative, once reserved for private universities, has become increasingly associated with the state-funded public universities as well, since state support for the public campuses has dwindled over the last 35 years. Many, if not most, state universities now receive less than 40 percent of their operating funds from the state whose name they may bear. For some state universities the support is below 20 percent (Chronicle of Higher Education, 2014), and the average state support for public universities is about 24 percent (Snyder & Dillow, 2013). Still, when the state declares a financial emergency the state universities are often required to cut their budgets or face having their funding reduced even more. When that happens state universities must consider the same factors that drive financial gains and losses as do the private universities.

Motives and Means

State university budgets are part of a very large and complicated political decision-making process. They are often used by the politically ambitious as symbols of fat in the state budget. What is framed as a state budget crisis may actually be a politically driven attempt to impose austerity measures on state employees or universities in particular. Similarly, private university trustees may insist that university administrators impose austerity measures as an assurance that the money they raise for the institution is not being overspent or squandered. Many university trustee members know little about the operation and needs of the university they oversee, so imposing an austerity program seems perfectly logical to them. Regardless of the circumstances that lead to the provost's dreaded announcement, budget reductions sometimes do occur and the deans will most likely be responsible for making those reductions happen within the academic affairs unit (June, 2014).

Purse Strings: Whose Budget Is It?

Sometime about halfway through my first year as a dean, when I was working for a small private university, I was approached by the provost to surrender 10 percent of "my" budget. As I recall, the reasons given for the cuts were vague, but I believe that the fundraising for the new building was not going as well as expected and they were a bit behind their financial target. I consulted with some of the more seasoned department chairs (there were nineteen), and decided to do an across the board cut of all the budget lines within my college, including those of my own office. That seemed to be the fairest thing to do under the existing circumstances, and the chairs seemed to be of the same opinion.

So, 10 percent of all the budget lines of my college were transferred to the provost's budget. I was immediately called into the provost's office and after considerable silence and some squirming, first by me and then by the provost, I was asked a difficult question. It was difficult for both of us, but I think it was especially difficult for the provost because the answer was probably already known. The question was, "Why would you not consider the personnel salaries of your college to be part of your budget?" The answer was obvious: I had been given absolutely no control over those funds and while I had significant authority in the hiring selection process, I had no input into the salaries that would be offered—outside of an occasional request for input by the provost; nor did I have any control over the assignment of positions in the college (called a school at that time). All of those responsibilities had been under the clear purview of the provost. (S)he held the academic affairs purse strings tightly, but suddenly wanted to hand them over to me when the cuts had to be made. The provost knew this was out of character for her/him, resulting in notable discomfort on her/his part. This situation also made the provost realize that (s)he had been overplaying her/his role relative to what normally takes place in higher education.

Trusting the Dean

This event was probably just one of several incidents that made the provost realize the importance and value of turning more responsibilities over to deans. It was not long after that event that the provost announced a major transformation of academic affairs. Instead of the undergraduate dean (my position at the time) being responsible for nearly all of the departments in the university, there would be four college deans, and the deans would have greater responsibility for budgets, personnel decisions, and fundraising.

There are three important issues raised by the previously described occurrence. One is that it is important to know what budgets you actually control when you take on a dean's role. A second important issue is that deans must be trusted by the higher administration. It is not as if deans are difficult to fire if proven to be untrustworthy. They serve at the pleasure of the president. There probably are not many campuses left where the deans don't have control over the personnel funds of their college, which means when large budget reductions have to be made the dean will most likely have to design a plan for eliminating positions. But deans should have full control of all funds related to their operation—in good times as well as in bad.

The third issue is whether budget cuts should be made across the board, that is, reduce the budgets of all of the departments by the same percentage, or whether some other method should be used. Obviously, the easiest method is to cut evenly across all departments by a specified percentage, as was done in the previous example. But that method is only easiest when budget reductions can be made without cutting personnel funds/positions. When faced with the prospect of having to cut personnel funds one needs to at least consider other options. My next example addresses that very situation.

THE 2008 ECONOMY COLLAPSE

When the United States economy collapsed in 2008 I held a deanship at a state university of about 19,000 students. By 2009 a state budget crisis was rapidly unfolding. In these kinds of situations rumors are followed by real budget reduction discussions at all levels of the university. Under these circumstance efforts have to be made to determine where the greatest costs lie and where the most positive outcomes can be found. This determination will likely be made across university units, across colleges, and possibly across departments within colleges. Hence, it is important for deans to be prepared to defend their college as well as determine how their own college budget will be reduced.

Building Arguments to Support One's College

Table 11.1 shows a comparison of the college I was administering (FFFF) with the other five colleges in the university at that time. The names of the colleges are omitted since the intent is not to reduce the accomplishments of others, but simply show the comparative successes of the college I was fortunate to be administering at that time. In reports including such data one does well to remind readers that all colleges have their own unique contributions, many of which are not measurable

Table 11.1 Major, Degree, and Credit Comparisons with Other Colleges (Academic Data Comparison—AY 2009–2010)

College	UG Majors	UG Degrees	GRAD Majors	GRAD Degrees	S:F Ratio	ADJ CRD/ FTEF	TOTAL FTEF	UG Credits	GRAD Credits
AAAA	2597	484	337	108	16.37	503	102.89	44,288	7,479
BBBB	1564	346	249	67	22.05	670	120.20	74,188	6,395
CCCC	2139	422	56	17	23.10	697	47.54	31,958	1,184
DDDD	905	278	628	166	12.64	408	82.58	19,414	14,281
EEEE	2807	389	142	43	22.39	612	131.53	76,722	3,760
FFFF	*2349*	*485*	*353*	*111*	*24.95*	*761*	*122.20*	*83,806*	*9,194*
Total	12,361	2,404	1,765	512	122	3,651	607	330,376	42,293
Avg.	2,060.2	400.7	294.2	85.3	20.3	608.5	101.2	55,062.8	7,048.8

by the usual assessment numbers. This is true of departments within colleges as well. But when hard decisions have to be made, something is needed to guide those decisions, something that relates to the very core of what keeps us alive: students. How many are there, where are they located, how well are they being served, and what are they costing us? It is not always as easy to answer those questions as one might think, but Table 11.1, constructed using numbers from the university's annual data-book, does a reasonably good job with the first two questions. The third and fourth questions will be answered within FFFF when comparisons are made between the departments of that college. Of course relative cost is important across colleges as well, but that is a matter best left to the provost. The first and third columns of Table 11.1 are based on declared majors, not intended majors, and not the entire student body, since many students don't declare their major until many of their degree requirements have been completed.

Focus on Cost/Benefit Ratios

Budget cuts are about money, so money cannot be divorced from the decision-making process. In academia students represent the financial base of the institution. So it makes sense to determine where most of the students are located and try to protect those areas. It also makes sense to look at the relative cost per student and cut those areas representing the greatest expense, keeping in mind the marketability of the programs and the overall return expensive programs might bring to the university in terms of prestige, recognition, and balance. These latter considerations are often given more weight than they deserve, but they should be looked at to whatever extent possible—most likely by the provost. It is far more feasible to compare departments within colleges than it is to compare the colleges within academic affairs. That point notwithstanding, Table 11.1 and what follows represent an example of how one might approach building a case for defending their college during a financial crisis. Deans have to use whatever data are available and build arguments from those data.

A dean's arguments for their college should take into consideration all of the various false realities that are known to be floating around. For example, in looking at Table 11.1 one might suggest that perhaps data for 1 year represent an anomaly. Constructing Table 11.2 shows that the data for the given year of Table 11.1 are consistent with the data over the previous 4 years. In fact, FFFF numbers are getting better with time, but generally are consistently higher than the other colleges. FFFF 4-year credit production averages are notably higher at the undergraduate level and in total, and so are the numbers for credit production per faculty member and the student-faculty ratio. The only category FFFF is not first in is graduate credit production, where FFFF is second only to College DDDD.

Table 11.2 Major and Degree Comparisons Using 4-Year Averages

College GRAD	UG Majors (4Y avg.)	UG Degrees (4Y avg.)	GRAD Majors (4Y avg.)	Grad Degrees (4Y avg.)	S:F Ratio (4Y avg.)	ADJ Cr/ FTEF (4Y avg.)	College FTEF (4Y avg.)	UG Adj Crds (4Y avg.)	GRAD Adj Crds (4Y avg.)
AAAA	2498.50	448	294.75	90	15.99	490.7	104.43	44,249	7,003
BBBB	1492.00	342	232.25	72	20.69	628.25	126.26	73,389	5,821
CCCC	2265.00	431	44.25	15	21.86	659.25	49.83	31,804	1,000
DDDD	911.00	210	590.25	176	12.04	388.00	82.36	18,646	13,285
EEEE	2764.75	375	134.50	34	21.39	600.75	139.03	80,150	3,297
FFFF	*2239.00*	*469*	*324.00*	*99*	*23.44*	*714.50*	*127.69*	*82,756*	*8,309*
Total	12,170	2,275	1,620	486	115	3,482	630	330,994	38,715
Avg.	2,028.4	379.2	270.0	81.0	19.2	580.3	104.9	55,165.7	6,452.5

Credits, Majors, or Both?

Another argument that sometimes surfaces is that the mission of FFFF is "general education" and that credit production is the isolated role of FFFF. This argument might suggest that FFFF produces the credits while the other colleges produce majors and graduates. Once again the university databook denies the validity of any such claim. While FFFF had the third highest number of UG majors at the time of the crisis and second highest number of GR majors (Table11.1), FFFF consistently has the highest number of graduates walking across the stage: both at the undergraduate level and overall (Tables 11.1 and 11.2). FFFF yields to College DDDD once again only on the number of graduate student degrees conferred, where FFFF is second. Thus, while the number of majors FFFF has is impressive, the number of FFFF graduates is even more striking. FFFF is consistently first in the university. The reason for the difference between the number of majors and the number of degrees conferred is probably a multivariate issue in itself, but the primary explanation is that most of the FFFF programs do not have the rigid pre-requisite, highly structured, curricula that many of the programs in most of the other colleges have. Students in other colleges are forced to declare their majors early while FFFF students can wait until later in their college career to declare their major. It is a common understanding that the reported number of FFFF majors is much lower than actually exists at many universities. However, it is not until college comparisons are made of the number of degrees conferred that a reasonably accurate understanding of the number of FFFF majors can be attained.

Who Draws the Students?

Finally, another dean might argue that students do not come to the university to major in FFFF—they make that decision once they arrive. While there is nothing wrong with that happening, since a large segment of all students who go to college are undecided about their major, it is not true regarding FFFF in particular. Here one can identify the exclusive qualities of some of the programs and their student application rejection rates—how they draw students from all over the world and so on. Hence, one should be comfortable arguing that FFFF brings more than its share of students to campus, takes care of those students, and many other students that later decide on a FFFF major. It also provides important general education (liberal arts) courses for all of the students who come to campus. Information on student successes is also pertinent: scholarships, paper awards, and graduate accomplishments.

There should also be striking statements that can be made about the faculty—albeit they might not always be comparative. For example, three FFFF faculty have won Distinguished Scholar awards (more than any other college) and there are many more that qualify. There were more books published recently than in any other college. The FFFF faculty is sought after in the local community and beyond for their expertise on a wide range of issues (and examples could be given). Examples of outstanding research could also be provided from the annual list of FFFF faculty accomplishments. Teaching awards and examples of teaching innovations could be cited.

Now Is the Time

The previous example of data and analyses is an important part of what deans may want to be prepared to do once budget reductions are eminent. If one has had reservations about the appropriateness of boasting about her/his college, which are normal healthy reservations to have, now is the time to put those reservations aside. This is a critical moment in the life of one's college. In addition to the data in the tables, a list of the college's various contributions and accomplishments is, of course, also important. It is good practice to compile such a list every year so as to be continually prepared to provide this important information as needed. Whether first or last on any dimension of success, one should be able to defend their college honestly and with sufficient evidence to make a positive impression.

MAKING THE HARD DECISIONS

When an actual serious crisis occurs nobody really knows the true magnitude of the problem right away, and this is especially true in a large state system that includes not only universities, but various other groups of public employees as well. In part, the crisis "reality" is being constructed as the political maneuvering evolves. The result is that the deans will probably be given a series of mixed messages from the provost who is getting mixed messages from the vice president of administrative affairs, who is getting mixed messages from the various state level offices to which (s)he must answer. Under the circumstances, it is tempting for a dean to take a wait and see stance, possibly still hoping that the crisis will blow over or simply disappear. Once reductions are announced to the deans the crisis is most certainly real in its consequences for college budgets and is not going away. If the dean does not take control of the situation right away the provost or some other higher administrator will, and the results might not best serve that college's integrity and faculty morale. The dean should know the college better than anyone else, having been watching all of the relevant data since her/his arrival. As the crisis evolves, the intentional dean will act quickly to arrive at a plan that will best serve the college overall.

Generating Plans

A prepared provost will continuously inform the deans as the crisis unfolds and deans will probably be assigned the task of coming up with a budget reduction plan for their college. Initially that plan might be something like 3 percent of the college budget, which is what my dean colleagues and I were asked to produce. A 3-percent plan should not involve personnel cuts of fulltime or regular part-time employees. Department budgets (including funds for temporary adjuncts) and the college office budget will suffer, but the fulltime and regular faculty positions should remain intact.

The just mentioned 3-percent budget reduction request became confusing, however, because just before the economic collapse the vice president for administrative affairs had requested a 3-percent reallocation "tax," which at that time was a pretty unusual request. The reallocation plan lingered, and to the surprise of at least some of the deans was an amount expected on top of the crisis-generated budget reductions.

The Crisis Can Grow

As time goes on and the "reality" of the budget crisis unfolds, the budget reduction percentage can grow into something more difficult to manage. When the required percentage reached approximately 7 percent at my university, it was no longer possible to execute this reduction without a plan eliminating regular part-time and fulltime fixed-term positions. The percentage representing this significant turning point will not be the same for all colleges everywhere because not all colleges have the same amount of non-personnel funds in their budget. Herein lies an unfortunate but important sub-lesson regarding budgets: it is advisable to keep non-personnel budget lines as flush as possible in good times so as to be better prepared for the bad times. This is not a recommendation I relish making because it implies the possibility of waste and/or turning back a lot of money to the general fund each year, neither of which are good administrative practices for a dean. But when large reduction numbers start getting thrown about it is important to have some cushion somewhere in the budget that will help protect the college's programs and corresponding faculty.

By the time the provost announced the final budget scenario and requested a 10-percent reduction plan, colleges were looking at about a 13-percent reduction of their budgets with the "tax" included. It thus became clear that avoiding fulltime tenure-track/tenured personnel reductions was not going to be possible. As it turned out, ultimately FFFF ended up with a higher percentage of cuts than the other colleges because of unfunded hires that occurred before I arrived—positions presumably funded out of budgetary play (see Chapter 6). Hence, FFFF was expected to reduce its budget by 16+ percent.

Making the Cuts: Timing Is Critical

The first response in this scenario, after cutting all non-personnel budgets to a bare minimum, is to stop all new hires, which I did immediately. Harsh criticisms from disappointed faculty members will most likely occur. This is normal. It takes a while for some people to absorb the full gravity of the situation. Start keeping a running tally of the reduction amount. The second response is to look at which faculty members and staff will be retiring or leaving for other reasons, and add those salaries to the reduction total. The third response is to identify fixed-term and other regular part-time positions that contractually, according to the collective bargaining agreement, would have to be released before tenured and tenure track faculty members could be released.

To help with this process the university eventually announced an early retirement incentive program, which did help somewhat, but it was clear from the beginning that it was not enough to get the FFFF reduction number up to where it needed to be. Hence, it became equally clear that I would have to come up with a plan that included faculty retrenchment, the academic and contractual word used for laying off faculty members, that is, cutting faculty lines, including tenure track and tenured lines if necessary.

THE MISERABLE "R" WORD: TO SAY OR NOT TO SAY

The provost wanted to avoid the word "retrenchment" as long as possible. (S)he was justified in her/his concern about using the big "R" word because once that word is used in a collective bargaining system a set of contractual guidelines must be initiated and union leadership becomes heavily involved—as they should be. Hence, it is prudent to wait as long as possible before taking that major step. But for the deans, life starts to get a little crazy. Department chairs hear things that may or may not be true and the dean's job is to set the record straight without causing a faculty panic and outward stampede of the best junior faculty members. There was also concern expressed (myself and another dean) about having enough time to be able to make our recommendations before the collective bargaining deadlines kicked in. So we pressed the provost to move forward on the retrenchment announcement. We were already moving in that direction within our colleges. Effective deaning requires recognizing and facing the inevitable.

Collective bargaining contracts typically require giving primary consideration to seniority when making retrenchment decisions, which can leave the more recent hires most vulnerable. Retrenchment clearly had to be handled carefully, but it had to be handled. As rumors of high budget cut numbers began to circulate among departments the faculty had to be brought into the process to whatever extent possible. As stated by Buller, "When you aren't candid in giving bad news in a bad situation, people will always imagine that the truth is even worse than whatever you would have told them" (2013: 193).

Nobody's Friend

I remember the meeting well when I announced to the department chairs that the budget reduction numbers had reached a point where it was no longer possible for me to come up with a plan that would not involve cutting faculty positions. I reminded them of the first meeting we had after I accepted the position of dean. At that time they were told that, from my perspective, I would have no individual friends and no enemies in the college, so that I would be able to make unbiased decisions. On the day that I announced that faculty positions would likely have to be cut I told them that this was the reason that I had not made friends with any of them. Deans must anticipate the possibility of the worst case scenario, because sometimes that scenario does become the reality. So I announced to the chairs that I would like to meet with each one of them individually to discuss the possibility of retrenchment, which I was able to do over the next several days.

During the meetings that I had with each of the chairs I asked them all the same question: "Would you prefer that we make the cuts across the board, which would mean each department would be diminished by the percentage required by the university; or would you prefer that we try to isolate the pain as much as possible by looking at departmental contributions and expenses?" It was also important to point out that taking the "across the board" approach would be complicated since the collective bargaining contract required targeting those with the least seniority. Whether that meant within each program, department, or college still had to be negotiated between the union and the higher administration. The outcome of that decision would make a dramatic difference in terms of which faculty positions would be lost, unless the FFFF chairs decided to localize the position losses.

The Question of Units

Before continuing the discussion about how the FFFF chairs responded to the question of whether they wanted to cut positions across the board or localize the cuts, it might be useful to look at the issue of units.

As it turned out, a university-wide contract interpretation was reached that allowed cuts to be made by units smaller than the university, college, and department levels. Programs would be the target. This means programs would be evaluated for retention, reduction, or elimination, with the last two options raising the possibility of faculty retrenchment. The preferred administrative position on what will constitute the evaluative unit for position reductions is that the finer the filtering process the greater one's ability to sift out those positions/(people) that are not serving the institution as well as they should. The reader will notice that I put "people" in parentheses. That is because the budget cuts due to financial exigencies are never supposed to be about the people in the positions, but the positions themselves and how to best save money. Budget reductions should not be used as an under-the-table way to address faculty performance or behavior. Using budget cuts in this way is a violation of due process, is dishonest, and is not really in the best interests of the college and university.

Identifying the Measurement Unit

So what about the unit? The question that is being asked is initially a methodological one. When assessing the faculty to find the most feasible and effective places to reduce faculty positions, what should the measurement unit and unit of analysis be (in this case they are likely to be the same): colleges, divisions, departments, programs, or individual positions? Typically the decision comes down to departments or programs. There is too much pushback among administrators to focus on colleges and divisions, and there is typically considerable pushback from the faculty with respect to focusing on individual positions. As alluded to previously, allowing that fine of a filtering system escalates the fear that the administration will simply use the budget reductions as a way to get rid of individuals they do not like. So administrators generally opt for programs as the measurement unit for determining position reductions. Dickeson, for example, begins with the assumption that it is programs that are the target, emphasizing the importance of maintaining the distinction between programs and the administrative units that contain them (2010: 91).

Are "Programs" the Best Unit Option?

Focusing on programs, theoretically, allows administrators greater ability to zero in on problem faculty (something that should not be done) than when focusing on departments. It also affords administrators the ability to say they have eliminated something, the cost of which looks good on paper. In actuality program elimination often has no immediate financial savings associated with it. Most programs are nestled within departments, some of which have many programs. Typically a faculty member in such a department is serving multiple programs at one time. Hence, eliminating one program within that department does not necessarily eliminate the faculty position, even if that faculty member plays a significant role in that program's operation—perhaps serving as the director. That is why I used the qualifier "theoretically" in the above sentence. Hence, more often than not the program elimination approach does not in itself eliminate faculty positions. As stated by Capaldi:

> universities are not managed by programs; they are managed by academic administrative units—colleges and departments and schools. And the main costs in a university are not programs but faculty members. If the same faculty member teaches in fewer programs, the university is being less efficient, not

more so. And if more programs are added without increasing the size of the faculty, the university is more productive, not less (2011: online, under academic programs).

Faculty members are typically rostered by department and hold seniority and rank within that department. This is especially the case in universities with collective bargaining. Departments create new programs and exercise considerable control over them. Deans work with departments to initiate or change programs under departmental control.

Hypothetical Example

A department with declining majors might take administrative advice to develop a new high demand program to better serve the institution and to better secure their existing programs and faculty. If retrenchment by programs occurs those who developed the high demand program might find themselves vulnerable because some of them are still teaching in the low demand programs—programs now targeted for elimination or reduction.

From strictly a management standpoint the above might seem like a clever strategy. Most likely some of the more senior and thus more costly members of the department are the ones targeted for retrenchment. However, taking this approach is punishing a department for being innovative and for following administrative advice. The very faculty members who are now targeted for retrenchment are the faculty members who had the foresight to create a new program that would increase the efficiency of the department and bring increased students and resources to the college. Punishing them with retrenchment sends a signal to all faculty members in the university that there is no benefit to being innovative and entrepreneurial. In taking the initiative to develop a new program, which is a lot of hard work, faculty members may simply be running the risk of making themselves more vulnerable instead of less, especially in a collective bargaining environment where seniority within a department should have a great deal of meaning.

Hence, this is a complicated issue and one that requires consideration of how college morale and future faculty cooperation will be affected—not just immediate managerial efficiency. Nobody would deny the importance of protecting successful high-demand programs. I believe the best way to do that is to protect the departments that produce and run them, which means protecting all of the wisdom and experience surrounding a successful program—not just the program itself. Departments that collect faculty positions and do no creative or entrepreneurial programming to support student demand and surrounding community needs should be the first targets of retrenchment. The creative mission-driven entrepreneurial departments should be left alone.

Preserving Departmental Integrity

It is within this framework that FFFF made its retrenchment decisions based on departments as the unit of analysis and not programs. Programs are parts of departments that are typically integrated into a multilayered fabric of curricula and faculty that create and preserve an organic whole. My advice to departments is to find and acknowledge that organic whole and protect it. And my advice to potential deans is to respect the department's need to be treated as one unit. Separating programs from departments is a false economy and could lead to long-term morale and productivity problems.

BUDGET REDUCTION PROCESS: CHAIR RESPONSES

When the interviews with the chairs were completed a clear majority of them had indicated a preference for isolating the pain, which meant identifying the departments with the lowest productivity and taking most of the faculty positions that needed to be eliminated from those departments. This outcome was announced at the next meeting of the chairs and they were asked how they would like me to proceed. The idea emerged that we should use the same criteria for eliminating positions as were used for adding positions. This is an approach promoted by others. For example, as stated by Buller, "In its essence, budget reduction does not involve any separate strategy than that used in planning an expansion" (2013: 193). Adding positions to a department in FFFF involved evaluating each position request on the basis of six criteria. Those criteria are discussed in Chapter 7 in the section on redistributing faculty position funds.

Criteria for Hiring = Criteria for Layoffs

I agreed to use the position assignment criteria as best I could with the understanding that some of the criteria might not be possible to use in this way since they either did not apply or were not directly measurable. It was also pointed out that cost would have to be considered more heavily since the process of retrenchment was about saving money, and that we would want to save the greatest amount of money toward our mandate while doing the least amount of harm to the college overall. It was emphasized that every department would most likely have to give up something despite the decision to localize the pain, and they should all be prepared for that as well. The six criteria as they appear in Chapter 7 are as follows:

1. The top priorities will be replacement of probationary faculty who were not renewed and the reauthorization of unsuccessful probationary searches.

2. A second criterion will be balancing student-faculty ratios in the majors across the college.
3. A third criterion will be balancing overall faculty responsibilities (reflected in Gen. Ed. Credits and/or service courses, student/faculty ratio, advising loads, internships, etc.) across the college.
4. A fourth criterion will be the centrality of the position to the departmental/programmatic mission and goals.
5. A fifth criterion will be the potential contributions the position can make to the college mission and goals, especially to potential contributions to enhance cultural diversity efforts in the college.
6. A final criterion will be the potential for program expansion based on previous or predicted success as reflected in increasing student demand, job opportunities in the field, quality and reputation of the program, and other indicators of success.

Compiling the Data

It is possible that every department chair assumed that the department(s) to be cut the most would not be their own. In fact, I suspected that most of the departments expected me to zero in on a particular department that most faculty members in the college did not think was needed and that had a long history of personnel problems. Personnel problems and public perception should not be the basis for making department reductions, let alone eliminating a department. The department in question did, in fact, serve an important mission in the college, and had a lot of students, both graduate and undergraduate. It was also one of the lowest cost departments on campus. If it had ended up on the bottom of the list it would have been eliminated, but I knew that it would not end up there. As dean one watches the numbers constantly and I knew the numbers for that department were quite good.

My understanding of the charge with which I was left was to arrive at a dataset that would help the college isolate the departments from where the bulk of the cuts would have to come. With the help of my assistant to the dean, relevant data were identified. Most of the data came from the university data book that is religiously compiled and published every year, and which is greatly underutilized most of the time. We had access to other data through the dean's office, including data related to the college mission and goals which have a heavy focus on diversity and student writing skills. To obtain additional data related to issues of "potential for program expansion" and "department centrality to college and university missions," the chairs were asked to write a brief statement making their best case for those items based on whatever data were available to them.[1] The assistant to the dean and I then evaluated and coded those statements, using our best judgment to create four qualitative variables. The values of these created variables could then be used as empirical indicators in the dataset.

Creating the Variable Matrix

Hence, all of the six general items from Chapter 7 as listed previously, except the first item which didn't pertain to budget cutting criteria, were covered by the created dataset. One can see reference to those items in the broad conceptual columns across the top row of Table 11.3. There were fifteen variables altogether. One variable that was created to control for the effects of seniority was eventually dropped because it was overly complicated and did not make much of a difference in the outcome. One very senior department would have been more favorably ranked as a result of this variable, but that change would not have affected their resource allocation. The department that ended up losing the most positions had a few senior faculty members, but most of the department consisted of relatively new hires.

The variables coded from the chair statements were coded conservatively with short scales allowing for the possibility of ties. We felt those variables were important, but did not want them to overpower the harder data taken from university records. They didn't. Most departments were pretty close on those indicators and the exceptions turned out to be inconsequential overall. Results were calculated with and without the four coded qualitative variables. The coded variables did not change the results in any way that affected the decisions guided by the data, so the results were presented to the higher administration without those variables included in order to reduce the likelihood of being accused of subjective bias. The departments that lose the most positions are going to make accusations of bias no matter what precautions are taken, but using only hard data from university records makes it more difficult for those accusations to have traction.

Another way accuracy and credibility can be improved is to involve the department chairs in the coding of the departmental statements, which was done. However, in a collective bargaining environment chairs, as members of the faculty bargaining unit, are normally discouraged by the union from participating in the budget reduction process to that extent. This practice helps protect the union in the event that grievances have to be filed. Hence, few chairs participated.

Maintaining the Conceptual Overview

Even with the qualitative coded variables removed, all of the general college level concepts were still covered in some way. For example, the issue of program potential was covered to some degree by the hard data variable that represented the amount of change that had occurred in the number of majors over the last

5 years. It was also covered by the special category represented by the last general column containing the cost indicators. Cost always has to be considered in the hiring process since a college cannot spend more money than it has; and cost certainly has to be considered when making decisions about which departments will lose positions. Expensive programs cannot be expanded or shielded from reductions unless the evidence for student enrollment growth is clear.

Another variable was eventually added under the general concept of student faculty ratios and departmental majors. It was the variable indicating the number of degrees granted per year within a department divided by the number of fulltime faculty equivalents. Since this variable was used to compare FFFF with the other colleges (see Table 11.1), it seemed reasonable that it should also be used to compare departments within a college. While it was not an outcome changer, it did turn out to be an important variable, validating the existing tendencies in the dataset in general. That is, knowing the number of degrees granted per faculty member strengthened our understanding of which departments are truly focused on appealing to student interests, student needs, and student service, keeping in mind that not all departments, especially smaller departments, have the capacity to draw a lot of majors. Departments that boast of high-demand markets, however, but have little to show for it in the way of majors and graduates, need to be looked at carefully in terms of the resources they claim to require.

WHO IS BEST SERVING THEIR STUDENTS?

While the number of majors and graduates (Tables 11.1–11.3, Columns 1 and 2) are highly correlated, they are not the same phenomenon. Some departments work hard to get their students through their program and some departments consider it a sign of their rigor if many of their students don't make it. I understand the theory behind the latter option, but have never found any evidence that anyone is well served by this approach to education: not the departments, nor the employers, and certainly not the students. To the contrary, I have seen departments with this approach to education bully and intimidate students. While there are all kinds of illusionary defenses relating to "preparing the student for the real world" and so on, I have found these defenses to be wanting. One's education is an important part of the real world, and our job is to make the educational experience rewarding and fulfilling for all of our students to whatever extent that is possible. If other people in the "real world" want to engage in forms of maltreatment we should not be accomplices to that highly questionable behavior.

While the number of majors and number of graduates are similar for most departments, such is not always the case. As an example of the important difference between the two, one might consider Department G. It is a relatively small department with a modest capacity to draw undergraduate majors, but they are well known for taking good care of their students and getting them through their programs. Hence, while last among the departments on the number of majors per faculty member, they are far from last relative to the number of graduates per faculty member. One might suggest that this is simply an anomaly of one particular year, but it actually is not. They take good care of their students and their students are graduated with consistency. Other departments, such as Department D, have a different pattern, offering programs billed as too rigorous for many of their students to master. Such programs are delivered in a way that tends to be discriminatory toward women, and thus upper level classes sometimes consist of men only. Nobody is well served by this type of behavior. There is nothing to be gained by making any subject matter seem more difficult to learn than it actually is. As educators our goal is to make learning easier, not more difficult.

Hard Data and Standard Indices

The need for quantification in prioritizing educational units has been emphasized by Dickeson (2010), but is generally conspicuously missing from recent works on deaning. If one cannot quantify the evidence upon which one is making serious retrenchment decisions, accusations of subjective bias will be impossible to refute, and those accusations will almost certainly come. Hence, as the previous section on data compilation suggests, the decision-making for the faculty reductions in FFFF was based on hard data primarily taken from university records, and those data represented the most common higher education variables typically considered in evaluating department and program performance. They also represented the mission and goals of the college, which were not only based on standard higher education performance expectations, but also on expectations appropriate for this particular type of college.

Deans of other types of colleges will want to be sensitive to the primary mission issues that drive their curricula and make sure that, to whatever extent possible, those issues are represented in the data used for important decision-making, such as budget reductions. In looking at Table 11.3 the reader is challenged to identify the departments that might be in the greatest peril. It should not be difficult.

Data That Answer Difficult Questions

The data in Table 11.3 show which departments are consistently working on the missions and goals of the college and the university. They also show which departments are most student centered. That is, Table 11.3 shows which departments are working the hardest to make their programs attractive and useful to students—which departments are drawing students and which are not. Who is going the extra mile to provide diversity courses and writing-intensive courses? Who is doing more with less?

Table 11.3 College FFFF Departmental Comparisons on Key Cost/Benefit Variables

Dept.	2. S:F Ratios-Majors			3. Bal. overall faculty responsibility		4. Dept.-Prg Centrality to missions and goals	5. Contribution to college mission and goals including contributions to enhance diversity			6. Potential for program expansion				Primary cost	
	Total Majors/ FTEF	Degrees/ FTEF	ADJ Cr. Hr FTEF	S:F ratio	Writ Inten. Cr.Hr./ FTEF	Centrality to missions & goals	Cult Div Cr. Hr./ FTEF	Fac Div Race-Ethn.	Fac Div Gend	5 yr % change majors	Cur chg-inno	Job opp.	Qual. Rep.	Sal cost per Cr.	Salary cost per major
A	18.45	4.74	843.9	27.25	0.00	1.00	377.37	31.58%	52.63%	4.7%	2	2.00	4	80	3628
B	25.46	6.63	811.8	25.09	4.86	1.00	50.22	5.88%	47.06%	20.3%	1	1.00	1	78	2347
C	1.32	3.36	686.8	19.75	11.44	2.00	148.34	16.67%	42.86%	53.3%	2	2.00	2	100	5460
D	13.86	6.42	875.8	27.87	4.31	3.00	214.68	25.00%	25.00%	_13.7%	2	2.00	5	67	3846
E	23.22	6.69	422.3	13.83	51.99	1.00	65.42	8.33%	75.00%	14.8%	1	1.00	2	151	2752
F	10.23	2.14	545.7	17.64	0.00	3.00	453.02	23.80%	61.54%	43.5%	2	5.00	6	104	5418
G	6.39	3.92	395.2	12.75	24.82	2.00	275.18	25.00%	100.0%	9.4%	1	6.00	1	120	7323
H	10.25	1.69	734.0	23.02	33.54	3.00	561.34	71.43%	28.57%	112.9%	1	5.00	7	77	5252
I	8.10	1.87	834.5	27.80	5.71	5.00	5.71	58.33%	16.67%	17.6%	5	1.00	9	89	9117
J	35.96	9.06	719.3	22.86	5.80	2.00	27.03	13.33%	26.67%	_0.8%	3	2.00	4	84	1615
K	15.04	4.55	726.5	23.59	60.17	1.00	530.34	27.27%	45.45%	_4.1%	2	4.00	6	84	3195

Indicator clarification: Column 1 = All declared majors divided by the number of fulltime equivalent faculty (FTEF); Column 2 = # of degrees conferred divided by FTEF; Column 3 = The adjusted number of credit hours divided by FTEF; Column 4 = Student faculty ratio based on class sizes; Column 5 = Number of credits designated as writing intensive divided by FTEF; Columns 6 and 7 should be self-explanatory; Column 8 = The percentage of the faculty officially from a racially or ethnically diverse group; Column 9 = The percentage of the faculty that are women; Column 10 = The average percentage of change in the number of majors over 5 years; Column 11 = The department's record on curriculum change and innovation; Column 12 = Opportunities for graduates to get jobs; Column 13 = Assessed overall quality and reputation of the department's programs; Column 14 = Total FTEF salary cost divided by the total number of credits produced; Column 15 = Total FTEF salary cost divided by the number of majors (most data taken from the official university data book).

Table 11.4 provides a different visual of the data in Table 11.3 by converting the values to the rank of departments on each of the variables in the dataset. The "sum" score on the far right of the table represents the total ranking, with the highest value equaling the lowest ranking department overall and the smallest value representing the highest ranking department overall. While the statistical perils of rank order data are fully understood, such as not adequately representing the actual distance between the real life values (which are close between departments in some instances), in conjunction with Table 11.3 the rankings are a useful tool. They show us more clearly and simply where the departments are relative to the data. If greater precision is desired one can always go back to Table 11.3. Looking at Table 11.3 carefully one can see what Table 11.4 reveals more readily: Departments I, F, G, stand out among all the departments as those with the lowest performance values overall. It is important to emphasize that the departments in FFFF were generally quite strong and healthy when the economy collapsed in 2008—many exceptionally so. With one possible departmental exception, the question was never, "how do we reduce our excesses?" The question was, "where are the most reasonable places to remove position lines in order to make the needed 16+ percent budgetary reduction?" Two of the three just identified departments were small and one was quite large. All three were targeted for retrenchment.

Lines Must Be Drawn

In addition to Departments I, F, and G, Department C was also ranked relatively low on many of the items and had an overall rank score that was fourth from the bottom—eight points below (lower scores are better) the third lowest ranked department. Department C was the only department that was disproportionately affected by having particularly senior faculty members. This impact appears in the last two right-hand variables (related to cost) where Department C ranked seven and nine respectively. The reader might recall that initially a variable was created to control for the effects of seniority, but it was dropped from the dataset because it added little value to the information and was overly complicated. Department C, having a relatively senior faculty, was the only department whose overall rank was negatively affected by the removal of that variable. Additionally, Department C's significant contribution to graduate education, their exceptional flexibility, and significant off-campus presence were also considered.

The information about Department C was taken into consideration when deciding just how far to go with the localization of the pain. How different was C from I, F, and G, and how much would that difference impact the morale of the college overall if C was chosen for retrenchment? I concluded that going up one more notch to include Department C might be a deal breaker in the quest to protect the integrity, balance, and thus the morale and general health, of the college. Combining this decision with the overriding objective of localizing the

Table 11.4 College FFFF Departmental Rankings on Key Cost/Benefit Variables

Dept.	2. S:F Ratios-Majors			3. Bal. overall faculty responsibility		4. Dept.-Prg Centrality to missions and goals	5. Contribution to college mission and goals including contributions to enhance diversity			6. Potential for program expansion				Primary cost		Sum
	Total Majors/ FTEF	Degrees/ FTEF	ADJ Cr. Hr FTEF	S:F ratio	Writ Inten. Cr.Hr./ FTEF	Centrality to missions & goals	Cult Div Cr. Hr./ FTEF	Fac Div Race-Ethn.	Fac Div Gend	5 yr % change majors	Cur chg-inno	Job opp.	Qual. Rep.	Sal cost per Cr.	Salary cost per major	Ranking Score
A	4	5	2	3	11	1	4	3	4	8	2	2	3	4	5	61
B	2	3	4	4	8	1	9	10	5	4	1	1	1	3	2	58
C	7	8	8	8	5	2	7	7	7	2	2	2	2	7	9	83
D	6	4	1	1	9	3	6	5	10	11	2	2	4	1	6	71
E	3	2	10	10	2	1	8	9	2	6	1	1	2	10	3	70
F	9	9	9	9	11	3	3	6	3	3	2	5	5	8	8	93
G	11	7	11	11	4	2	5	5	1	7	1	6	1	9	10	91
H	8	11	5	6	3	3	1	1	8	1	1	5	6	2	7	68
I	10	10	3	2	7	5	11	2	11	5	5	1	7	6	11	96
J	1	1	7	7	6	2	10	8	9	9	3	2	3	5	1	74
K	5	6	6	5	1	1	2	4	6	10	2	4	5	5	4	66

pain to whatever extent possible, only the three lowest ranked departments were included for retrenchment and those departments were identified exclusively using the data provided in Tables 11.3 and 11.4. This is important. If deans are unable to identify exactly how the budget reduction decisions are being made they are rightfully suspect of making decisions for the wrong reasons: friendships; favored and disliked department chairs or faculty members; chair/faculty lobbying; ideology; discrimination; and so on. Having a carefully worked out method does not guarantee that the above accusations will not be made anyway.

Accusations Will Be Made

I was accused of being biased against a discipline of one of the departments targeted for retrenchment. And one other department chair whose faculty was not targeted for retrenchment challenged my decision-making. Ignoring my initial statement that everyone would have to give up something, this chair felt (s)he should not have to give up a position vacated by a retirement, despite the fact that every department gave up the equivalent of at least one position. Given the magnitude of the expected college reduction, this chair was clearly not being reasonable. The chair and I met with the associate provost and I reviewed the data and the initial statement I had given to all of the chairs. Finally, after much complaining and objecting the decision seemed to be accepted. The accusation from the retrenched department did not go away, however, and that ended up being the source of much discussion between the faculty union and the higher administration. To my knowledge nothing significant came of those discussions. At least I was never called to testify and never heard anything to suggest that a formal grievance was filed.

THE RESULTS

As forewarned, all departments that were not targeted for retrenchment lost the equivalent of at least one position, and some lost two. This was done through early retirements, canceled searches, not renewing fixed term appointments, and combining and eliminating part-time positions. While this was cumulatively a lot of positions, no fulltime departmental colleagues were lost who had not decided to leave on their own. Hence, the damage to each department was relatively minor compared to the magnitude of what had to be done overall. And the faculty of these non-retrenched departments eventually came to recognize they were getting by without notable damage to their programs.

Retrenched Departments

As it turned out, the two smallest departments of the three targeted for retrenchment preempted their losses at the last minute through unexpected retirements and resignations. These two departments were actually among the smallest in the college and each lost the equivalent of 1.5 positions. The 1.5 positions do not seem like a lot, but that figure represents 27 and 33 percent of Departments F and G respectively. Both departments had just added positions with recent hires, which they were able to keep. The loss was much different than it would have been if the retrenchment had actually taken place, since retrenchment requires starting layoffs at the bottom of the seniority roster. The damage done to these two small departments was significant, however. Being small in the first place is what led to some of their low numbers. For example, it is difficult for a department of four to have high credit production if all of the faculty members must use most of their credit load to service the courses needed for their majors—courses that typically have low numbers of students. Both departments were trying to do what they could to get their numbers up but it was extremely difficult given that they also had well-respected graduate programs they worked hard to protect by selecting only a few good students each year and taking good care of them. One of the two departments, experiencing decreasing numbers of majors, was in the process of significantly diversifying its curriculum in order to broaden its market toward a new category of prospective students. It is for these reasons that I advised the university to replace the positions for these departments as soon as possible. Both departments represented disciplines that were central to FFFF and eliminating them from the university curricula was clearly not a consideration. Yet, the departments could not be expected to continue providing their programs without adequate staffing.

A Different Scenario

The third department targeted for retrenchment (Department I) represented a different picture. The department seemed to have gained a number of positions over a relatively short period of time by creating an impression of a high demand market for its programs. When the data failed to support that impression the department found itself on the retrenchment list. It was one of the largest departments in FFFF and seemed to be uninterested in being in the college. It had previously been in another college and seemingly would have preferred to remain there, but was moved to FFFF prior to my arrival because it failed to meet some of the goals of their previous college. Similarly, Department I did not seem to be making an effort to meet the mission and goals of College FFFF either, which is reflected in the data of Tables 11.3 and 11.4. The department was advised accordingly long before the 2008 economic collapse, but to no avail.

Department I appeared to be staunchly committed to primarily two activities: (1) increasing the pay for its faculty members; and (2) increasing the number of faculty in the department. There did not appear to be enough focus on student recruitment and retention, the marketability of their programs, or the welfare of the college/university. Yet, Department I had managed to create a public reality of its importance and demand that now appeared to be significantly inconsistent with the actual data. Since some of their courses were required by other majors (most outside of FFFF) and since they were considerably overstaffed for servicing their own majors, they could offer a lot of medium-sized sections of lower level courses that almost always filled. This gave them one of the highest credit production numbers in the college (third in the college). Because they were able to have so many filled medium-sized service courses that more than statistically compensated for their small sections offered for their majors, they also maintained a high student-faculty ratio (second in the college). Of course, these two variables are basically one in the same. They maintained a high student-faculty ratio because of the outside demand for primarily one of their lower level courses—a course with content that could be taught by departments outside of FFFF. In fact, the content of that course was also being taught in another department in another college, but over the years Department I was able to protect an exclusive claim to students in certain outside majors needing that content. There was no academically or fiscally sound justification for that claim.

Strong on Two Variables Is Not Enough

Unfortunately for Department I there were fifteen variables in the dataset that were used to make the retrenchment decisions, and they had the lowest or second to the lowest scores on six of them. One of the most important variables on which their score was second to the lowest was the number of majors per faculty member. And their salary cost per major was predictably the highest (lowest rank) in the college. This was partly a function of their failure to draw majors and partly a function of the artificially inflated demand for their discipline, resulting in their faculty being comparatively and significantly overpaid. While claiming to be a high demand field they did not have many students wanting to get into their programs, unlike a number of other programs in FFFF that had to turn many students away. So one couldn't help but wonder, "Where is the demand in this supposedly high demand discipline?" A reasonable conclusion was that it did not exist and that the university, perhaps like many universities, was being tricked into paying far more for its faculty in this area than it should have been paying. It is important to remember that faculty pay across departments is a zero-sum game. In any given year there is only so much money to distribute for positions and the more one department requires for its positions the less money there is for positions in other departments.

Mitigating Curriculum Issues

The challenge ahead was difficult, but seemed obvious. Much of the content of the high demand credits of Department I was the actual domain of another lower cost underutilized department. Transferring some of that I credit load to that other department would assure that retrenchment would not impact the curricula of other departments in the university. Deans of two other colleges were approached and discussions commenced on how that could be achieved. Eventually the shift began, which involved changing or waiving program requirements in another college. Hence, a large portion of the lower level credits offered by Department I could now be covered by other departments, creating a theoretical credit vacuum in Department I large enough to eliminate five Department I faculty positions. As stated by Buller,

> Deans need to approach budget cuts as they might approach a game of chess: studying the implications of each decision several moves hence. Although it is obvious that every budgetary cut will have consequences, you don't want a cut to have unanticipated consequences (2007: 191).

Implementing the Reductions

The five most junior members of Department I were identified for retrenchment and notified accordingly. Among these five faculty members were some excellent scholars and thus a significant loss to the college in that regard. This, of course, was the most difficult action I had to take in my career as a dean. While confident that it was the right decision based on the right rationale and data, it was nevertheless extremely difficult and painful to carry out. The professional lives of five faculty members were at stake and deans should not take such matters lightly. Contrary to what some might claim, it should never be easy to fire someone and such actions should always be a last resort.

The good news is that the positions of some of the retrenched faculty members were spared by a budget rebound at the state level. With the vacating of still other positions due to retirements and relocations some of the retrenched faculty members were able to keep their positions. But Department I is smaller and, hopefully, wiser than it once was, focusing more on the importance of serving a wide base of student majors.

CONCLUDING COMMENT

Regardless of how careful deans are when making these difficult decisions, the faculty members on the receiving end of the bad news are most likely going to see the process and the outcome differently than the administration. No matter how methodical the dean is and how many times the faculty is shown the data and provided a thorough explanation of what took place, the department(s) most affected are going to be angry and expend a lot of energy creating and projecting a completely different reality than what has occurred. The data will be attacked and it is likely that the dean will be attacked as well, including her/his scholarly work. This is to be expected. It is why deans must remain neutral without allegiances to anyone.

Realize that faculty members typically have extraordinary intelligence and skill. Some may even anticipate that they could be facing problems and set up the dean as their enemy in advance—accusing the dean of having a negative bias toward them or their department before hard decisions are ever made. It is important for deans to make sure they do not fall into this trap, which could cause them to blink when the most difficult times arrive. No enemies and no friends—just keep moving forward with data and integrity and let the hard decisions fall where they must.

It is, however, important for the reader to keep in mind that all of the programs in College FFFF remained intact and that the vast majority of the departments were relieved that they did not lose more than they did, given the magnitude of the college's (as well as state's and university's) financial losses. Many chairs and faculty members expressed appreciation for the methodical, data-driven approach that was taken in the budget reduction process. When all was said and done the morale of the college overall seemed high, and I left that position, as I did my previous deanship, with tremendous support and positive regard from the faculty in general.[2]

NOTES

1 Measuring a department's contribution to the university is discussed by Gary S. Krahenbuhl (2004: 89–93) who offers a scheme for using qualitative ratings on numerous items to arrive at a cumulative annual score. Krahenbuhl used those data to help determine resource allocation across departments, but they would also be useful to determine where budget reductions should occur.

2 According to the provost, the faculty survey in my last year of my first deanship was the highest score of any dean ever at that institution. A faculty survey at the second institution was distributed by the Union during the retrenchment. It was not nearly as positive since turnout was low and a large segment of the responses came from the retrenched department. More important, however, were the many individual extensions of good will and support. Being fair and honest does have its rewards.

REFERENCES

Buller, J.L. (2013). *Positive academic leadership: How to stop putting out fires and start making a difference*. San Francisco: Jossey-Bass.

Buller, J.L. (2007). *The essential academic dean*. San Francisco: Jossey-Bass.

Capaldi, E.D. (2011). Budget cuts and educational quality. *Academe* (November-December). Retrieved February 29, 2016 from www.aaup.org/article/budget-cuts-and-educational-quality#.VtPq-dC2F0o.

Dickeson, R.C. (2010). *Prioritizing academic programs and services: Reallocating resources to achieve strategic balance*. San Francisco: Jossey-Bass.

June, A.W. (2014). It all comes down to the dean. *Chronicle of Higher Education*, 61 (13), 19–22.

Krahenbuhl, G.S. (2004). *Building the academic deanship: Strategies for success*. Westport: Praeger Publishers.

Snyder, T.D. & Dillow, S.A. (2013). *Digest of education statistics 2012*. (NECES-U.S. Department of Education). Retrieved January 6, 2015 from http://nces.ed.gov/pubs(2014)/(2014)015.pdf

The Chronicle of Higher Education. (2014). 25 years of declining state support for public colleges. *The Chronicle of Higher Education,* (March 3, 2014). Retrieved August 28, 2016 from www.chronicle.com/interactives/statesupport

Chapter 12

Knowing When to Move On

HOW LONG?

As one might have gathered from reading this book, deaning can be pleasurable, rewarding, and yet quite difficult at times. It is not an easy job, and if someone finds they are having an easy time of it they most likely are not adequately addressing their responsibilities. An intentional dean works hard and takes risks to make a positive difference, frequently solving problems and sometimes going out on a limb for the faculty and students of their college. Hence, the life of a dean is typically pretty short. For example, education deans/heads serve for about an average of four and a half years (Robbins et al., 1994), and the median tenure of a law school dean is reported to be 3.19 years (Rosenblatt's Deans Database, 2010). Tenure for deans in general shows higher figures, but they are still low. As stated by Bright and Richards (2001: 248), "The half-life of a Dean is actually less than four years," and Tucker and Bryan (1991: 24) suggest the "standard appointment now for a Dean is between five and seven years," while "Few Deans serve more than ten years"(1991: 24–25). Wolverton and Gmelch (2002: 125) state simply that "Deans serve an average of six years." And Buller (2015: 555) supports this figure when he states that "Deans and Provosts serve on average for about five to six years," with Gerdes (2014: 135) echoing the five to six year estimate.

Measures of central tendency are difficult to interpret because so many deans drop out after the first or second year, and it is unclear as to whether many of those people would be included in the cited data. Once a pattern is set, deaning becomes less stressful. But many new deans find themselves asking why they would want to continue doing this job when they could be more comfortable lecturing and reading term papers while sitting out on the porch with a cold beverage.

Should I Stay or Should I Go?

Assuming a dean makes it past the initial "hazing," how long should a dean stay in their position? There are a number of possible simple one line answers to that question: for as long as one can take it; for as long as one can survive; for as long as one is still doing some good; until one is asked to leave; until there is a faculty vote of no confidence; and so on. There should be a better way of approaching that question—albeit there is no certain answer that fits everyone. I had the pleasure of working with a person who was, perhaps, the longest serving dean in the United States—35 years, which is off the charts for a dean's tenure. So is 20 years. And, as noted by Tucker and Bryan earlier, 10 years is exceptional.

The earlier estimated survival rates, ranging about 4–7 years, make the dean's tenure a relatively serious and delicate issue because there also seems to be a minimum number of years that is expected for deans to have served in order for others to consider them "legitimate" deans. For example, if it becomes known that a dean is applying for provost positions in the second year of their appointment, (s)he may experience some criticism from the other deans—not to mention from the higher administrators if they find out about it. The magic minimum legitimacy number is probably somewhere around 3 years, which does not leave a very large window for deans to plan and implement the rest of their career. Generally there seems to be a decreasing marginal utility associated with staying beyond the 7-year mark relative to future higher level administrative success.

What Constitutes a Healthy Tenure?

A healthy tenure is when a dean is creating positive outcomes for the college, whether it is for the future of the college as a contributing university component or for the current programs, faculty, and students of the college. There is no rule about how much a dean should accomplish at any one particular time—beyond the minimum expectations of meeting the various deadlines. A dean's positive contributions may decrease over time but still be comparatively and beneficially high. It is important, however, for a dean to monitor how rapidly circumstances are changing. How much energy is being expired to achieve goals that would have taken less energy earlier in the tenure? How receptive are higher administrators and the college faculty to the dean's ideas and initiatives? When a new dean is hired there is typically a cautious honeymoon period where the higher administrators and faculty leaders are supporting (as well as testing) the person they played a role in hiring. Once new deans have their agenda in place and have made it over the first few hurdles (roughly 6 months to a year), it seems that their activity and productivity levels increase toward a plateau which can be expected to stabilize for an indeterminate period of time.

There are many forces acting upon a dean's position, some of which over time may tend to destabilize their productivity plateau and thus the dean's ability to accomplish goals. A decline may begin gradually in a relatively inconspicuous manner or abruptly, depending on what causes the destabilization. What are some of the causes of the destabilization of the dean's productivity plateau?

DESTABILIZATION OF THE PRODUCTIVITY PLATEAU

Exhaustion

An intentional dean is one who takes chances and puts a lot of energy into their work. It is easy to set too fast a pace and burn out quickly. In the best of colleges there is a lot to do and only so much time in which to do it. Going back to the early part of this book the reader may recall being advised to assure a certain amount of compatibility between oneself and the higher administration as well as the mission of the institution before accepting a position. As documented by Wolverton, Gmelch, and Wolverton (2000), "fit" is an important variable in the success and longevity of a dean. That issue comes full circle when the dean has spent as much energy as can be mustered and yet, due to insufficient support, fails to accomplish some of her/his most basic goals.

Even with support, however, there comes a time when the desired energy level cannot be maintained. It is sometimes difficult to recognize exactly when this is happening. It might be seen in others but not in oneself. Hence, it is important for deans to be continuously monitoring themselves (Murray, 2014) by asking basic questions about their own accomplishments and what those accomplishments may have entailed. A good time to do this reflexive thinking is when one is preparing one's self-evaluation for the annual personnel meeting with the provost. Rather than simply doing a routine fill in the blanks report, one should seriously consider, for her/his own personal record, the relative difference between what has been done during the past year in comparison with previous years. Deans should be sensitive to their own "staleness"—to borrow a term used by Buller (2007: 394). That is not to suggest that every year should be filled with great and miraculous accomplishments, but the pulse needs to be strong and steady. Deans should not be afraid to take their own pulse.

Long-Term Stabilization Is Possible

The dean mentioned earlier, who had the distinction of serving for 35 years, was exceptional. (S)he was my mentor for my second dean's position, and (s)he certainly did not seem to be exhausted—albeit only (s)he would know. Her/his retirement was announced along with a multi-million dollar gift that (s)he received for her/his college—a gift (s)he had nurtured for many years. A person who defied most of the socio-demographic and cultural norms of administration, her/his productivity plateau seemed to remain stable over the long haul. (S)he became a dean at an early age and routinized many of the responsibilities in a way that helped her/him enjoy the position over a long period of time. (S)he probably didn't intend to be a dean that long, but given her/his appreciation for the institution and the college, it turned out that way.

Exhaustion doesn't befall everyone who finds their way into a deanship. There are other possible factors impacting a dean's productivity and longevity, and occasionally someone completes a full and robust career as a dean.

Formal Complaints

It is difficult to remain productive when time and energy are consumed with defending oneself in grievance hearings or within legal investigations. I was fortunate to experience very little of this kind of diversion during my deaning career, but some deans find themselves going from one complaint hearing to another. The provost for my first deanship informed me when I accepted the position that I would be sued—that all of her/his deans had been sued at least once. I was careful enough and fortunate to never have that experience in either of my positions as dean. While it is sometimes the case that deans create these circumstances by the way they respond to events within their college and by their failure to read and internalize important institutional documents, the causes of complaints against a dean are not the current issue. Constantly defending oneself is grueling, time-consuming work and not pleasant for anyone. The processes and even the outcomes can be quite devastating for all involved. Under these circumstances a dean's agenda gradually shifts away from her/his goals for improving the college toward defending oneself. It becomes difficult just to carry out the perfunctory deadline-based activities of the job. I saw examples of this problem in dean colleagues, but encountered much more as a faculty leader and grievance officer.

Personal Stresses Related to the Job

Stress is one of the main factors leading to the decision to step out of a dean's position (Gerdes, 2014; Wolverton & Gmelch, 2002; Wolverton, Gmelch, Montez, & Nies, 2001; Wolverton, Gmelch, & Wolverton, 2000). Gerdes discusses research completed with Christopher Zappe showing that the average deans' responses related to stress ranged between moderate and very high stress levels. Wolverton, Gmelch, and Wolverton (2000: 204) identify seven dimensions of stress related to being a dean: (1) administrative task (what deans have to do), (2) provost/supervisor-related, (3) faculty/chair-related, (4) personal time-related, (5) scholarship, (6) salary and recognition, and (7) fundraising. Institutions that want to have vital and productive deans should take measures to alleviate/reduce stress related to these factors. Too many institutions take good deans for granted and, once hired, abandon and/or exploit them. While unqualified and ineffective deans should be counseled out of their positions or let go if necessary, intentional deans, deans who have the strength and courage to lead, should be supported. If higher administrators want to keep good deans there are ways, most of them pretty obvious, of addressing the previous list of stressors. The dilemma higher administrators face, however, is whether to risk faculty (and possibly public) criticism for using funds to add administrative support when academic departments may need faculty positions.

Stressors are Interrelated

Various dimensions of stress are interrelated. For example, while the dimension noted called "administrative task" was found to account for a lot of the stress related to the dean's daily responsibilities (Wolverton, Gmelch, Montez, & Nies, 2001: 22), it is largely a result of not having enough time to do all that needs to be done. "Scholarship," "fundraising," "faculty/chair-related," and "personal time-related" stresses similarly result primarily from insufficient time to complete all of the necessary responsibilities. On the other hand, "provost/supervisor-related" and "salary and recognition" stressors are most directly related to what Wolverton et al. (Wolverton & Gmelch, 2002; Wolverton, Gmelch, Montez, & Nies, 2001) identify as the lack of fit between the dean and the environment in which (s)he finds her/himself. Conflicting management styles, incompatible educational and/or world viewpoints, disparate opinions on what the dean's work is worth—all of which should be determined before accepting a deanship—can be energy draining and quite stressful. Of course, time issues are also environmental to some extent, since campuses provide different levels of support for deans to perform their various responsibilities.

Space limitations prevent discussing each of the seven stressors mentioned earlier, so only one will be explored directly: "personal time-related." In discussing this source of stress the importance of "time" and possible corresponding remedies can be addressed. As noted, most other identified dimensions of stress are arguably also time related. For a dean to remain an active scholar, raise external funds, and solve departmental disputes, all while performing the more routinized aspects of the dean's role, requires time. Without sufficient time, either the quality of results or the dean's personal life will have to be sacrificed.

Deans Have Families Also

The demands of being a dean, and the time required of deaning, can be hard on family relationships. It is difficult to stay focused on one's agenda at work if important related personal matters are not resolved at home. Long days and weekend events at work often cut into what should be quality family time. To minimize family-related stress, the best time to become a dean is when one's nest is empty, which apparently is what happens most of the time since only about one-third of deans have children at home (Wolverton & Gmelch, 2002: 105). But even with an empty nest there can be issues related to spouse and life partner relationships. People may have elderly parents who need care, and/or grandchildren who want to see them. The more one can integrate family members into one's deaning position the less likely it will seem as if the person in the dean's role has abandoned their family. Bringing children to the office often and bringing one's entire family to university events helps mitigate the distance between what the dean is doing when away and the perceptions of the dean's loved ones.

In addition to bringing the family to the dean, the dean must be brought to the family. Higher administrators can help alleviate stress in their deans by making sure they have time to be involved in the daily lives of their loved ones. As a faculty member I ran a continual shuttle service for my four kids: picking them up and dropping them off as needed throughout the day. I cannot imagine doing that as dean. Nearly every hour of every day was blocked off with meetings and appointments. This is why most deans don't have children at home and another reason why going into deaning late in one's academic career is recommended. But it doesn't have to be that way. If faculty members can spend time with their family, deans should be able to do so as well.

Working Together to Relieve Stress

The relative rigidity of a dean's life and the absence of truly "free" time are what keep many highly qualified faculty members from wanting to move into administration. Having a life outside of one's job should not only be possible, but it should be expected. For this to happen, higher administrators, deans, and their staff all need to be on the same page regarding the routine integration of family activities/events into the daily calendar of the dean. Effective deaning is not a 9–5, 5 days a week job any more than an effective professorship is, and higher administrators should not try to squeeze more responsibilities into a dean's non-existent "9–5 day." From a management standpoint the question should not be, "how can I demand more time from my deans?" It should be, instead, "how can I draw better deans to the institution, help them become effective and happy, and thereby increase their desire and ability to stay in the job for a reasonable length of time?" If a dean is going to have a 10–14-hour day, the days need to be more loosely bundled than they currently are.

Higher administrators should also do what they can to provide an ample number of vacation days to deans and deans should be encouraged to use all of them. My last provost was supportive in this way, and it paid off for both of us. (S)he had a more effective dean after I returned from vacation, and I was able to maintain a healthy relationship with my spouse, which in turn improved my deaning. I took nearly all of my vacation days each year and encouraged the new deans to do the same. It helps immensely, even with the occasional panicked emails and phone calls from office staff while away.

Changes in administrative culture relative to managing deans would most likely help alleviate some of the personal time-related problems deans experience. When pursuing a dean's position one might raise questions about how close or far the institution is from a culture supportive of deans and their personal lives. In the current *status quo* environment, however, I can only advise deans to protect their time and manage it carefully. Take full advantage of vacations and holidays—both for spending time with loved ones and for continuing one's scholarship. By doing most of one's scholarly work at home one can also be available to her/his family. I was able to continue writing, present papers, and even do some publishing throughout my decanal career—albeit I had an empty nest and a commuting relationship with my spouse.

The reader should not interpret this section to mean that deans should not work hard and be expected to accomplish a great deal. In fact, if deans are valued and treated accordingly they will most likely be more productive than if treated in a draconian managerial style. It should also be stated that sometimes there are personal time-related problems and other stressors that simply cannot be resolved. There is nothing to be ashamed of under these circumstances. When this happens, leaving the deanship serves everyone's best interests.

Dual Professional Relationships

Since it is difficult for two professionals to find positions in the same city, especially if it is a small city, some deans and their intimate partners may end up commuting long distances—possibly half-way across the country or more. The difficulty of commuting may eventually wear on the couple, and the person in the dean's role may find it hard to maintain a consistently high level of performance. External forces can make already challenging commutes even more challenging. When the planes hit the Twin Towers in 2001 the difficulty of the 1,500-mile commute between my spouse and me ballooned significantly. I was able to complete the core curriculum transformation project and help complete the university's college restructuring project. But I could not imagine taking up new challenges and continuing to do my job at a high performance level with the added strains that distance and travel suddenly presented. Against much internal pressure to stay, I turned in my resignation and went back to the classroom at my previous university from which I had a leave of absence.

After a couple years a dean's position opened at a university in a city just a 2-hour drive away and I was fortunate enough to be selected for that position.

My spouse, knowing the time commitment of my position, did most of the commuting. She had more flexibility in her scheduling and could often craft long weekends to spend with me. It worked out quite well.

The point being made in this brief section is that commuting relationships are difficult under most circumstances, and while it is certainly possible to make such conditions work well, it doesn't take much to destabilize such an arrangement and make doing a high-stress job, like deaning, even more stressful and difficult.

Other Remedies for Stress

Chapter 9 was ended with a recommendation that deans seek out and attend Bodhisattva Peace Trainings to help them more effectively deal with the difficulties of dealing with disciplinary issues and corresponding processes. The same recommendation could have been made at the end of Chapter 11 on austerity, and it can be made again now in regard to assessing a dean's longevity. But there are other ways of dealing with the stress related to the most difficult aspects of deaning. Quality relaxation time away from work, as described previously, is critical. And nurturing personal relationships goes along with that relaxation. Having hobbies and regular recreational activities also help mitigate stressors. A healthy physical state is crucial to having a healthy mental state and both can be greatly assisted with physical exercise and a healthy diet. I have benefitted greatly from various forms of exercise and a vegan diet over the last 23 years.

Stress is also greatly mitigated by deans being amply prepared for their job. This book has been crafted to assist toward that objective, and other books exist for that purpose (see references). There are, however, organizations that help prepare deans as well. The Council of Colleges of Arts and Sciences (CCAS), and the American Conference of Academic Deans (ACAD) are two such organizations, each having their own conferences and workshops. These organizations are well known for their ability to engage deans in real life problem-solving scenarios (e.g., CCAS, 2012a, 2012b). I recall looking forward to those small group analyses/discussions when I attended the conferences.

Important also is a dean's ability to stay active in their academic field of scholarship. Continuing to attend and participate in those conferences helps a dean keep her/his bearings as an academic and helps one remember what her/his job is all about. Higher administrators tend to discourage this kind of activity. The discouragement is based in part on the idea that new deans have to be broken from their faculty past and fully socialized and assimilated into the administrative "side" of the academic enterprise. This "us-them" kind of thinking is counterproductive. Staying active in one's discipline provides deans with a familiar professional escape that is centering and reinforcing. It is a retreat in the fullest sense of the word.

Changing of the Guard

Anyone who has ever had a new boss knows how disruptive just the idea can be—not to mention the actual operational changes that may occur. This is certainly true for deans when a new provost is appointed. More often than not changes are made to which the deans must adapt. If these changes are sufficiently large in magnitude or number, deans may find themselves having to compromise and possibly rethink their agendas for their college. Under these circumstances it may become difficult to remain productive and make the contributions a dean would want to make. If, for example, a new provost changes the way the budgeting for the colleges is handled it could negatively impact on the ability of the deans to manage college departments. Indeed, sometimes new provosts are hired specifically for such reasons, that is, to shift resources away from the deans' control into the general fund so the president has more discretionary money. Such moves are often also accompanied by a change in the vice president of administrative affairs position.

Protecting College Resources

Summer school funds are a good example of where the budgeting process can be quickly changed in a way that makes a dean's life considerably more difficult. Many universities have a practice of splitting summer school money between the general fund and the colleges. There is usually a formula that determines the way the money will be divided. This practice of splitting the summer income is based on two assumptions. The first is that if there is not a robust summer program at the university the illuminated and air-conditioned buildings will simply be a financial drain. A formula that generously channels money back to the colleges assures a healthier academic component within the university as well as some money going back into the general fund to pay the bills. The second assumption, triggered off the first, is that a healthy incentive for the deans to manage summer school effectively will provide maximum assurance that the desired robust summer program will occur. If a new provost, or vice president for administrative affairs, decides (s)he want the summer formula changed, or possibly even done away with altogether, that could dramatically reduce the discretionary money available to the deans, and thus negatively impact on the dean's agenda/productivity. There are not many circumstances under which deans should consider drawing a line in the sand (while packing up their office perhaps), but this could be one of them.

Non-Success

Few factors destabilize a dean's overall productivity more than failure to accomplish a specific important goal, especially a goal directly mandated by the higher administration. A dean should know that if (s)he was brought into a position for a particular reason and did not fulfill that objective, (s)he will most likely not be retained. Whether the charge is to solve an ongoing problem with a particular department, turn the college around on an important issue (such as diversity), increase fundraising, or organize a major curriculum transformation, the higher administration will expect it to be accomplished within a reasonable period of time. If the expectation is not fulfilled, deans can assume that, at some point relatively soon, they will be encouraged to seek a position elsewhere, or possibly face being fired.

Don't Oversell Yourself

There is a sub-lesson related to this issue that takes us back to the early part of this book dealing with the process of applying for a deanship. It is important to be honest about one's strengths in the application process. One should not sell oneself as having a notable skill based on a minor sideswipe with a particular issue. A dean's worst nightmare might be an expectation to accomplish something about which (s)he actually knows little. If the president says to the provost, "look, the chancellor keeps beating up on me because we have insufficient diversity on this campus, and I want you to turn this around," the next dean's position will likely be filled by someone who is an expert on diversity. Whoever that person is had better make sure what they wrote in their application and said during their interviews was not an exaggeration. They had better know a lot about diversity, and the diversity experience they identify in their CV had better be real and significant. The same would be true of any major challenge for which one could be hired. Honest strengths can bring fulfillment and satisfaction while exaggerated qualifications can quickly bring disappointment and pain.

ONWARD AND UPWARD

Partly because a dean's job is challenging and generally known to be a short-tenure position, many deans consider deaning a stepping stone to a higher status and/or better paying position—either internally or at another university. The most obvious target is a position as a provost, but there are others, such as associate provost, dean at a more prestigious university and/or of a bigger college, or even a presidency. As discussed early in this book, moving into higher administrative positions is not a good reason to become a dean. If a dean, from the beginning of her/his tenure, has as a primary goal moving into a higher level position, her/his ability to make hard decisions may be impacted. Her/his personal goal of moving "up" might overshadow her/his desire to do what is best in each situation. The ultimate "intent" (with an emphasis on *ultimate*) of the intentional dean should not be focused on fulfilling one's own ambitions, or for that matter even promoting the university *per se*. "Institutions of higher education are conducted for the common good and not to further the interest of either the individual teacher or the institution as a whole" (AAUP, 2015: 46). Depree (1992: 138) supports the AAUP when he states, "Leaders learn how to make a commitment to the common good." And he continues by adding, "We will progress toward the common good only if we as individuals are intentional about pursuing it."

Timing Matters

While becoming a provost or president is not a good reason to become a dean, it is a common and generally positive reason for deans deciding to leave their position. If a dean decides to make the move "upward," the best time to leave is while still reasonably well liked by both higher administrators and the faculty. This typically means sooner rather than later since serious deaning often requires upsetting increasing numbers of people over time. Being a good problem solver can easily be taken for granted as time goes on, but denying one person tenure could turn nearly an entire department against a dean forever.

In addition to leaving before the faculty "ax to grind" list is too long, one might consider applying for positions following a major accomplishment, such as leading a curriculum change, a new program development, or a major fundraising success. Under these circumstances one maximizes the chances of having external opportunities for attaining a new position. It is possible, and even likely, that a dean will have both factors in operation at the same time when considering a move: people who are unhappy with one or more of the dean's decisions, and the dean's significant accomplishments. These two conditions often go hand in hand. It is generally difficult for a dean to bring about a major change without upsetting someone or some group of people who then might work against the dean thereafter. The dean's hope under these circumstances is that there are far more people satisfied with her/his work than dissatisfied, and that this condition will be evident as the dean applies for other positions.

And the Agenda?

Earlier in this book a lot of time was spent discussing the importance of agendas. Deciding to leave isn't just about successes and failures and the number of years served. Before a dean leaves (s)he should be thinking about how much of her/his agenda is fulfilled. There is no expectation that deans will be able to accomplish everything they set out to do. Some disappointments are almost guaranteed. However, one should ask with seriousness whether one has done enough. Has a sufficient amount of her/his agenda been completed to be able to comfortably leave the rest behind and hope that someone else will pick up the ball? Or, are there unresolved issues that the dean has the capacity to complete. Deans have agendas to help them organize their time toward making specific contributions for the betterment of the college and the world in general. They shouldn't take that responsibility lightly.

WHEN THE CONVERSATION CHANGES

One of the qualities of deaning that makes it interesting and fulfilling is its unpredictability. Each day presents new challenges, holding the potential for memorable victories, and sometimes (hopefully not often) defeats. The unexpected usually starts out as a problem, quickly becomes a challenge, and if all goes well, ends with a successful solution. Throughout all of this, on a daily basis, there is a general context of activity that is positive and constructive. The questions generally remain the same: What problems/needs have emerged today, who are the people affected by the problems/needs, and how can I help deliver effective solutions? On a daily basis the dean's conversations are with the faculty of their college, and deliberately so, since an effective dean spares the busy provost from getting involved in the daily activities of her/his college. Discussions with faculty members about what can be done to improve conditions in their departments are generally value-added conversations. Often times college or university funds are being channeled into a department or program and those resources help produce a better outcome in some way. Students have increased opportunities, faculty members can deliver their classes more effectively, research opportunities have been expanded, and life in academia is on a positive win-win trajectory.

Universities do not exist in a vacuum. They are greatly impacted by the political and economic conditions surrounding them. This is especially true of institutions that we used to call state universities, and which we now might more accurately call state assisted universities. When political environments become hostile to public higher education, whether at the state or federal level, there can be negative financial consequences for campuses and even entire university systems. Under these circumstances university administrators are caught in a difficult game of pleasing their "bosses" at the state level while trying to minimize the damage to their campus. Private universities have similar challenges, but with a slightly different set of players.

Impact of Budget Crises on Deans

While the budget reduction process was discussed in Chapter 11, it must be revisited briefly relative to the impact it might have on the dean's decision to leave. Many scenarios could be constructed, quite real in their consequences, to depict the direct and indirect effects of financial crises on the ability of deans to complete their agendas. When financial crises occur, real or otherwise, and universities must significantly cut their budgets, the dean's conversations change dramatically.

There is still much to be done in the way of daily problem solving, but the general focus shifts away from an agenda designed to add value to departments and the college. The subtext of most conversations now revolves around deciding what is the best way to protect the value that is already there? How does one deliver what the institution demands financially and yet protect the programs and faculty that are so vital to the delivery of a quality education?

What Shall We Talk About Today?

When a university is in financial crisis mode much of the time at the dean's council meetings is spent discussing the various scenarios that could unfold. What if the state does X, or what if the chancellor does Y? What will be the size of the expected reductions and how can colleges best go about fulfilling those expectations? Will all of the colleges be expected to give the same proportionate amount or will some colleges be protected more than others? There will most likely be discussions about how this experience could make the colleges/university stronger in the long run, and there could be some small piece of twisted truth in that speculation. How often universities are actually made stronger through budget reductions would probably be a great doctoral dissertation. However, if not handled carefully, as it often times is not, a major budget reduction could lead to program damage and morale problems that have lasting negative consequences for colleges and universities. That possibility should be part of the conversation as well.

It is important to keep in mind that the greatest university expense is faculty salaries, which fall within the domain of the college dean's budget. Colleges are, for the most part, the spokes in the academic affairs budgetary wheel. And the provost, acting under the influence and pressure of other higher administrators, is the hub of that wheel. During a budget crisis provosts can shorten all the spokes proportionately, shorten some and not others, or shorten some spokes and lengthen others. Another approach available to the provost is to remove one of the spokes altogether or simply shorten just one spoke enough to cover the impending deficit. The latter two options are dramatic and will likely cause a lot of blowback from the faculty leadership. Either option could mean eliminating several programs in one college rather than weakening many across the entire campus. These possibilities will likely be part of the conversation during a budgetary crisis.

When Responsibility Shifts

If responsibility shifts to the deans, which is likely to happen, the same conversation taking place at the dean's council will now take place in the college chair meetings. Those conversations were discussed as a matter of process in Chapter 11. Similar to the provost, the dean's office is a hub as well. The departments are the spokes of the college wheel. And the dean has all of the same options as the provost but now the discussion is about departments rather than colleges. The provost knows that the deans have the greatest awareness of where the strengths and weaknesses are within the colleges. A smart provost will set out some general guidelines and then challenge the deans to come up with the necessary reduction plans to make budget. That was done at the university where I was located during the financial crisis, and that reality eventually drove most of the conversations from that point onward—whether in the deans' meetings with the provost or the chairs' meetings with the dean. When given the decision-making authority, some deans are able to meet the provost's challenge and some are not, forcing the provost to step in and make decisions in areas (s)he would prefer to avoid.

Does the Dean's Life Change?

The point being made by revisiting the unpleasant realities of reducing college resources is that budgetary crises are just that: crises. They are messy, sometimes brutal, and are almost certain to have lasting negative effects on a deanship. The conversations deans will have following the announcement of a major budget reduction will be quite different to the conversations they have under normal circumstances. Even conversations that are not directly about the crisis itself are likely to have that topic as a hidden or not-so-hidden subtext. The dean's challenge is to keep the faculty informed, but not frighten them toward a mass exodus or major workday disruption. The work of the college must go on as smoothly as possible, and the deans can play an important role as shock absorbers for their faculty. It is a grueling and somewhat ominous responsibility. Hence, it is wise for a dean to understand and accept this reality, and prepare for it.

Protect Your Credibility: Prepare to Leave

One of the best ways to prepare for the impact of a budget crisis is to simultaneously prepare to leave when the crisis is over. This is the promise I made to the provost and associate provost on one of the saddest days of my career, shortly after the announcement of the university's budget crisis. The implication is not that deans cannot survive and continue being effective following a major budget crisis. The message is more so that it is going to be extremely difficult for a dean to recover if the budget reduction process is executed boldly and in the best long term interests of the college.

As the shock absorber for the college the dean can expect to receive psychosocial damage inversely related to the stability of the overall college after the budget cuts are made. According to DePree (1992: 139) it is the leader's job to "bear the pain . . . if you are bearing the pain properly as a leader, . . . you ought to have the marks of the struggle." Keeping relative balance within a college that must be significantly reduced typically requires making some of the most difficult and painful decisions a dean will face. The marks will be there. Making such decisions with courage and with the common good in mind will have a physical and mental impact on even the strongest of administrators.

How Clean Can You Make It?

Keeping the budget-reduction process based on data, keeping it clean, and keeping it college centered are extremely important objectives. The decision-making process cannot contain the slightest concern about what the dean's life will be like when the dust finally settles. Even more importantly, there cannot be any suspicion on anyone's part, either in the faculty or among the higher administration, that what the dean is doing is related to her/his own self-interest. If deans make an early commitment to leave once the crisis is over they are free to follow whatever process is needed during the crisis to minimize the damage to the college, preserve morale, and quickly get the college back on track to a quick and full recovery. The dean's credibility is critical to the preservation and stabilization of the college (Kouzes & Posner, 2003: 14).

FINAL COMMENT

One might argue that taking such a position of committing to leave is easier for some than others, and that may be true. If one is reasonably close to being able to retire, as I was when the economy collapsed, theoretically the decision to leave is easier since one would not have to find another job. But in reality, when I turned in my resignation there were plenty of job opportunities for me. Furthermore, when I retired from my dean's position, as communicated to many friends and relatives at the time, I was seriously considering going back into administration after a short break. As has been emphasized previously in this book, once a dean has established a successful record of leadership and college administration other position opportunities will be there. I have had many invitations to apply for positions since my retirement. Instead of pursuing those invitations, I decided to write this book from a number of relaxing beautiful locations. I greatly enjoyed my work as a dean but writing this book has also been a very rich and rewarding experience. I hope it is of value to others.

REFERENCES

AAUP (American Association of University Professors). (2015). 1940 Statement of principles on academic freedom and tenure. *Policy Documents and Reports*. Baltimore: John Hopkins University Press, 45–52.

Bright, D.F. & Richards, M.P. (2001). *The academic deanship: Individual careers and institutional roles*. San Francisco: Jossey-Bass.

Buller, J.L. (2007). *The essential academic dean*. San Francisco: Jossey-Bass.

Buller, J.L. (2015). *The essential academic dean or provost.* San Francisco: Jossey-Bass.

CCAS. (2012a). A case of tenure denial. *CCAS case study for inclusion in New Deans Seminar*. Retrieved September 1, 2016, from www.ccas.net/files/ADVANCE/Case%20 Studies/Tenure%20Denial_NDS.pdf

CCAS. (2012b). A question of equity in hiring. CCAS case study for inclusion in New Deans Seminar. Retrieved September 1, 2016 from www.ccas.net/files/ ADVANCE//Case%20Studies/ Equity%20in%20Hiring _NDS%281%29.pdf

DePree, M. (1992). *Leadership jazz*. New York: Dell Publishing.

Gerdes, E.P. (2014). When to move on, ready or not, in L.L. Behling (Ed.), *The resource handbook for academic deans* (pp. 135–140). Hoboken, NJ: Jossey-Bass.

Kouzes, J.M. & Posner, B.Z. (2003). *Academic administrator's guide to exemplary leadership*. San Francisco: Jossey-Bass.

Murray, K. (2014). Self-Assessment, or how do I know if I am succeeding?, in L.L. Behling (Ed.), *The resource handbook for academic deans* (pp. 127–130). Hoboken, NJ: Jossey-Bass.

Robbins, J.H. et al. (1994). Who is leading us toward quality professional development? *Meetings of the American Association of Colleges of Teacher Education*, Chicago, IL. Retrieved August 23, 2016 from http://files.eric.ed.gov/fulltext/ED367632.pdf

Rosenblatt's Deans Database. (2010). *Average and median current length of service of current deans.* Retrieved September 9, 2015 From www.law.mc.edu/Deans/stats.php

Tucker, A. & Bryan, R.A. (1991). *The academic dean: Dove, dragon, and diplomat*. New York: Macmillan Publishing Company.

Wolverton, M., Gmelch, W. & Wolverton, M.L. (2000). Finding a better person-environment fit in the academic deanship. *Innovative Higher Education*, 24 (3), 203–226.

Wolverton, M. & Gmelch, W.H. (2002). *College deans: Leading from within*. Westport: Oryx Press.

Wolverton, M., Gmelch, W.H., Montez, J. & Nies, C.T. (2001). *The changing nature of the academic dean.* New York: Jossey-Bass.

Index